The only way God's people will stand and overcome in the days ahead is by the power of the Spirit. There are few people more qualified than Stephen Strang to share what that means. *Spirit-Led Living in an Upside-Down World* is a much-needed guide for believers to live, thrive, and prevail in the end-time. It is spiritual, accessible, practical, authoritative, and dynamic, an essential resource for those who are serious about living a victorious life.

—RABBI JONATHAN CAHN
NEW YORK TIMES BEST-SELLING AUTHOR

Spirit-Led Living in an Upside-Down World is about the gifts and the fruit of the Holy Spirit. It seems as though no one is writing books about the power of the Holy Spirit in our lives, and it is so very needed in this upside-down world that is on a downward spiral of morality. This book needs to be read and studied with your Bible while you meditate on the scriptures provided throughout the book. Stephen Strang does an excellent job of introducing you to the Holy Spirit and showing you how to hear from Him and know Him intimately. I highly encourage you to read this book and discover how the Spirit of the living God lives within true children of God in order to lead them to think, speak, and act according to the Word of God.

—KENNETH COPELAND
HOST, *BELIEVER'S VOICE OF VICTORY*

In the face of an increasingly adversarial culture, believers tend to settle for a hunkered-down survival mode. Stephen Strang's newest book claims that is not what God wants for us. In a down-to-earth, readable style, Strang reminds us that the Spirit-led, Spirit-filled life of power is the joyful path of sanity in a world of craziness.

—MARK RUTLAND
FOUNDER, NATIONAL INSTITUTE OF CHRISTIAN LEADERSHIP

I am no stranger to the attacks of the enemy. Being a Christian has never been easy, but today's chaotic and openly hostile environment accounts for more stress, discouragement, anxiety, and depression for believers than ever before. Stephen Strang has been faithful in bringing the gospel to the world. In this book he combines the wisdom and experiences of his personal faith and journalism career with a divinely inspired vision to encourage the Christian community to experience the transforming power of the Holy Spirit. The result is his passion for the reader not only to spiritually survive but to thrive in a world turned upside down. Everyone needs this book.

—JIM BAKKER

HOST, *THE JIM BAKKER SHOW*

Nothing changes us like the power of the Holy Spirit. I've witnessed this in my own life and in the lives of countless others. The supernatural often seems natural to the anointed man or woman. If ever we needed this kind of power, it's today. In this important book, Stephen Strang reminds us that no matter what happens in the world around us, the Holy Spirit empowers us to overcome. Written by someone who has spent more than forty years chronicling the move of the Holy Spirit in *Charisma* magazine, this book will help you discover how to be led by the Holy Spirit and inspire you to experience His power in a fresh, new way.

—R. T. KENDALL

FORMER PASTOR, WESTMINSTER CHAPEL

You need only to read the daily headlines to see how far America has fallen from its original ideals. Our beloved "one nation under God" is barely recognizable as the country most of us remember. But this is no time to hang our heads and declare defeat! With the help of the Holy Spirit, we can reclaim this great nation for God and pass the torch to our children and our children's children. Stephen Strang reminds us of the difference we can make when we come together in the power of the Spirit to sow righteousness instead of discord and goodness instead of evil.

—MARIO MURILLO

EVANGELIST

Stephen Strang's newest book will equip you for your new assignment. All hands on deck! We are about to see the largest soul-winning revival in history—greater than all the moves of God put together!

—SID ISRAEL ROTH
HOST, *IT'S SUPERNATURAL!*

If there's a man alive who can truly take the pulse of America and its people today, it's Stephen Strang, publisher of *Charisma* magazine. He is a student of America's spiritual history and has spent many years interviewing virtually all the movers and shakers in the Pentecostal-Charismatic and wider evangelical communities. In this wonderful book, Stephen tells the stories of people like us, people we know and admire, people who have experienced supernatural answers to prayers and God's guidance in these troubled waters and are thriving today. And he shows how simple it can be to have the same experiences. God loves us all equally and offers us each the ability to live and succeed with His Holy Spirit guiding us through the trials we face. You'll want to give this book to everybody you know.

—PAT BOONE
SINGER AND AUTHOR

After coming to Christ during the Jesus movement in 1971, someone told me there's "something more." That's when I learned about being filled with the Holy Spirit. Jesus told the early disciples to remain in Jerusalem until they receive what Luke 24:49 calls "power from on high"—and that's what happened. The same gift of the Holy Spirit is offered to us. Whether you are a new believer, a seasoned saint, or someone who is still searching for the truth, *Spirit-Led Living in an Upside-Down World* will serve as a primer (or a reminder) of all that God intends for you: to live in the fullness of His Spirit day by day. In these pages you'll hear from many of God's choice servants in the twentieth and twenty-first centuries—such as Fuchsia Pickett, Jack Hayford, and Reinhard Bonnke.

—MIKE BICKLE
FOUNDER, IHOPKC

We know we live in an upside-down world. We see the problems of our culture everywhere we look. Yet Stephen Strang reminds us that all is not lost. God has sent His Spirit into our contemporary world, and He is empowering His church by the Spirit to become a revolutionary force so great, so inspired, so anointed, and so radical that we will change our world. This book will take you on an exciting journey. God wants to use you as a contemporary revolutionary, and Stephen Strang inspires you with revolutionary faith and a revolutionary message that can and will change our world.

—BISHOP TOMMY REID
NIAGARA COMMUNITY OF CHURCHES

Stephen Strang reminds us that the Holy Spirit is not the idle member of the Trinity but is the third member of the Godhead who lives inside believers, and our relationship with Him is vital for Christian living. Enjoy the journey of what it means to live a Spirit-led life.

—DOUG CLAY
GENERAL SUPERINTENDENT, ASSEMBLIES OF GOD

Stephen Strang earned his place in the hall of trusted Charismatic voices decades ago. He affirms his position there with *Spirit-Led Living in an Upside-Down World*, revealing a heart and mind wholly devoted to the Lord. His words will encourage anyone who finds themselves dismayed at the state of our nation, reminding readers that there is a holy power available to heal us if we will only make ourselves available to Him.

—SAMUEL RODRIGUEZ
LEAD PASTOR, NEW SEASON; PRESIDENT AND CEO, NHCLC

For more than four decades Stephen Strang has demonstrated his unique grasp on how the Spirit-filled community can coexist and even thrive alongside a seemingly deteriorating culture. *Spirit-Led Living in an Upside-Down World* is Strang's latest perspective that is sure to capture the same pattern of excellence and thought-provoking insights as previous contributions.

—TIM HILL
GENERAL OVERSEER, CHURCH OF GOD

This is an important book to read—right now, at this moment. The church and all Christians are under full attack by satanic forces that all but take your breath away. And the church could not be less prepared. Stephen Strang, having published two thousand books and almost a thousand issues of *Charisma* magazine since the 1970s, stands alone in his firsthand knowledge and insights into how we got here—and how we can overcome every ungodly thing that's happening to us today. God is the same yesterday, today, and forever! And the power of His Holy Spirit is just as real and available to us today as it was with Christ's disciples. You need only to read this book to know how quickly you can enjoy the comfort and power of the Holy Spirit in your own life.

—BARRY MEGUIAR
PRESIDENT, MEGUIAR'S CAR WAX; FOUNDER, IGNITE AMERICA

Drawing from a host of prominent leaders in the Charismatic movement, Stephen Strang offers a kaleidoscope of dramatic experiences, memories, and quotes about how the Holy Spirit moves in a person's life—and in the life of the church—to comfort, empower, strengthen, anoint, and come alongside. If you're longing for more—deeper joy, lasting peace, more victorious power—come drink from this deep well of wisdom about the third person of the Trinity. *Spirit-Led Living in an Upside-Down World* will be food for your soul.

—EVANGELIST ALVEDA KING
FOUNDER, SPEAK FOR LIFE

I highly recommend Stephen Strang's new book, *Spirit-Led Living in an Upside-Down World*. In a culture that is upside down and eroding before our eyes, this book will inspire you and give you thought-provoking insight on how to ask the helper, the Holy Spirit, for guidance in difficult times. We can still have righteousness, peace, and joy despite all the challenges the world may present. May you use this book to find power for living—it is yours for the asking.

—GORDON ROBERTSON
PRESIDENT, THE CHRISTIAN BROADCASTING NETWORK

This book's chapter on deliverance had me on edge as I read it in one sitting while rejoicing that I wasn't the only one hearing the truths written in it. *Spirit-Led Living in an Upside-Down World* is a recommended read to every believer looking to walk in higher levels of the anointing.

—APOSTLE ALEXANDER PAGANI
FOUNDER, AMAZING CHURCH

Stephen Strang's perspective of Spirit-led living is both helpful and encouraging. This book helps the reader understand not only what spiritual gifts are but also how they are accessible to the believer and their relevance today. *Spirit-Led Living in an Upside-Down World* is filled with numerous examples, and Stephen Strang communicates in a way that anyone can understand conceptually and practically the keys to being empowered by the Holy Spirit in the twenty-first century. I remember when I came to faith, not knowing much about spiritual gifts. I desired to have a book like this. Now it's here!

—HUBIE SYNN
AUTHOR AND PROPHETIC MINISTER

Many books are published about deliverance from evil spirits, but not enough is said about how the Holy Spirit brings daily deliverance to the life of the believer—as in resisting the devil so he flees from you. That's easier said than done: we can't resist the devil in our own strength! But Jesus promised to send us the Helper, the Comforter, the One who empowers us to resist the enemy. In these pages, get reacquainted with the Holy Spirit as Stephen Strang takes you on a journey through the Holy Spirit's purpose, gifts, and fruit—and how life in the Spirit will make you salt and light to a world in desperate need of Jesus.

—BISHOP GEORGE G. BLOOMER
PASTOR, BETHEL FAMILY WORSHIP CENTER

SPIRIT-LED
LIVING
in an
UPSIDE-DOWN
WORLD

STEPHEN E. STRANG

CHARISMA
HOUSE

SPIRIT-LED LIVING IN AN UPSIDE-DOWN WORLD by Stephen E. Strang
Published by Charisma House, an imprint of Charisma Media
600 Rinehart Road, Lake Mary, Florida 32746

Visit the author's website at SteveStrangBooks.com.

Cataloging-in-Publication Data is on file with the Library of Congress.
International Standard Book Number: 978-1-63641-139-2
E-book ISBN: 978-1-63641-140-8

23 24 25 26 27 — 65432
Printed in the United States of America

Most Charisma Media products are available at special bulk-quantity
discounts for sales promotions, premiums, fund-raising, and educational
needs. For details, call (407) 333-0600 or visit www.charismamedia.com.

Portions of this book were previously published by Charisma House as *Old
Man, New Man*, ISBN 978-0-88419-697-6, copyright © 2000.

*I dedicate this book to the late Jack Hayford, who
exemplified the Spirit-led life and was more of an example
of integrity in the Pentecostal world than anyone I've known.
He was the editor of the* Spirit-Filled Life Bible; *wrote
more than five hundred songs, including "Majesty"; and
influenced me more than anyone else in the past thirty years.*

TABLE OF CONTENTS

FOREWORD

By Benny Hinn

WHEN I WROTE *Good Morning, Holy Spirit*, I shared my personal story of getting to know the Holy Spirit in an incredible, life-changing, intimate way. The same morning that I woke up and said, "Good morning, Holy Spirit," I asked Him to show Himself to me so I could know Him better. He directed me to learn about Him in 1 Corinthians 2. I opened my Bible, and my eyes fell on verses 9 and 10, which tell us that "'eye has not seen, nor ear heard, nor has it entered into the heart of man the things which God has prepared for those who love Him.' But God has revealed them to us by His Spirit. For the Spirit searches all things, yes, the deep things of God" and reveals them to us.

In that moment, I knew that this precious person I was talking to was the One who could tell me everything I needed to know about God. He is the revealer of who God is, who Jesus is. A great journey began in my life that I never knew existed. From that day forward, before I would read my Bible, I would say, "Holy Spirit, You are the author of the Scriptures. Help me to understand them." Before I would pray, I would say, "I am just dust. How can dust talk to the Lord? Holy Spirit, help me talk to Him. Help me pray." This went on for a whole year, and it became such a fellowship. I began to understand that this blessed person, the Holy Spirit, is more beautiful than beautiful, more glorious than glorious. He became more real to me than any person or anything around me.

He stayed with me that way for a whole year, and then one day as I was talking, His presence suddenly lifted. At this time, I was a teenager, and I attended the Catacombs, a Christian youth group in Toronto led by Merv and Merla Watson. I told a leader there what happened to me, and she said, "I'm glad He left." I was shocked. "What do you mean?" I asked her. "I'm glad He left you, because now you will have to search for Him with all your heart. Now you will grow." I learned that day that as precious as it is when the Spirit's presence descends upon us and stays with us, it is when we search for more of Him that we grow.

On a personal note, I first met Stephen Strang in the 1970s in Orlando, Florida, around the time he started *Charisma* magazine. He and I were such good friends in those days that he was at my bachelor party and wedding to Suzanne! We have remained good friends over the years.

It is my privilege to write the foreword for his book *Spirit-Led Living in an Upside-Down World*. Because of our relationship, I know that his mission for all these years has been to publish materials about the Holy Spirit that encourage people to know Him and experience His presence and power in their lives. And I also know that books on the Holy Spirit can open us up to encountering Him in new ways.

I pray that as you read this book, written by my dear friend Stephen Strang, you will seek the Holy Spirit with all your heart. Whether you're just beginning your journey with Him, as I was back in Toronto, or you're seeking to know Him afresh and anew in your life, I challenge you to diligently search for Him as if your life depends upon it—because it does. We need Him so very desperately. We need Him more now than ever before. As the days ahead look darker and darker, He is our hope and strength, and He will tell us everything we need to know to be prepared and to fulfill everything God wants us to do.

And I can assure you that as you seek Him, you will find Him. There is always more of Him to discover and learn about. He is waiting for you. He longs to fellowship with you and become more real to you than anything else in your life, just as He did to me all those years ago and still does even more strongly and deeply today.

The reason the Holy Spirit is here is to make Jesus, the Son of God, more real to us in our lives, to give us a love for the Lord we've never known, and to glorify the Lord Jesus in and through our lives.

—BENNY HINN
EVANGELIST, TEACHER, AND BEST-SELLING AUTHOR

A WORD FROM JACK HAYFORD

THE HOLY SPIRIT, the third person of the Trinity—Father, Son, and
Holy Spirit—is somewhat of a mystery to most people. Referred to
for centuries as the Holy Ghost, His person has been surrounded
by a dimension of unreality, if not spookiness, for a long time.

When someone comes to God the Father and willingly receives the
gift of life through Jesus the Son, the first thing that happens is the Holy
Spirit enters that person's life. Jesus described Him as a "Comforter"—
One who will remain beside you to help, counsel, teach, and strengthen
you.[1] His entering is only a beginning, though, and the sensible believer
in the Lord Jesus will keep open to the Holy Spirit's increasing desire to
expand the evidence of God's purposes in his or her life.

The fullness of the Holy Spirit, the fruit of the Holy Spirit, the gifts of
the Holy Spirit, and most of all, the abundant, flowing love of the Holy
Spirit are all expressions of God's intent in giving us His Spirit. In other
words, to simply realize that the Holy Spirit entered when I received
Christ is to grasp a precious truth. But I need to see more—to want more.
The practical development of God's work in my life requires that I give a
growing place to the Holy Spirit's working within me.

The Comforter has come, and His mission is to help us move forward
as growing sons and daughters of the Most High God.

If you haven't yet done it, allow the Lord to open in you a conduit
of His Holy Spirit, an ever-flowing stream of living water. This fulfills
His promise, which is to you personally as much as it is to every other
believer in the body of Christ: "You shall receive the gift of the Holy
Spirit."[2]

Jesus wants you to be filled with the Holy Spirit. He is a miracle
resource of power, flowing from an unending source. "Spirit fullness"
can strengthen you when you're under attack, provide refreshment

through daily prayer and praise, and release a flow of Christ's ministering, healing power in you and through you to others.

Ask Jesus to fill you with the Holy Spirit. With praise in your heart and on your lips, come into His presence, and by faith receive His promise because "the promise is to you."[3] Expect His miraculous touch upon you as He answers your invitation.

Continue daily in a fresh walk in Holy Spirit fullness. Ephesians 5:18 tells us to "be filled with the Spirit," but a more accurate translation of that verse is, "Keep on being filled with the Spirit." You cannot be sustained by drinking only once. But having been satisfied initially, keep coming daily to King Jesus' pool, the Holy Spirit's never-ending fountain of living water.

Having begun this life by the power of the Holy Spirit, how shall we grow in this new life? The answer is rather obvious: by the power of the same Spirit! But most of us are slow to understand this fact.

Paul asked the Galatians, "After starting your Christian lives in the Spirit, why are you now trying to become perfect by your own human effort?"[4] We all need the same reminder: New birth isn't the end of God's program for us. His Spirit has started something by His power that He wants to advance with our partnership.

Now, everything I have said up to now is probably easy enough for you to acknowledge. Any honest believer will be quick to say, "I need to grow," or "I want to grow." But the pathway to growth is usually cluttered with obstacles, and the obstacles are usually hangovers from our past—past lifestyle, past habits, past attitudes, past sinning. We will not "grow out of" such things naturally. It's the partnership with the Holy Spirit that is all-important to our spiritual and emotional growth.

In other words, the results of our past all too often remain part of our present reality. The fact that you sinned in the past can be seen in its remaining fruit. Of course, you can be absolutely certain that God has forgiven it all—this is a bright truth of your new God-given inheritance! But of equal certainty is the continuing presence of many personal problems bequeathed to you from your past. Your salvation solves the problem of your relationship with God, but it doesn't always dissolve the problems in your life. It opens the doorway to solutions, but it is only by walking through that door and patiently pursuing that way that those problems will finally be resolved.

If patience during God's waiting periods is trying for even the most mature believer, how much more so is it for those of us still discovering that our receiving of the Holy Spirit rarely includes an immediate change of circumstance?

Over the years, I have had many people say to me, "Pastor, since I've been filled with the Holy Spirit, I feel different, but it doesn't seem like much else has changed." They go on to express their concern that a week, two weeks, a month has passed, and yet dramatic events still aren't filling their days "like all those people" they've heard testify.

I usually seek to comfort them with two facts:

1. My experience with dramatic testimonies is that they are honest but usually abbreviated. People report in a condensed version things that took much longer to come about. Don't feel like a second-class Christian when time seems to be passing by and action seems slow.

2. God is never in a hurry. Yes, the presence of the Holy Spirit within us does bring an instant witness; He's there and He's at work.[5] But remember this: the gifts and the fruit of the Spirit aren't unwrapped with haste and grown at a moment's notice. If things aren't happening fast, that's normal.

The relevance of our learning to recognize that God's delays are not denials is that such understanding can defuse the tendency to feel unworthy (condemned) simply because things aren't happening as quickly as we think they would if we were somehow more acceptable to God.

The simple fact of the matter is that the Lord has quiet times of dealing with our souls. When they come, be of good courage. If you have opened yourself up to the Holy Spirit, be patient. The Holy Spirit knows what

He's doing, and a little more time won't make Him falter or fail. God doesn't have to dash about busily in order to prove Himself. He's the One who's in charge, not you. Don't compensate by getting busy yourself, or most likely you will have to undo your work.

Some time ago, after the passing of a family member, I was moved to do a study on God's activities in the dark. I was amazed at the number of major events in the Bible in which victory was wrought in the midst of darkness:

- Creation's light burst into the darkness of chaos.[6]
- Jacob wrestled all night and gained a new identity.[7]
- Israel's Passover deliverance took place in the night.[8]
- Gideon's battle unto victory began in midnight hours.[9]
- Jesus' cross was immersed in a sky of inky blackness though it was midday.[10]

Even when Jesus comes again, it will be as a "thief in the night"[11] and during an era of history predicted as one in which "darkness shall cover the earth and deep darkness the peoples."[12]

This truth can bring brightness and exhilaration to your soul. The Holy Spirit is ministering to your need now. Whatever the apparent darkness, God never forsakes the works of His hands.[13] Rather than allowing the darkness of waiting to become a shadow of doubt, and instead of letting a cloud of questioning deceive you into believing you are the victim of God's apparent inactivity or unconcern, learn this wisdom: *Dark times are intended for your rest.* When they come, lean back and recline in the everlasting arms of the Almighty. Allow the Holy Spirit to work out and through what He's surely doing. I guarantee you that when morning comes, you'll be surprised!

Years of pastoring have taught me that the healing and deliverance of human souls can only be preserved where responsible obedience is manifest by those receiving the Holy Spirit's rebuilding within them. Jesus' words to the restored include this advice, which we are wise to heed:

> Now you are well; so stop sinning, or something even worse may happen to you.[14]

> When an unclean spirit goes out of a man, it goes through dry places seeking rest. Finding none, it says, "I will return to my house, from which I came." When it comes, it finds it swept and furnished. Then it goes and brings seven other spirits more wicked than itself, and they enter and dwell there. And the last state of that man is worse than the first.[15]

These are hard words. But Jesus also said: "Neither do I condemn you. Go and sin no more."[16]

What should we do with all this?

Well, for one thing, thank the Holy Spirit that He is jealous enough to crowd you against the wall. Give thanks to God that He cares enough about you to not allow you to wander off the narrow but joy-filled pathway of holiness and true abundant living.

When you feel overwhelmed by the circumstances of life, ask Him to show you what He's doing. He wants to get your attention. He will not allow you to be defeated by your enemies or your own wayward human impulses.

Then, once you hear His voice saying, "Come," return to Him. Go back. He will bring the power of the cleansing blood of Jesus that not only carries away the stains of sin but also filters out whatever is toxic to this new life. He will identify the hidden works of darkness. He will dissolve bondages. He will not permit you to continue to grieve the Spirit. He is your permanent helper.

He who has come to help you see your life rebuilt will also come to see your life advanced into His purposes. He will respond to your every prayer, and He will nurture your soul, reminding you of His loving character and His clear truth.

The Holy Spirit will restore, establish, strengthen, and settle you, today and every day of the rest of your life.[17]

Jack Hayford, who passed away while I was writing this book, was the longtime pastor of the Church on the Way in Van Nuys, California. He later served as chancellor of King's University (formerly King's College and Seminary) and was a man I greatly respected. As a way of honoring his legacy as a respected authority on the Holy Spirit, I added this brief excerpt from his book Rebuilding the Real You: The Definitive Guide to the Holy Spirit's Work in Your Life, *which was the best seller of all the Jack Hayford books I had the privilege of publishing.*

—STEPHEN E. STRANG

Introduction

THE WORLD IS UPSIDE DOWN

S OMEONE HAS SAID that living the Christian life is not *difficult*; it is *impossible*—that is, *without the power of the Holy Spirit.*

Never has that statement been truer than today. It's never been easy to be a Christian, but now segments of society are openly hostile to anything religious. And the culture is pulling us down, luring our children away from God, and worse. It's as if the onslaught will never end.

Even though we live in what many believe is the greatest country in the world, there's a feeling almost everywhere that something is seriously wrong in America. Morality is on a downward spiral. Pandemics and riots have people living in fear. A new expression—wokeness—is now part of the national lexicon to describe the extreme liberal views that have infiltrated every institution of our culture.

It seems the world is upside down. The Judeo-Christian values our nation was built on, such as the sanctity of life and individual rights, are eroding before our eyes.

The days we live in are dark, and they seem to be getting only darker. Yet there is a power so great it can help you not only survive but also thrive in this crazy world. It's a power that comes from God Almighty through the third person of the Godhead, the Holy Spirit. It's the power that took the teachings of a young carpenter from Galilee, turned upside down the most ruthless empire of its era, and overcame the paganism that went with it.

Two thousand years after the Day of Pentecost, when the Holy Spirit was poured out and the church was birthed, this power can still give you joy and peace, release miracles, and make you victorious no matter what. Even though this power seemed all but dormant for almost two millennia and some Christians say it ceased after the days of the apostles, I believe it has been restored to the church and is currently at work in the earth, just as the Bible says. It's available today to help you understand the future, have faith to believe for miracles, and experience unspeakable peace no matter your circumstances. Understanding some simple truths can unlock this power and help you navigate the chaos that I call an upside-down world.

My hope is that *Spirit-Led Living in an Upside-Down World* will help you experience this power and know the Holy Spirit intimately. I've come to realize through my study of Scripture and personal experience that the Holy Spirit's power is there for the asking—even if others misuse or ignore it. It's there to give you victory over the forces of evil, help you stand strong when the culture wants you to compromise, and provide tools to help you prosper in spirit, soul, and body.

But this book is more than an intellectual exercise. This power is not found through logic, so I can't persuade you. It's something you must experience in the depths of your soul. This power is spiritual, which is why we need an awakening like those that have come throughout history at critical times like the ones in which we live.

The church must be revived. There must be a spiritual renewal, and this happens when individuals are convicted of sin, experience the power of the Holy Spirit, and get so excited they turn their own worlds upside down! Some people get so zealous others accuse them of being so heavenly minded that they are no earthly good! That's too bad. Each of us must be that heavenly minded!

I've heard church folk joke that when some people receive the Baptism of the Holy Spirit, their doctrine changes and they get so on fire they need to be locked in a closet until they settle down! Actually, the opposite is true. Those staid people should get some of this power.

But what about you? Are there things in your life with which you are not satisfied? Are you trying to live for God, but you continue to battle unhealthy behaviors or habitual sins that have dogged you for years? Maybe you are disappointed with your life, career, marriage, or health. Maybe your walk with God is not all you dreamed it would be.

Many are discouraged, battling disease, or in need of deliverance from addictions. You may be one who needs a financial miracle, restoration of your marriage, or the spiritual return of a wayward child. If so, this book is for you.

As Christians, we believe the Bible gives us power to change and that we should follow what it teaches. The culture doesn't agree. People want us to think we are wrong and they are right. They call this gaslighting, which is pressure to think we're the crazy ones and others are right. Gaslighting has now become part of the woke culture. It's so prevalent, in fact, that the *Merriam-Webster* dictionary designated it the Word of the Year for 2022. We must understand this so we don't conform to what an unbelieving world tells us to believe and how it tells us to live.

While struggles exist, there is a realm in the Spirit where we can live above the problems. There is a place in God where we can experience the power of the Holy Spirit. That is what this book is about. It is to help you move from where you are to where you can be in Christ. Of course, we never really arrive spiritually. But as we grow spiritually, we can begin to soar like eagles—not stay around the barnyard with all the turkeys, or, worse yet, wallow in the mire like a bunch of pigs.

THERE IS HOPE

With God's help, you do have the power to change. No matter where you are in your Christian walk—whether you're a new believer or someone who has followed Jesus for a long time—there *is* hope that you can experience the power of the Holy Spirit and attain your full destiny in Christ.

You might know me as a Christian journalist, or you may have never heard of me and just found this book. It doesn't matter. This book is not about me. I am just opening my heart and life to tell my story and inspire you to experience the Holy Spirit in a deeper way that improves your life.

I'm the first to admit I don't have all the answers and am continuing to learn. Writing this book has forced me to dig deep to define these truths, and I found I grew as a result. I'm neither a theologian nor a minister. I'm a journalist and businessman who has had more than my share of problems over the course of my life. But I can truthfully say that my life in the Spirit has been as the apostle Paul wrote: "exceedingly abundantly beyond all that we ask or imagine."[1] And if I can experience that, you can too.

I remember the testimony of Fred Price, who gravitated to the Word of Faith movement because when he came into Pentecostalism, he heard talk of power but didn't see it in action. I heard him say that life in the Spirit doesn't remove us from the sinful environment around us any more than using an oxygen tank when we scuba dive keeps us from getting wet. But just as scuba gear allows us to exist in an underwater environment that ordinarily would kill us, so the Holy Spirit enables us to live in this sinful world without being ensnared by it.

That's what gives me hope for all of us living in this upside-down world right now. I sincerely believe that what I write in this book will help you connect with God in new, fresh ways; be a powerful influence on your family, friends, and community; and deepen your faith so you're able to move mountains. Plus, I hope this book motivates you to allow the Spirit to uncover your heart's deepest desires and empower you to overcome the challenges keeping you from fulfilling your dreams and purpose in life.

But there's more. One of my favorite verses says we are children of God if we're led by His Spirit.[2] So get ready for the ride of your life. The Holy Spirit might lead you in the craziest ways, such as when He told Philip to go to the Gaza road, where he met the Ethiopian eunuch, a divine encounter that led to the gospel going to that part of the world.[3] Life in the Spirit is a God adventure; if you let Him, He will help you accomplish things you never thought possible.

Many people are bored with life, and others live in fear of COVID-19, mass shootings, civil unrest—the list goes on and on. But it doesn't need to be that way. Don't be discouraged. Instead, realize that getting to know the Holy Spirit will be the most fulfilling thing you'll ever do. I want this book to not only show you how to get to know Him but also inspire your faith.

Let me repeat: No matter how bad things seem to get in the world, there's a power to help believers overcome. It's the power of the Holy

Spirit. This is something you won't read about in the mainstream media or even hear preached in most Protestant churches. Even many whose theology includes believing the Holy Spirit is still at work in the world, just as He was in the first century, don't understand this power or how to appropriate it to help them navigate life. Yet this wonderful power helps us be victorious through life's difficulties and overcome evil.

As a journalist, I have covered the work of the Holy Spirit worldwide. But this is not just an occupation for me. Long before I ever wrote about any of this, God was doing a work in my life, teaching me and forming me into the man I am today. From a powerful church-camp experience where I received the Baptism in the Holy Spirit to crying out to God as a college student running from the call of God on my life, I have come to know the Holy Spirit. He became real to me, and I saw the power He gave me to overcome sin in my life and that got me so excited that I was witnessing to people on my university campus and discipling other students.

All these years later I wonder if what happened is exciting enough for a book. I mean, my experience wasn't like David Wilkerson's in *The Cross and the Switchblade* or John Sherrill's in *They Speak With Other Tongues*. Or was it? Was my experience simply the path God chose for me, knowing it would cause me to trust Him in a way only the Holy Spirit could empower me to do? Thankfully, I've been able to rub elbows with, interview, and know many notable Christian leaders from the 1970s to today. Wilkerson and Sherrill were two who had a powerful impact on my life, and there are many others you will meet in this book. I've learned from them and been inspired.

But as wonderful as that has been, it also let me see (often up close and personal) their weaknesses and shortcomings—something that could have discouraged me many times. My longtime mentor Jamie Buckingham was open about the struggles in his life and ministry that resulted in heartbreak and scandal. Yet it was that crushing that led to him being open to the Holy Spirit, and his relationship with the Holy Spirit totally changed him, to the point that for more than twenty-five years, until his untimely death, some considered him the conscience of the Charismatic movement.

I remember some highly publicized ministry scandals. In some cases, I knew the people involved personally. As I questioned how to cover those events in *Charisma,* I knew I must not only help Christians learn from the scandals but also explain to an unbelieving world that those who pursue the Holy Spirit aren't perfect.

So why write a book like this now? Most readers would agree that something is seriously wrong in our world today. As my good friend Mario Murillo put it in his book *It's Our Turn Now,*

> Those in power in our nation operate with arrogant impunity. They no longer hide their intentions. They use their power to destroy anyone perceived as an enemy of their agenda or who threatens their power.
>
> The media is a malicious mouthpiece of these tyrants. The media has sold its soul to radicalism and will tell whatever lie it takes to protect its agenda.
>
> What about our children? Woke leaders have made it clear that parents should not be in charge of their children's upbringing in our nation because the federal government has seized that role. I fear that teachers have turned into activists, classrooms have turned into indoctrination camps, and what was once education has turned into nothing more than government grooming.
>
> And don't even get me started on whether we'll ever have free elections again! If our current leaders hang on to power in the next election, they will know they can take tyranny to the next level. At that point, everyone who has posted something on social media against Wokeness will be hunted down.[4]

So what are believers supposed to do? We can almost get discouraged just thinking about it. Yet those who follow Jesus and are led by God's Spirit must find a way to live amid this madness. At one level, we must survive, especially when governments are talking about implanting microchips they can use to track people and force us to become a cashless society. Years ago, I couldn't imagine how people all over the world could be made to take what the Book of Revelation calls "the mark of the beast." Now I see that it could happen with the use of microchips. And we saw how passively much of the population went along with "the shot," or the so-called COVID-19 vaccines, even though the vaccines had not proved to prevent the virus and there are many credible reports of the shots being dangerous and killing many who received them.[5]

To make matters worse, next came the "great reset," where global elites began working to establish a one-world government under the guise of economic recovery after global COVID-19 shutdowns.[6] What was once considered conspiracy theory became reality before our eyes, leaving many to wonder if we are catapulting toward the end of time.

In schools, some want to teach young children that it's OK to think they are boys even if they were born girls, or vice versa. And this isn't just in America but in the entire Western world as the culture rejects the Christian principles that previously defeated paganism. Now it seems the culture is going in the opposite direction, as Jonathan Cahn pointed out in his book *The Return of the Gods.*

Some of this has infiltrated the church. Previously conservative congregations are now espousing woke doctrines that are actually communist principles. And even though we have religious freedom and freedom of assembly, we saw how quickly churches were closed during the COVID pandemic while liquor stores, abortion clinics, and in some states even marijuana dispensaries were allowed to remain open.[7] This leads me to one conclusion: we need the Holy Spirit's power in our lives today more than ever before.

EXPERIENCING TRUE POWER

I have been a Christian for most of my life and was taught to believe in miracles and the literal truth of the Word of God. Yet growing up, I saw sincere, godly Pentecostals talk about power but never experience it, much as my friend Fred Price witnessed. They believed the Bible says physical healing is for today, yet they rarely experienced healing or saw miracles.

In the 1960s, as political figures were assassinated and riots broke out in the streets, a vast outpouring of the Holy Spirit was under way in mainline churches and among Roman Catholics. This is also when thousands of hippies and drug addicts were turned on to Jesus in a revival that became known as the Jesus movement.

This all happened as I was coming of age. I remember how high-energy the new Charismatic movement was as people began to understand God's power and leave dead churches. These believers were so passionate all they talked about was Jesus and how He wanted everyone to have this wonderful experience.

These new Charismatics were, as I remember, just learning about healing, deliverance, and how to walk in faith, believe God, and get a vision for what He wanted them to do. Around that time, I started *Charisma* magazine.

At the time, I was disillusioned with the legalism and small-mindedness I saw among Pentecostals. I was a newspaper reporter making less than $10,000 a year. Yet as my faith grew, I experienced the power of the Holy Spirit and developed a vision for my life to encourage the Christian community to experience the power of the Holy Spirit to radically change their world.

I had the privilege of getting to know many national and global leaders of Pentecostal and Charismatic ministries. As a result, I've devoted my career to reporting on what the Holy Spirit is doing in the world.

I've lived long enough to see the rise of the discipleship movement, the Word of Faith movement, the prophetic movement, and the mushrooming of independent Charismatic churches in African American and other minority communities. In the 1990s, stadiums were full of men influenced by the Promise Keepers men's movement. If you were in the Pentecostal movement in the nineties, you probably remember the revivals that went on for several years, including what critics called the "laughing revival" led by Rodney Howard-Browne in Lakeland, Florida; the Brownsville Revival (also called the Pensacola Outpouring) in Pensacola, Florida; and the Toronto Blessing in Canada.

In the mid-1990s, Hillsong worship burst onto the scene, and a new, modern form of praise and worship infiltrated most Protestant churches. Yet the culture seemed unchanged. If anything, it got worse.

Other times in history have been as bad as, and worse than, today. Yet the church survived; people got saved, lived Christian lives, tried to influence others, and often had victories. It's like we see in Hebrews 11, which lists the who's who of the Old Testament, men and women "who through faith subdued kingdoms, administered justice, obtained promises, stopped the mouths of lions, quenched the violence of fire, escaped the edge of the sword, out of weakness were made strong, became valiant in fighting, and turned the armies of foreign enemies to flight. Women received their dead raised to life again."[8]

But Hebrews 11 goes on to say: "Others were tortured and did not accept deliverance, so that they might obtain a better resurrection. Still others had trials of mocking and scourging, and even chains and imprisonment. They were stoned, they were sawn in two, were tempted, were slain with the sword. They wandered around in sheepskins and goatskins, while destitute, afflicted, and tormented. The world was not worthy of them....These all have obtained a good report through faith, but they did not receive the promise."[9]

Every believer lives with this tension. We can experience wonderful victory and yet also have terrible things happen. In good times and bad we must have the power of the Holy Spirit. We don't know what life will hand us. We must be ready for anything.

Since you're reading this book, I assume you're looking for answers. We know that everyone, no matter how blessed they seem, faces major problems in life. I hope you also know that those whose lives may not seem to be blessed can have an abiding joy and peace that come only from the Lord. Each of us must follow the Lord as He is revealed in His Word through all the seasons of life. Yet we need pastors, mentors, coaches, and brothers and sisters in Christ to help us navigate life's ups and downs and grow in the Spirit.

Let me assume those roles as you read this book. I hope not only to paint a picture of how bad things are but to inspire you to believe the Holy Spirit can give you discernment about all the current events leading to the end of time. Come on a journey with me as I share my understanding of what Spirit-led living means and stories from my life and others who have experienced the power of the Holy Spirit.

In many ways this has been the driving force behind our company's publishing more than a thousand issues of *Charisma* and other magazines, and more than two thousand books. That merely says I haven't just researched this topic in a library, but rather, out of those millions of words, I've tried to distill the very best into what you're reading now. The examples in this book can help us make sense of and navigate this upside-down world and discover what Spirit-led living looks like today.

This book full of spiritual advice I hope will improve every area of your life—from your relationships to your personal sense of fulfillment—and help you find an even deeper spirituality. To that end, I do a deep dive into what spiritual gifts are. Have they faded away, or are they operating more strongly in today's world than at any other time in history? Are there signs all around us today pointing to the end-time? And if so, what can we do to be ready and occupy until He comes? How can we help prepare others spiritually, financially, and practically for what lies ahead?

How have past Pentecostal and Charismatic movements shaped the Spirit-led community today? Is there a coming revival, and are we prepared for it in our personal spiritual lives?

I wrote this book because I'm concerned about the condition of the world and I see Christians becoming discouraged. I have sometimes been discouraged too, which has forced me to seek God for more power to navigate all the changes in the culture. I'm not writing theories. I've lived this. And I've learned it's possible to experience God's power to have a more fulfilled life and overcome spiritual attacks. I have a burning desire to let the world know that the Holy Spirit can help people survive and thrive spiritually, even when the world is upside down.

—STEPHEN E. STRANG
ST. AUGUSTINE, FLORIDA
DECEMBER 16, 2022

Chapter 1

FOLLOW A PATH DIFFERENT FROM THE WORLD'S

WE LIVE IN a world where evil is called good and good is called evil. Right is considered wrong, and wrong is considered right. Everything is being turned inside out and upside down. But if you have a personal relationship with God and are being led by His Spirit, you can stand strong and thrive, even in an upside-down world.

What do I mean when I say we can be led by the Holy Spirit? Spirit-led living is following a different path from what the world says you should pursue. It's having different values, goals, and measurements for success from those dictated by the world. Spirit-led living is freedom from guilt, condemnation, and shame. It is boldly stepping into the future without fear.

Spirit-led living is knowing who you are in Christ and having confidence that the Holy Spirit within you is greater than anything you face in this world. It is knowing God intimately, which results in learning to hear His voice. Spirit-led living is following God's leading so you can fulfill every bit of potential He has designed for your life. And Spirit-led living is the peace of knowing that no matter what following Him costs, it will be worth it.

Living in the Spirit isn't easy, but it's not something we must accomplish by ourselves. The Holy Spirit fuels us by His power. He gives us spiritual gifts that enable us to gain victory in life and minister to the world. And as we surrender to Him, His fruit becomes more and more evident in our lives.

I do not want to do *anything* without the presence of the Holy Spirit. Living a Spirit-led life is the key to moving forward successfully in this upside-down world and accessing the fulfilling life God has planned for us.

If I were addressing a group of young people eager to progress in life and the things of the Spirit, I would explain that when I say "Spirit led," I'm not speaking of mere human intuition or gut instinct. Mood, diet, and even hormones can influence these natural, sometimes helpful, prompts. This makes them undependable at best, and they may even be misleading. Rather, being Spirit led is being guided by the Spirit of God, the third person of the Trinity, the navigator abiding within the core of the born-again believer.

We *must* be Holy Spirit led. When we give the Holy Spirit full rein in our lives, He transforms us.

- The Holy Spirit helps us be more than we are. We find many biblical examples of this: the Spirit turned a shepherd boy into a king, a murderer into a deliverer, and fishermen into disciples.

- The Holy Spirit helps us say more than we know. When He anointed Peter, who had denied knowing Jesus just seven weeks before, three thousand who heard him speak were saved and baptized.

- The Holy Spirit helps us do more than we can. We accomplish far more with Him than our natural abilities enable us to do.[1]

You may ask, "How do I become a person who is led by the Holy Spirit?" It starts with getting to know the Holy Spirit the same way you would get to know a friend. Think of your relationships with friends or your spouse. How did you get to know them? By spending time and talking with them. To get to know the Holy Spirit, you spend quiet time waiting for Him to communicate with you in your spirit. He desires to commune with you and to lead and guide you in all things.

Being led by the Spirit isn't something we do passively; it's a conscious decision we make to be different from a world that thinks those who live according to the Bible are backward and out of step. It's a choice to trust God's Word and stand against the woke culture that rejects what Scripture says about marriage, sexuality, and even gender. It means staying married and raising your kids according to biblical values, and having integrity in all your relationships, both personal and professional. It means speaking up on moral issues and not just going with the flow. It means not being intimidated into silence about transgenderism or drag queen story times at libraries. And it means realizing that reaching others for Christ is our main responsibility.

Being led by the Spirit isn't a matter of being conservative, and it's not a political position. I use those examples to convey that when we live by the power of the Holy Spirit, we don't just go along to get along. We live a different way.

Decades ago the culture at least had a facade of religiosity. It was good for business to go to the right church and make people think you were a good person. Of course, there was a lot of hypocrisy, and Christianity in those days was very shallow. But today the tide has turned. It's not easy to walk a different way when the culture not only doesn't support Christianity but pulls us away from God instead of toward Him.

This happens in every aspect of life—entertainment, education, government, and business, where there are so many ways to compromise and be dishonest. The family is being shattered, and even the church is becoming more and more reprobate. Some denominations embrace homosexuality in the name of diversity. Even some evangelical churches are pushing ungodly woke doctrines such as critical race theory and gender fluidity, even though the Bible clearly says God created us male and female.

How do we not only survive but thrive in such an upside-down world? It is only by the power of the Holy Spirit, and this book is a road map to help you discover what that means. But first we must get to know who

Transformed by the Power of the Spirit

Although I was raised in a fine home, supported and loved by wonderful Jewish parents, I had become a wretched human being as a teen. I started getting high at fourteen years old and was shooting heroin at fifteen. I stole money from my own father on several occasions and, of course, lied about it to his face. I caused my parents untold grief and pain.

I had such a reputation for wickedness that the first time I attended a Pentecostal church service, in August 1971 at the age of sixteen, a young woman who knew me from high school wrote this in her diary: "Antichrist comes to church." Although the people were very loving to me, I left the church with no thought of ever returning. But those believers started praying for me regularly. And suddenly, instead of being proud of my sins, I was tormented by them. This was the convicting power of the Holy Spirit.

Then, on November 12, 1971, I agreed to attend another service, where I responded to the altar call to receive Jesus. But I was not yet willing to repent. I was planning to smoke a large quantity of PCP that night and then shoot a large quantity of cocaine. So I prayed, "God, if You don't want me to do this, let it have no effect on me!" And that's exactly what happened.

the Holy Spirit is as well as what the Bible says about His power, His gifts, and the fruit of walking with Him.

WHO IS THE HOLY SPIRIT?

The first step to becoming Spirit led is to have the right understanding of the Holy Spirit. Many people, even some Christians, view the Holy Spirit as an impersonal force that represents God. But the Bible describes Him in personal terms, not as a mere concept that represents spiritual power or God's presence. So exactly what or who is the Holy Spirit?

The editors of the *FireBible* wrote that throughout God's Word, the Spirit is revealed as a distinct individual. He is a divine person, they wrote, who is fully God and has personal characteristics all His own, which means He thinks, wills, and has the capacity to love and enjoy personal companionship. He was sent by the Father to bring believers into a close, personal relationship with Jesus.[2]

We were made by God with a built-in desire to have a relationship

I did all the drugs I had (enough for several people), my heart started to pound, and then nothing. The drugs had zero effect. I knew then that something was going on.

For the next six weeks, I lived in constant conflict, going to church one day and using drugs the next. Then, at a service on December 17, 1971, I received a deep revelation of God's love for me. I saw myself covered in filth from head to toe; then Jesus washed me clean and put white robes on me. But I kept going back and playing in the mud! At that moment, I told the Lord, "I will never put a needle in my arm again," and I was free from that moment on. Two days later I said I would never get high again. By His grace, I never went back!

Today, by the Lord's mercy, I have earned a doctorate degree in Near Eastern Languages and Literatures from New York University. (Yes, my testimony is literally from LSD to PhD.) As the man who once huffed diesel gas to get high, I have now taught at eight leading seminaries, written more than forty books, and contributed to prestigious academic works such as *The Oxford Dictionary of Jewish Religion*. I have also preached the gospel around the globe and trained thousands of ministry-school students. This is the transforming power of the Holy Spirit. It is as dramatic as it is lasting.
—MICHAEL L. BROWN, PHD, HOST, *ASKDRBROWN* RADIO SHOW

with Him, and Jesus came to earth to give us that opportunity. Jesus in turn gave us the Holy Spirit to fulfill that desire. The editors of the *FireBible* go on to write:

> Because He is God, the Holy Spirit is omnipresent (everywhere at the same time), omniscient (all-knowing), and omnipotent (all-powerful). He is also loving, forgiving, merciful and persistent. When people sense things about God "in their hearts" or consciences, it is often the work of the Spirit prompting them toward God or leading them into a closer relationship with God. In light of these truths, we should treat Him as a Person and understand that He is the infinite living God, worthy of our worship, love, and surrender.[3]

Before Jesus ascended to heaven, He promised to send "another Counselor, that He may be with you forever."[4] The Holy Spirit was poured out on the Day of Pentecost and now lives inside every believer, convicting us of sin and enabling us to live holy lives.[5] He imparts God's love and reveals God's truth. He fills us, frees us from sin, empowers us to witness, equips us to fight Satan, provides comfort and encouragement, helps us pray, enables us to worship, gives us special gifts, and develops His fruit in our lives.

THE FRUIT OF THE SPIRIT

The one word that differentiates Christianity from the other world religions is *love*. Other religions demand rituals and behaviors that follow a rigid set of rules. But when one is welcomed into the family of God, it is His love that invites us. We love Him because He first loved us.[6]

A favorite chorus we used to sing in the early days of the Charismatic movement was one titled "They'll Know We Are Christians by Our Love." That's no easy feat. As humans, we have a wicked nature. We are hurt, and then we hurt others. So how does our nature change so we love? The answer is the Holy Spirit.

I love the way evangelist Kenneth Copeland puts it in his *Word of Faith Study Bible*: "Love is not a feeling. Love is a Person. God is love.[7] He has faith, but He is love. Love is a spiritual force and along with the other spiritual forces, the fruit of the re-created human spirit abides in every born-again believer by the Holy Spirit." Love "moved Jesus to heal the sick, raise the dead, cast out devils and walk on water. And it was the mighty power that raised Him from the dead."

He adds this encouraging statement: "When you settle it in your heart and make the quality decision to live by this God kind of love, there is no demon in hell that can stop you because the power of God's love in you *never* fails!"[8]

In fact, when the apostle Paul lists the fruit of the Spirit in Galatians, the first one is love, followed by "joy, peace, patience, gentleness, goodness, faith, meekness, and self-control."[9] This is what Spirit-led living looks like. If we become mature, Spirit-led Christians, our lives will exhibit these traits.

Respected Bible teacher Fuchsia Pickett was a dear friend, mentor, and prolific writer. Toward the end of her life, I had the privilege of publishing several of her books. She wrote that she believed Paul used the singular verb *is* to describe the fruit of the Spirit because "love is the single channel through which the fruit of the Spirit flows."

She said the other eight characteristics listed are all different facets of love, which she believes Paul intended as *the* fruit of the Spirit. "So the fruit of love works in our lives and manifests its beauty in eight different ways," Pickett wrote, emphasizing that these eight traits, borne out of love, are the evidence that a Christian is living life by the power of the Holy Spirit.[10]

D. L. Moody, the American evangelist who founded Moody Bible Institute, also described the eight subsequent characteristics in Galatians as flowing from the first one, love:

> Joy is love exulting; peace is love reposing; long-suffering is love untiring; gentleness is love enduring; goodness is love in action; faith is love on the battlefield; meekness is love under discipline; temperance is love in training.[11]

Pickett explained that the fruit of love cannot be produced by our efforts. It is the result of the love of God being "shed abroad in our hearts by the Holy Spirit who has been given to us."[12] This love produced by the Holy Spirit is much more than human affection. According to Pickett, "It is God's very character, who He is."

Pickett wrote that in the same way Paul clearly taught that we should not administer the gifts of the Spirit without love—going so far as to say those who operate in the gifts of the Spirit without love are *nothing*[13]— neither can we truly display the remaining fruit of the Spirit in our lives without love. She wrote:

> Among all the words in the Bible, this simple word *love* stands alone as the supreme description of the very essence of the Christian life. Love binds all other virtues of the fruit of the Spirit together. It is the common denominator of Christian character. One cannot love completely and fail to cultivate the other

virtues. To be filled with the Holy Spirit and display the fruit of the Spirit in our lives is to be filled with love.[14]

Jack Hayford, the longtime pastor of the Church on the Way and later the chancellor of King's University, was a man I greatly respected. For many years, he had a mentoring role in my life. I spent time in his home, and he visited mine. I even had the privilege of serving on the university's board of trustees. I dedicated this book to his memory.

Hayford elaborated on the fruit of the Spirit in the *Spirit-Filled Life Bible*, saying the Holy Spirit "removes abrasive qualities from the character of one under His control."[15] He went on to say that Spirit-led living is a call to character more than to the Charismatic gifts. In fact, all believers are called to exhibit these nine characteristics—especially when our patience is tried or the pressures of life pile up.

"These virtues are characterized as fruit in contrast to 'works,'" he writes.[16] So only the Holy Spirit can produce them and not our own efforts. When the Spirit fully controls the life of a believer, He produces these graces: the first three (love, joy, and peace) concern our attitude toward God. The next three (longsuffering, kindness, and goodness) apply to how we deal with others. And the final three (faithfulness, gentleness, and self-control) have to do with our Christian conduct.

Jesus told us to judge a tree by its fruit. That means people will know we love the Lord and are empowered by the Holy Spirit when they see the fruit of the Spirit in our lives.

THE PERSON AND WORK OF THE HOLY SPIRIT

For the serious student of the Bible, it can be exciting to try to find the Holy Spirit in every book of the Bible. In the very first verses of Genesis, we find the Holy Spirit hovering over the earth. He moves through the creation of the universe and every form of life upon the earth, breathing the very breath of life into humanity and forming us in His image.

The first few sentences of the Bible say, "The Spirit of God was moving over the surface of the water" and that God said, "Let there be light."[17] In other words, the Holy Spirit was present from the start.

We find the Holy Spirit throughout the Old Testament. For example, the Spirit of God came upon these men:

- Joshua: "The LORD said to Moses, 'Take Joshua the son of Nun, a man in whom is the Spirit, and lay your hand on him.'"[18]

- Gideon: "The Spirit of the LORD enveloped Gideon. He blew a ram's horn trumpet, and the Abiezrites assembled behind him."[19]

- Samson: "The Spirit of the LORD began to move upon him....Then the Spirit of the LORD came mightily upon him, and though unarmed, he tore the lion in two as one might tear a young goat in two. However, he did not tell his father and his mother what he had done."[20]

- Saul: "And it happened, that when he turned his back to go from Samuel, that God gave him another heart. And all those signs came to pass that day. When they came to the hill, a group of prophets met him. And the Spirit of God came upon him, and he prophesied among them."[21]

All these men were granted power the moment they needed it so they were able to do more than they could without the Holy Spirit. Being empowered by the Spirit of God allowed them to operate at an exceptional level, far beyond their natural abilities. But during the Old Testament time period, the Holy Spirit produced only a transitory effect—when He came upon someone, the power was there, but when He left, the power left with Him.

In the New Testament, Jesus told His followers to wait in Jerusalem for the promise of the Father. He told them what they were waiting for: the *Baptism of the Holy Spirit*. Jesus said, "You shall be baptized with the Holy Spirit not many days from now."[22]

Think about it. The last thing Jesus said to His disciples before ascending to heaven was, "You shall receive power when the Holy Spirit comes upon you. And you shall be My witnesses in Jerusalem, and in all Judea and Samaria, and to the ends of the earth."[23]

After Jesus told His disciples to wait in Jerusalem, the Scripture says 120 people did so for fifty days after Passover—about ten days after Jesus ascended to heaven. That day—the Day of Pentecost, which the church celebrates every year—was the birth of what we now call the Christian church.

In his classic work on the Holy Spirit, *They Speak With Other Tongues*, John Sherrill writes,

> The promise of some kind of new relationship with the Holy Spirit weaves like a thread through the New Testament....The Jews, for a while, thought that John the Baptist might be the promised Messiah. But John told them, "There cometh one mightier than I after me, the latchet of whose shoes I am not worthy to stoop down and unloose. I have indeed," he said, "baptized you with water; but he shall baptize you with the Holy Ghost."[24] The baptism with the Holy Spirit, John was saying, would be the distinguishing mark of the Messiah.[25]

Toward the end of His earthly ministry, Christ began emphasizing the Holy Spirit "would be the Comforter of the disciples, standing by them in trouble, leading them into truth, taking Christ's place when He was gone."[26]

Sherrill then recounts what happened on the Day of Pentecost and goes on to explain:

> From this infilling with the Holy Spirit the Church dates its beginning. It was new, small, surrounded with enemies, and yet this young Church had power: to heal, to convince, to spread. The churches that evolved with the passing of time kept in their traditions a vestige of this early dependence on a specific filling with the Holy Spirit as the source of their power. Roman Catholics, Lutherans, Episcopalians all preserve, in their confirmation services, the idea that it is at this moment that the

confirmee receives a special gift of power to be an effective Christian.

But groups like the Wesleyan Methodists and the Holiness people glimpsed the fact that this ceremony of confirmation was often just a ritual, and often failed really to impart power. They stressed the baptism as an experience that did not come automatically but had to be sought over and over, if necessary, until the Christian was certain he or she had been filled with the Holy Spirit.[27]

Sherrill says throughout the second half of the nineteenth century, interest grew in an experience with the Holy Spirit sometime after conversion. This school of thought set Charles Parham and his students on a quest to discover if such an encounter with the Holy Spirit was possible and if any evidence of such an experience existed. I'll discuss what happened to Parham and his students later.

For now, let's revisit the question "Who is the Holy Spirit?" Theologians say the Holy Spirit is the third person of the Godhead: Father, Son, and Holy Spirit. The early church fathers settled this doctrine in AD 325 at the first Council of Nicea.

Just because the Holy Spirit is the third person of the Trinity does not mean He is less important than the Father and the Son. The *FireBible* editors have this to say about the importance of the Holy Spirit's role:

> Many Christians have not even considered how different things would have been had there not been the presence of the Holy Spirit from the very beginning. Without the Holy Spirit there would be no creation, no universe, no human race.[28] Without the Holy Spirit there would be no Bible,[29] no New Testament[30] and no power to effectively communicate the message about Christ.[31] Without the Holy Spirit there would be no way to have faith in God, no way to experience spiritual salvation or renewal, no way for Jesus' followers to live in holiness (i.e., moral purity, spiritual wholeness, separation from evil and dedication to God). In fact, there would be no Christians at all in the world.[32]

The Holy Spirit is so important that ever since He was poured out on the Day of Pentecost, He has been ready and waiting to give help to every single Christian who has ever lived. When the Holy Spirit lives within a human being, that person becomes a new creation, a new being. Jesus called this experience being born again. When you are born again, you are born by God's Spirit into a new family—the family of God. You are no longer only a human being. I like to think you have a new DNA, a brand-new identity. You are now a child of God.

Someone might ask, "Well, aren't all people God's children?" In one sense, yes. All humans are created by God. We are made in the image and likeness of God. But all people are not God's children in a *personal* way, as individuals.

The Old Testament refers to God as Father only fifteen times. Often this reference as Father is in a corporate way; God is the Father of Israel. God as our Father in a personal way is realized only through God's Son, Jesus Christ.

The good news of Jesus Christ is so simple that a child can hear the message, receive His gift of salvation, and be born again. God sent His Son to shed His blood and die for the sins of every person who ever lived or ever will live. Jesus rose from the dead in victory, and He is alive. You are saved when you confess your faith in Jesus and receive Him as your Lord and Savior. You might say, "It can't be that simple. You don't know all I've done." It's not easy; Jesus paid the supreme price for it. But it *is* simple. First John 1:9 tells us, "If we confess our sins, He is faithful and just to forgive us our sins and cleanse us from all unrighteousness."

If you haven't made Jesus your Lord, I encourage you to read appendix A, which will explain how you can receive the gift of salvation. That's where Spirit-led living starts because, as I've said, the Holy Spirit comes to live within us at salvation. But we can experience an even deeper infilling called the Baptism of the Holy Spirit. This equips us to live in the fullness of His power and begin an intimate relationship with Him through which we learn to hear His voice, as we'll discuss in the next chapter.

LIVING IT OUT

Read Galatians 5:22–23:

> But the fruit of the Spirit is love, joy, peace, patience, gentleness, goodness, faith, meekness and self-control; against such there is no law.

Think about it:

1. What does Kenneth Copeland mean when he says, "Love is not a feeling. Love is a Person. God is love"?

2. How does the following statement by D. L. Moody apply to your life: "Joy is love exulting; peace is love reposing; long-suffering is love untiring; gentleness is love enduring; goodness is love in action; faith is love on the battlefield; meekness is love under discipline; temperance is love in training"?

3. In the same way Paul clearly taught that we should not administer the gifts of the Spirit without love, how does love bind all the other virtues of the fruit of the Spirit together, as Fuchsia Pickett wrote in this chapter?

4. How does the Holy Spirit help us be more than we are? If He turned a shepherd boy into a king, a murderer into a deliverer, and fishermen into disciples, how does He help us become what we must become despite our limitations and backgrounds?

Chapter 2

LEARN TO HEAR GOD'S VOICE

MILLIONS HAVE EXPERIENCED the power of the Holy Spirit since the Day of Pentecost, when tongues of fire rested on those in the Upper Room and the disciples began to speak in a heavenly prayer language that made onlookers think they were drunk at nine o'clock in the morning. In his sermon in Acts 2, Peter said they were witnessing what Joel prophesied: the Spirit of God was being poured out on all flesh, and the sons and daughters of Israel were prophesying.[1] But there was more to the outpouring of the Holy Spirit than just what people saw and heard. A power caused three thousand to believe that day and begin a movement that spread worldwide and continues today.

The Roman Empire tried to crush that odd Jewish sect as it had quashed many others before it. But they were unsuccessful. The Roman Empire is gone, replaced by the Christian church, which exorcised the paganism of the Romans and the Greeks before them. Today, Christianity is the dominant religion in both Italy and Greece. While the Spirit's power seemed to ebb and flow and even go underground for generations, the Holy Spirit has been at work throughout history and has made Himself evident in our generation.

God wants nothing more than to pour out His Spirit on our sons and daughters, no matter how much it seems evil is increasing around us. Today's world is not that unlike the pagan world of biblical times. Babies were sacrificed to Molech in places such as Caesarea Philippi, a region Jesus often visited and the site where He asked His disciples, "Who do you say that I am?"[2]

Sexual perversion and temple prostitution were common in the known world, even in pious Israel. And if contending with pagans weren't bad enough, the religious people of the day persecuted the early believers. It reminds me of Christian denominations today that not only deny the gifts and manifestations of the Holy Spirit but hound out of their midst anyone who dares to believe or teach about them.

And today, with the advance of the Left and a one-world government, it seems we are racing toward the end of time. It's enough to discourage even the strongest believer. But it's not about us. We had no choice but to be born at this time. We don't control world events. All we can do is trust in God, believe His Word, and experience the amazing power of His Spirit, which not only will help us stand up to and get through all this evil but also will help us experience joy and peace in the midst of trials, as the apostle Paul did.

Just before his execution, Paul wrote these timeless words:

> For I am already being poured out as a drink offering, and the time of my departure has come. I have fought a good fight, I have finished my course, and I have kept the faith. From now on a crown of righteousness is laid up for me.[3]

Paul encourages us that this crown of righteousness is not just for him "but also to all who have loved His appearing."[4] That is you and me.

Mark Batterson tells his readers in *The Circle Maker* that it's "imperative...you come to terms with this simple yet life-changing truth: God is for you. If you don't believe that, then you'll pray small timid prayers; if you do believe it, then you'll pray big audacious prayers. And one way or another...it will change the trajectory of your life."[5]

My prayer life has been greatly affected by Batterson, who is himself a powerful Spirit-led leader. I knew his late father-in-law, Bob Schmidgall, who had one of the most powerful Pentecostal churches in the nation from the 1970s until his untimely death in 1998.

Books about prayer like Batterson's are important because experiencing the Holy Spirit begins with prayer. It's how we commune with Him and enter His presence. But knowing the Holy Spirit involves more than just prayer. Even non-Christian religions incorporate some form of prayer. Through this book I want to encourage you not only to experience the Holy Spirit's power in your prayer life but to exercise it by increasing your faith to see miracles, cast out evil spirits, and live in the glory of God—something my friend Sid Roth, host of the *It's Supernatural!* TV program, will talk more about in a later chapter. The Holy Spirit empowers us not only to pray but also to see results!

But there's more. The Holy Spirit prompts an awareness of deep worship and empowers us to understand how the gifts of the Spirit can operate not only in the church but also in our lives. The Holy Spirit shows us how we can become free of the things that bind us and overcome spiritual strongholds, offenses, and unforgiveness. Benny Hinn, who wrote the foreword of this book, makes this point in his book *Mysteries of the Anointing*:

> It might surprise you to read this, but I have come to believe that prayer in and of itself is not necessarily powerful. After all, religious people pray. Even well-meaning Christians try to put a spiritual label on things they are doing in the flesh, even spiritual practices such as prayer, fasting, and praise.
>
> The problem is, there is no power in those things when they are done in the flesh. There is only power in the presence of Jesus. When we commune with the Lord, there is power. As we spend time with Jesus and He becomes real to us, there is real power....
>
> Read this clearly: I am not saying you shouldn't pray. The Bible says we can make our requests known. But there comes a time when we finish our prayer lists. What do most people do when they're done asking God for things? They say amen and walk away. Imagine that. They are in active communication with the Creator of the universe, and they do all the talking and *none* of the listening! That is when they lose. That is the definition of *visiting* instead of *dwelling*. So when you finish your prayer list, be quiet long enough for God to quicken you, to ignite you.[6]

Hinn goes on to share what he has learned about what he calls "practicing the presence of the Lord," which includes spending time daily waiting on the Lord and worshipping Him for who He is. I encourage you to read his book and apply the deep insights he shares from a life lived in pursuit of God's presence. It is sure to enrich your walk with God and increase the level of the Spirit's presence and power in your life.

In many ways I want this book to accomplish the same thing. And learning to hear God's voice is a good place to start.

UNDERSTAND HOW GOD SPEAKS

As a publisher, I know that for many years one of the most in-demand topics for Christian books has been how to know you're hearing from God. People want to know if the Lord speaks to us today. And if He does still speak, how does He do it? Some wonder if God has ever spoken to them, if they've never heard His audible voice. Others wonder if they are really just listening to their own thoughts and feelings when they seek an answer from the Lord. Still others fear they might be hearing demonic voices seeking to lead them astray.

Are there concrete ways to recognize the voice of God or the leading of the Holy Spirit?

As Christians, we know we can hear from God through His Holy Word. We also hear from His prophets, which is how God spoke to His people, the Israelites, in the Old Testament. It wasn't until Jesus sent the Comforter in the person of the Holy Spirit that each of us could hear Him speak in our inner spirit.

One of the best explanations of this way of hearing God comes from Kenneth E. Hagin, who used down-to-earth humor to teach an entire generation of Christians about faith. "Dad Hagin," as he is affectionately called by those who knew him, is remembered for founding what is now Rhema Bible Training College and mentoring a young Kenneth Copeland. Many refer to him as the father of the modern faith movement. But I believe his understanding of the Holy Spirit is one of his greatest legacies.

He believed each person had to be led by the Spirit of God through what he called an "inner witness." This is where you understand God's will without hearing a still, small voice—it's just a knowing. No longer did someone need to go to a prophet to hear from God, as King Saul did when he sought counsel from the prophet Samuel.

While someone with a prophetic gift may confirm what you know is God's will, Hagin said he believed Christians who chase after prophets for a "word" end up on the spiritual junk heap. Hagin used to say that if Christians would simply believe the Bible and practice the Word of God, it would cut out 99 percent of our need for counseling. If you go to man for help, he may just be telling you out of his own mind what he thinks. It's far better to go to the great Counselor all believers have inside us.

"Every Christian has the Spirit of God, who is the guide," Hagin said.[7] In John chapters 14 through 16, Jesus tells His disciples that He will give them another Counselor "that He may be with you forever; even the spirit of truth."[8] The Comforter comes in the name of Jesus and will teach you, guide you into all truth, and show you things to come.[9]

The Greek word for the Holy Spirit, *paraklētos* (or Paraclete), can be translated into many terms, including Helper, Comforter, Advocate, Strengthener, and Counselor. Each of these words reveals a role the Holy Spirit fills in our lives. This is the scriptural foundation for believing the Holy Spirit's chief purpose is to be our lifelong guide and if we follow Him, we are actively engaging in Spirit-led living. Instead of God being some remote, stern figure in the sky, as many religious people seem to view Him, He speaks to us and guides us through His Holy Spirit, which means God is anything but impersonal. He is a personal God who will guide us if we'll just listen.

The Bible tells us there are three parts to us: spirit, soul, and body.[10] Hagin used the following scriptures to establish the fact that not only do we have a spirit man, but the Holy Spirit guides us through that inner man.

- "For as many as are led by the Spirit of God, these are the sons of God."[11]

- "The Spirit Himself bears witness with our spirits that we are the children of God."[12]

- "The spirit of man is the candle of the LORD, searching all
  the inward parts of the heart."[13] Another translation reads,
  "The spirit of man is the lamp of the LORD."[14] That means
  God will enlighten or guide us through our spirits—not
  through our intellect or our physical beings.

Hagin taught that most people seek guidance through every means
except the way God said it would come. "We sometimes judge how God
is leading us by what our physical senses tell us. But nowhere in the Bible
does God say that He will guide us through our senses," Hagin said.
"Sometimes we look at our circumstances from a mental standpoint and
try to reason things out. But God does not guide us through our intellect. Proverbs 20:27 says, 'The spirit of man—[not the mind of man or
the soul of man]—is the candle of the Lord.'...This means that God will
enlighten us—He will guide us—through our spirit."[15]

To understand that God guides us through our spirit, we must first
know what our spirit is. The spirit never dies. It's eternal. Peter tells
Christian wives not to let their adorning be outward but to "let it be the
hidden nature of the heart"[16]—which corresponds to what Paul calls the
inner man. Hagin explained that what Paul calls the "inner man"[17] and
Peter calls the "hidden nature of the heart"[18] is the spirit of man, or who
we really are. When the Bible speaks of the heart, most of the time it's
speaking of the spirit—the inner man, or the real man.

Hagin also made an interesting observation about the way people
often misquote 1 Thessalonians 5:23, where Paul said, "I pray to God that
your whole spirit, soul, and body be preserved blameless unto the coming
of our Lord Jesus Christ." Hagin said Paul was praying for the church at
Thessalonica, and he began with the inside and worked his way to the
outside: spirit, soul, and body. Hagin said many people put the words in
the wrong order and say, "Body, soul, and spirit." He believed they put
the body first because they're more body-conscious than anything else.

Hagin said other Christians are more soul conscious than Spirit conscious.
What's the difference between the spirit and the soul? Hagin preached that
most people think the soul and spirit are the same, but they can't be. The

Bible says, "For the word of God is alive, and active, and sharper than any two-edged sword, piercing even to the division of soul and spirit."[19] If the soul and spirit can be divided, they can't be the same thing.[20]

If we're going to be led by the Spirit of God, we need to become Spirit conscious. Many people understand the soul to be the seat of our mind, will, and emotions. But our spirit is who we really are. It's the part of us that resembles our heavenly Father. We are made in the image of God, and God is a Spirit.

We need to think of ourselves as spirit beings possessing souls and living in bodies. That is who we are. We have souls and live in physical bodies, but we are spirit beings. And when we accept Christ, the Holy Spirit comes to live within us. This is why believers can expect to be led by the Spirit of God, because the Holy Spirit dwells inside us.

If you're a believer, God's Spirit communes with your spirit, so you must learn to listen to your spirit. Hagin said he practiced doing this from a young age, and eventually he learned to listen to his spirit. The Holy Spirit will bear witness with your spirit, and that inward witness is how He leads you.

TEN WAYS GOD SPEAKS

If we position our hearts to hear from God, we will find that He is almost always speaking to us. Jennifer LeClaire is a former senior editor of *Charisma* magazine. She leads Awakening House of Prayer and is a prolific author and gifted speaker. She identifies ten ways the Holy Spirit speaks to us.

1. The Holy Spirit speaks through supernatural wisdom. So follow Solomon's example and pray for wisdom. And when you receive it, don't reason it away by letting your mind rule over your heart.

2. The Holy Spirit speaks through dreams by night and visions by day. To know if a dream or vision is from God, measure it by these three guidelines: (1) it won't contradict

the Word of God, (2) God will give you an immediate interpretation, and (3) you won't be able to shake it; it will stay with you and you will be compelled to pray about it or seek counsel about its meaning.

3. The Holy Spirit speaks through our surroundings. God can and does speak to us through nature and through practical, everyday situations and circumstances.

4. The Holy Spirit speaks through peace. This can be helpful if you're making a major decision. Even while your soul is wrestling with what to do, you'll have peace in your spirit about the way forward.

5. The Holy Spirit speaks through the Bible. This is the best place to start when you need to know if God is speaking. He will always speak through His Word. If you apply its words to your life, you'll be in a position to receive more truth and wisdom.

6. The Holy Spirit speaks through our conscience. This is the inner witness Kenneth Hagin spoke about.

7. The Holy Spirit speaks through a sudden flash of inspiration. Sometimes people just have a sudden "knowing" in their spirit that they can't explain. Make sure it lines up with biblical principles when this happens, but pay attention when you get these flashes of inspiration.

8. The Holy Spirit speaks through impressions. You might have a feeling in your spirit that you should do or say something. You might describe it as something God put on your heart. You haven't actually heard the voice of God, but you have a strong urging to follow through with what He is prompting you to do.

Supernatural Peace in a War Zone

I've learned that the Spirit-led life is a journey. Each day, I am filled with that distinct awareness of the Holy Spirit's presence in me. It doesn't look the same for everyone.

I've trusted Father God to mold and shape my life into the purpose He designed for me. I don't get to pick what circumstances I face, but I can choose to completely trust Father God as the potter because I will always be the clay. Because I've been baptized in the Holy Spirit, I know I have power to handle whatever comes my way. I knew this even when I was in a war zone.

A few years ago I was deployed to Afghanistan. I was told the area I was assigned to was less dangerous because there was less likelihood of engaging enemy contact. But that changed before I got there. Instead of being the least dangerous region, it was classified as the most dangerous. I didn't tell my wife this—she would have worried too much. Instead, I clung to Psalm 118:6: "The LORD is on my side; I will not fear. What can people do to me?"

I prayed for guidance and that God would protect me and the soldiers assigned to me. I had a witness of the Spirit that I would be fine and

9. God sometimes speaks in an audible voice. If this happens, meditate on the words He speaks to you and pray about how they will come to pass in your life.

10. The Holy Spirit speaks in a still, small voice. It can be so quiet that you miss it if you are not paying attention. It can be so subtle that you don't believe it's God. Learn to tune in and trust this voice when you sense it.

LeClaire says, "The Bible is the bottom-line authority on all things, but some situations are not covered by the Bible, like job choices or ministry turning points. We need to hear from the Lord for ourselves and others." If you are walking in obedience to God but still aren't sure you're hearing from Him, LeClaire says it's possible you haven't tuned in to one of these modes of communication. "We need to pay close attention and establish a pattern of how He speaks to us most often," she advises. I pray protected. I held to that word from the Holy Spirit, even though I didn't know what was in front of me.

Within days of my arrival, the enemy began rocket attacks on my location. Some attacks were more unnerving than others, but I stood on the promise given to me before I arrived in country: He would never leave me, and both my men and I would be safe.

Then it came. One night while taking a rocket barrage, I just went to bed instead of going to the bunker. I prayed, "If I am going to die tonight, that's fine, but please, Lord, take care of my wife." The Lord was my protector, and He was faithful that night, even as debris fell all over my tent and location. You see, I've learned that Spirit-led living is required in all circumstances—not just in the easy places but all!

There have been times when the problem seemed insurmountable, but I have learned to walk moment by moment, trusting and placing my confidence in my heavenly Father. He will be your protector too. Listen to the Holy Spirit and discern His voice for you. Remember, "He who dwells in the secret place of the Most High shall abide under the shadow of the Almighty. I will say of the LORD, 'He is my refuge and my fortress; My God, in Him I will trust.'"[21]

—COLONEL EVAN J. TRINKLE, US ARMY (RET.)

the Lord will open your spiritual ears to hear His voice so you will be led by the Spirit.[22]

LEARN TO KNOW THE SPIRIT'S WAYS

R. T. Kendall is the former pastor of Westminster Chapel in London and has written more than seventy books, many of which we've published through Charisma Media.

Kendall's book *The Sensitivity of the Spirit* talks about the many things that can grieve the Spirit. He even goes so far as to say, "The easiest thing in the world to do is to grieve the Holy Spirit."

In Ephesians 4:30, Paul warns us not to grieve the Holy Spirit, and Kendall believes the next two verses are very telling. Right after he spoke of the possibility of grieving the Spirit, Paul articulates that we are to

get rid of all bitterness, rage and anger, brawling and slander, along with every form of malice. Be kind and compassionate to one another, forgiving each other, just as in Christ God forgave you.[23]

Kendall says it is significant that bitterness tops the list. He writes, "Bitterness, or resentment, is one of the chief ways we grieve the Holy Spirit. Sadly, resentment always seems justifiable the moment it surfaces. We often do not realize at the time that we are grieving the Spirit. He quietly flutters away with no announcement or fanfare."

Holding on to bitterness is not the only way we can grieve the Spirit, but since it's at the top of Paul's list, we would be wise to examine our hearts regularly and practice what Kendall calls "total forgiveness" anytime we find bitterness or resentment lurking there.

Kendall offers a few more tips to avoid grieving the Spirit.

1. Learn to listen to the Spirit's voice. Listening is an art, and very few people truly learn to do it. Most of us do much more talking than listening, but it would be wise to practice listening for the Spirit to speak before we make a move.

Awakened to the Still, Small Voice of the Spirit

My husband abandoned me with a two-year-old baby in 1999. I shook my fist at God and demanded answers for the injustice. He was silent. Fast-forward four months, and my life was in shambles. I was arrested for a crime I didn't commit. I was facing five years in prison—a sentence that would have left my daughter essentially orphaned.

Helpless and hopeless, I finally cried out to God—and He delivered me from the enemy's plot to destroy our lives. I surrendered my heart to the One who created me. It was in this setting—a county jail filled with all manner of violent criminals—that I heard the still, small voice of God for the first time.

I'll never forget my experience. The Holy Spirit told me I would be released in forty days. Being a new convert, I had no idea that the number forty was a symbol of testing and trial, but every time I opened my Bible, I read an account that revolved around that number: the Israelites' forty years in the desert, Noah's experience with the forty-day flood, Jesus' forty days in the wilderness.

This seemed impossible, considering that the judge had refused to allow me bail three times—and that this same judge was on vacation well after the fortieth day of my captivity. All I can say is, "But God." On the fortieth day,

2. Learn to accept the Spirit's silence. Remaining silent is God's prerogative, according to Kendall, and He doesn't tell us all we would love to know. But we must trust that He tells us all we need to know, when we need to know it.

3. Learn to wait on the Spirit. Kendall says sometimes waiting is the hardest thing to do, but silence is God's holy ground. While we wait on the Spirit, we must take off our shoes and worship Him. Never assume He is communicating when He isn't.[24]

MAKE ROOM FOR THE SPIRIT

Sadly, most Christians are not taught to listen to the Holy Spirit. In fact, few churches—even Pentecostal and Charismatic ones—practice the fullness of the Spirit, meaning they don't allow all the gifts and expressions of the Holy Spirit to operate. Early Pentecostals who experienced the Holy Spirit at Azusa Street were excited. They worshipped for hours. Their services were wild. They emphasized living holy, and sometimes

without ever being tried or convicted or standing before an earthly judge, I was released, just as the Holy Spirit told me I would be.

That was the beginning of a beautiful friendship with the Holy Spirit that has opened the door for me to receive all His benefits: His leading, comfort, truth, grace, and much more. The Holy Spirit is so faithful! He never fails to speak to my heart at critical moments. He is quick to warn me when I am heading down the wrong path. And He always has a word for me in due season when I am careful to maintain a listening ear and a watchful heart.

God has restored my life in beautiful ways, more than making up for the injustice of being abandoned, falsely accused, and imprisoned. Today, I lead a global prayer movement, have written best-selling books, and had the honor of serving as senior editor of *Charisma* magazine.

As my relationship with the Holy Spirit has developed over the years, I've learned plenty about how He speaks and what He likes to talk about. If you're listening, it's not difficult to hear Him. He communicates through faint impressions, dreams, visions, circumstances, nature, other people—and of course through Scripture. Most of the time, though, He speaks in the still, small voice I first heard in the county jail.

—JENNIFER LECLAIRE, LEADER, AWAKENING HOUSE OF PRAYER

when they were overcome by the Spirit's power, they fell to the floor and even rolled around. Holy Roller was a term of derision used by Christians from more "dignified" churches. In hindsight there may have been some "wildfire." But it's like a country preacher once said, "I'd rather have wildfire than no fire at all!"

Consider how "wild" the birth of the church was in AD 33. The first Pentecost was an abrupt, heavenly invasion. It wasn't planned in a staff meeting; it came "suddenly."[25] The noise from a mighty, rushing wind was not on the program; neither were flames of holy fire.

No one in that prayer meeting in the Upper Room in Jerusalem expected to speak in a supernatural language. Certainly, Peter didn't expect to give his sermon; I'm sure he was surprised when three thousand people were converted. The church was born in a moment of unearthly, unimagined strangeness.

In a recent article, J. Lee Grady, *Charisma* senior contributing editor, eloquently asked: "How would we respond today if God wanted to repeat the miracle of Pentecost in one of our carefully scripted Sunday meetings? I wonder if we would embrace the wildness of that Acts 2 moment. Would we welcome the holy chaos? Or would we tell the Spirit to sit down and behave Himself? If God wants to do this miracle again, will we make room for it?"

Grady's answer is that he fears we have enacted so many human controls that the Spirit is totally left out of our Sunday experience. If we don't give Him free rein, worship can become a man-made ritual that is stripped of God's power.

The apostle Paul warned us not to quench the Spirit.[26] *Quench* means to extinguish a fire. Many of our churches today have been equipped with state-of-the-art fire extinguishers that do a professional job of eliminating any risk of a holy outbreak. Here is Grady's list of the five most common ways we quench the Holy Spirit:

1. **We ignore the Holy Spirit.** Many churches today make no mention of the Spirit. He is, as author Francis Chan says, the "forgotten God." We play it safe by focusing on Jesus and

salvation—yet we forget that Jesus talked repeatedly about the Spirit. And it was Jesus who told His followers that they must be "clothed with power from on high."[27] We are not being faithful to Christ if we don't take people into the deeper waters of the Spirit that He Himself promised.

2. We limit the gifts of the Holy Spirit. There are thousands of churches in this country that teach that the gifts of the Spirit no longer function. Even though the apostle Paul said, "Do not forbid speaking in tongues,"[28] and, "Do not despise prophecies,"[29] speaking in tongues and prophecy are off-limits—along with healing and miracles.

It was a lack of faith that created the doctrine known as cessationism. Respected Bible teachers have convinced whole sectors of the church that God no longer operates supernaturally. Christianity has been reduced to an intellectual argument, devoid of power. And even in churches that wear the Pentecostal label, we have created such tight controls on our meetings that the gifts can't function.

3. We misuse or abuse the gifts of the Holy Spirit. We Pentecostals and Charismatics have sometimes quenched the Spirit more than Evangelicals who deny His power. We have whacked people to the floor to prove our "anointing," manipulated audiences with mood music, used fancy titles to fake apostolic authority, and manufactured counterfeit miracles to con people into giving offerings.

God forgive us. We cannot use the Spirit or His gifts to achieve our selfish agenda. Either we submit to His plan, or He withdraws and lets us play our silly games.

4. We misrepresent the Holy Spirit. How often have we heard, "Thus says the Lord," or, "God told me this," when the Spirit had nothing to do with the message we cooked up on our own. When we give the Spirit credit for messages that did not originate with Him, we take the Lord's name in vain. We have allowed polished, unbroken preachers to mislead us with flattery, manipulation, exotic visions, and promises of wealth.

5. We divide the Holy Spirit. When the apostle Paul corrected the Corinthians for quenching the Spirit, he addressed sexual sin and the abuse of spiritual gifts. But first He challenged them on the way they were treating one another. "Is Christ divided?" he asked.[30] We grieve the Spirit when we judge one another, build walls, divide ourselves racially, follow personalities, or create camps according to our pet doctrines.

The secret of Pentecost is found in Acts 2:1: "They were all together in one place." Can that be said of us today? We are divided between Black and White, White and Hispanic, Republican and Democrat, Protestant and Catholic, denominational and nondenominational, evangelical and Pentecostal. We are fragmented and weak. We have quenched the Spirit with our disunity.[31]

Part of the reason I'm writing this book is to inspire each of us and the entire church to pray for a new Pentecost. As Grady says, "Let's throw away our fire extinguishers and invite a fresh, heavenly flame to engulf the church."[32]

If you're hungry for more of God's Spirit, keep reading. In the next chapter we'll discover a key to reclaiming the fire that first fell on the Day of Pentecost.

LIVING IT OUT

Read Ephesians 4:30–32:

> And do not grieve the Holy Spirit of God, in whom you are sealed for the day of redemption. Let all bitterness, wrath, anger, outbursts, and blasphemies, with all malice, be taken away from you. And be kind one to another, tenderhearted, forgiving one another, just as God in Christ also forgave you.

Think about it:

1. What do you think Mark Batterson means when he says it's "imperative...you come to terms with this simple yet life-changing truth: God is for you"? How would believing this truth change the way you pray?

2. Have you experienced God's leading you through an inner witness? If so, describe it. If not, write what you will do to practice listening to your spirit, as Hagin instructed.

3. Have you ever noticed a pattern of how the Holy Spirit speaks to you most often? Which of the ways the Lord speaks discussed in this chapter have you personally experienced?

4. Have you ever grieved the Holy Spirit? Reread Ephesians 4:30–32, and list the things you need the Spirit to remove from your heart so you don't grieve Him.

Chapter 3

RECEIVE THE BAPTISM
IN THE HOLY SPIRIT

THE BAPTISM OF the Holy Spirit has long been the subject of much debate within the evangelical church. In fact, for decades this doctrine separated Pentecostals from their evangelical brethren. The Baptism in the Holy Spirit is, Pentecostals believe, a renewal of first-century Christianity, when the Holy Spirit was poured out on the church on the Day of Pentecost. This gave the disciples such power and boldness that within one generation they had turned the known world upside down.

I was taught growing up that a power came from this experience—and I experienced that power and its lasting effects for myself. I know firsthand that being baptized in the Holy Spirit adds a wonderful and welcome dimension to a Christian's walk.

It gives a believer access to the power source that enables us to live pure, godly lives that are pleasing to the Father. It does not eliminate the need for the spiritual disciplines, such as prayer, Bible reading, and fellowshipping with other believers. Nor does it immunize a person from sin. But there is something within the Baptism of the Holy Spirit that confers power.

In other countries, missionaries of all denominations have found that those who receive the Baptism of the Holy Spirit have the boldness needed to confront demons, making their efforts to spread the gospel more effective. The power of the Holy Spirit at work in the country of Argentina has been the catalyst for one of the fastest-spreading revivals the world has ever known. Literally thousands and thousands of individuals have been set free from sin, delivered from bondages, loosed in evangelism and soul winning, and healed of disease—all by the power of the Holy Spirit.

In little more than a century, beginning in 1901 when the modern Pentecostal movement began, the number of Christians who have come to believe in the power of the Holy Spirit has grown to more than 644 million worldwide, making Pentecostal-Charismatic Christianity the fastest-growing religious movement in history.[1] And while some wring their hands about the waning influence of Christianity, the Charismatic movement is growing faster than the population growth of the world.[2]

I believe the first-century followers of Jesus provide a key in learning to become mature Spirit-led believers. They had walked and talked with Jesus; they had seen the miracles. Yet when He was taken to be crucified, none of the Twelve were there except John. The other disciples cowered behind locked doors. Then they received word that Jesus had been raised from the dead and later saw Him ascend into heaven, at which time He told them to wait in Jerusalem until they received power from the Holy Spirit to be His witnesses.

Can you imagine how those 120 people gathered in that Upper Room must have felt? They had lost the One they thought would rise up and overthrow the evil rule of Rome in their country. And rather than dying a hero's death, Jesus died the death of a traitor. He left them alone, discouraged, brokenhearted, and unable to do anything about it. Rather than ruling in dignity, they were cowering in shame and fear.

But ten days after Jesus ascended to heaven, on the Day of Pentecost, the people heard a sound like a mighty, rushing wind and saw something over each person's head that looked like tongues of fire. And as they prayed, they did so in languages they didn't know. People from around the world were in Jerusalem, and they heard the men and women in that Upper Room speaking in their native languages.

The Holy Spirit came with mighty power and transformed the lives of every person in that Upper Room. The second chapter of Acts tells us the disciples began to speak in other tongues as the Spirit gave them utterance. That encounter with the Holy Spirit gave them power to then leave that Upper Room and boldly proclaim the gospel in their city, country, and even the world. In describing the work of these early believers, Acts 17 says they "turned the world upside down."[3]

Those men and women never forgot how they felt before that day in the Upper Room. And they never forgot what changed them. They testified to everyone they met about the Holy Spirit and what He had done in their lives. They saw every encounter with an unbeliever as an opportunity to pass on that power for godly living.

Shortly after they left the Upper Room, Peter and John encountered a poor, lame man begging for food near the gate of the temple. All that man thought he needed was a little money to buy some food. But fresh from an encounter with the Holy Spirit, Peter knew what he really needed, and he gave the man much more than he expected.

We read in Acts 3: "Peter, gazing at him with John, said, 'Look at us.' [I imagine Peter thought what happened to him in that Upper Room was written all over his face!] So he paid attention to them, expecting to receive something from them. Then Peter said, 'I have no silver and gold, but I give you what I have. In the name of Jesus Christ of Nazareth, rise up and walk.'"[4]

The power Peter, John, and the rest of the 120 received in that Upper Room enabled them to heal the sick, raise the dead, cast out demons, spread the gospel, and establish churches. Once the Holy Spirit resided in their lives, they were fearless in life and in the face of death.

I once heard a secular speaker tell a group of business executives that it is impossible for an adult to change unless that change is accompanied by a significant emotional experience. The speaker went on to say employees often will change unwanted behavior in the workplace when faced with a significant emotional experience—such as the threat of being fired.

Maybe that works in a secular workplace, but this idea of what it takes for an adult to change may have a spiritual application. I have observed that for adults who accept Christ, it is often difficult to change unless they experience something significant and emotional. This frequently occurs at the time of salvation when there is true, heartfelt repentance, often with tears, and they express sorrow for their sin and plead for forgiveness and eternal life. Sadly, however, when the gospel is presented on an intellectual basis and a person is counseled to ignore his feelings and accept Christ on faith alone, that sort of conversion all too often doesn't "stick," and the person later goes back on his commitment to follow Christ.

Another way to look at this is to realize that what I am identifying as an emotional experience happens only when a person comes to what people describe as the "end of themselves." A person must be so tired of how he is living that he is willing to change, turn to God, and ask the Holy Spirit for help.

I know there is vast power available to help us change—it is the power that comes from the Baptism in the Holy Spirit. Not only does the baptism give us the power to change, but it also gives us power in many other areas. These include

- power to hear God's voice,
- power to pray and see results,
- power to manifest the fruit of the Spirit,
- power to love,
- power to minister,
- power to speak beyond what you know,
- power to take authority over circumstances,
- power to take authority over the evil one,
- power to see people delivered from the evil one, and
- power to do miracles.

THE SPIRIT BRINGS LIFE CHANGES

Being baptized in the Holy Spirit doesn't guarantee that someone will live a holy life—but it does guarantee the person will have the *power* to live a holy life. We've all seen the headlines about Christian leaders who have fallen into sin. Being baptized in the Holy Spirit does not obliterate free will and choices, but it does make available to us the power we need to live a life of miracles—and often the greatest miracle is the transformation of our own hearts.

I received the Baptism of the Holy Spirit when I was eleven while attending an Assemblies of God youth camp in Iowa. I can remember the late-night altar services in which I felt the presence of God and cried out for this baptism experience I had heard about all my life. I see now that I understood only a little of what the Baptism of the Holy Spirit is all about.

Yet I left that youth camp totally convinced God was real and that somehow He had a plan and purpose for my life. I can see now that this experience was the bedrock that brought me back to God after a difficult time later in my teens.

Even though receiving the Baptism in the Spirit was a very dramatic experience, I started rebelling at age fourteen and was up and down in my walk with God until I was twenty. At various times I would recommit my life to serve Christ at a youth camp or during a dramatic church service. However, often it was just a matter of time before I was back to my old ways.

Now I understand it isn't that easy to lose out with God. But many sincere Christians at that time seemed to believe if you weren't 100 percent holy, you were on your way to hell. In my case, I never turned my back on God. I stayed connected to church and even gave offerings because I believed that was the right thing to do. But I was pulled by my own carnal nature and the culture during the turbulent hippie era.

Unhappy with the up and down, I finally called out to God and said, "This has to work." This was the same time millions of youths, many of them from the drug culture, were coming to Christ in what we now call the Jesus movement. It did "work," of course. I was discipled during that season of my life and taught how to look to God for strength to serve Him. And I haven't looked back.

Obviously, the experience of being baptized in the Spirit is not a cure-all—unless we allow it to be. But I am convinced that being empowered by the Spirit in this unique way gives Christians a far greater chance of staying true to their commitments and overcoming stubborn sin habits.

THE SPIRIT BRINGS HEALING

Often when a believer is baptized in the Holy Spirit, more than sin bondages are broken. In Fuchsia Pickett's case, she received the Baptism of the Holy Spirit and a physical healing at the same time.

Afflicted by a hereditary disease and forced to wear cumbersome braces, she nevertheless had an intense longing for more of God. Despite the progression of her disease, she pastored a church and taught in Bible school. But eventually the disease reached a point where she was fitted with a body brace and scheduled for surgery to fuse her back together to keep her from hemorrhaging. While waiting at home for the surgery, she persuaded a friend to drive her to a Pentecostal church she had never visited.

During the service, she felt God nudge her and tell her to go forward for prayer. She resisted but finally dragged her weakened body forward and asked the minister to pray for her.

He anointed her and prayed gently in the name of Jesus. "It changed my life—and my theology—totally," she writes. The Lord spoke to her, asking, "Are you willing to be identified with these people—to be one of them?" She said, "Yes, Lord, I will be identified with these people." Then she asked to say something to the audience. "I am going to live. Jesus just told me so," she told them with tears running down her face.

> Suddenly the power of God struck the base of my neck and coursed through my body. The miraculous, healing power of God put me back together instantly. It was the infinite, triune, omnipotent God who touched me that morning. I was made every whit whole inside my organs, my blood condition, and my bones. And when He turned me loose, I ran and danced and shouted. I had been struck by resurrection power, which healed me and set me free.

Pickett's divine teacher had come to fill her with Himself and to split open the veil between her soul and her spirit. He healed her miraculously, even though at the time, she did not believe the doctrine of healing. For the first time in her life, she began to understand, through revelation, the same Scriptures she had studied and taught faithfully for many years. The Scriptures came alive to her, not as information but as power that was working in her and transforming her life.[5]

THE SPIRIT BRINGS A PRAYER LANGUAGE

Jack Hayford tells the story of how he received the Baptism in the Holy Spirit as a young college student after some years of doubt and skepticism. He had heard all the warnings: Don't seek an experience for its own sake! Look out for deceiving spirits! Beware of manipulation, emotionalism, and suggestiveness! Don't let sensationalism about the supernatural catch your fancy! Hayford says there were enough obstacles to block any Christian from pursuing a freely open, fully available, spiritually vulnerable moment in the presence of our precious Savior. But he was both hearing and desiring—both understanding and feeling—the truth he was being presented. When the invitation was given to go forward for prayer, he went.

In those moments of prayer, God put a four-syllable non-English phrase in Hayford's mind, but he did not speak it. In fact, he did not speak the phrase for three more years because of his expectation that speaking in tongues would be a supernatural seizure of the tongue rather than a voluntary cooperation with the Holy Spirit. He had to get past several blocks in his own willingness to receive the baptism.

When he did speak those four syllables, and many more, at the close of a service, he says he "sensed that Jesus Christ had filled me with the Holy Spirit, but I had also experienced a release into a beautiful language of praise and prayer."

That experience did not turn out to be a one-night spiritual thrill ride as he had feared. It instead became a "naturally supernatural" part of Hayford's everyday communion with God that allowed him to express with more liberty his love for God.

WHY TONGUES?

Speaking in tongues has long been among the most controversial of the gifts of the Spirit. If cessationists, those who believe the gifts of the Spirit ceased in the first century, or non-Christians criticize Pentecostals, it's almost always over this.

Even in Pentecostal circles, tongues is controversial. For the Assemblies of God, speaking in tongues is the "initial physical evidence" of the Baptism in the Holy Spirit. When the Charismatic renewal came along, many new leaders said if someone had received the Baptism in the Holy Spirit, they would speak in tongues but it wasn't the only evidence of the infilling of the Spirit.

I like the way Fuchsia Pickett describes the importance of tongues in her book *Walking in the Spirit*. She notes that there were seventeen different nationalities in Jerusalem on the Day of Pentecost. At creation, God made one language until men decided to build the tower of Babel and become as God, and so pride entered their hearts. Then God confused their languages and scattered mankind across the earth. From the time of the building of the tower of Babel to the Day of Pentecost, nothing brought people together in one language.

Pickett writes:

> On the Day of Pentecost as the disciples had humbled themselves to wait for the promise of the Father, God had a message for all mankind. He didn't deliver His message through confusion; every man heard it in his language. Now for the first time since Babel the body of Christ can speak the same language, a heavenly one. The language of the Holy Spirit is the only language that is not a part of the curse. It is a language of the heavenly world coming from our spirits by the power of the Holy Spirit.[6]

As I child, I remember grownups tarrying for days, months, or years to receive the Holy Spirit. The word *tarrying* comes from Luke 24:49, where Jesus told the disciples to "tarry in the city of Jerusalem until you are endued with power from on high."[7] But in the modern day, tarrying became a form of spiritual procrastination, as people who didn't know how to speak in a heavenly language sought the gift.

While old-time Pentecostals seemed to agonize over receiving this wonderful gift because it was the crucial "proof" that they were Spirit filled, the neo-Pentecostals seemed to take a more relaxed approach. They embraced it as a prayer language, and that is what it is widely called today. It's a way to speak to God spirit to Spirit. The apostle Paul said, "The Spirit helps us in our weaknesses, for we do not know what to pray for as we ought, but the Spirit Himself intercedes for us with groanings too deep for words."[8] When we pray in tongues, the Holy Spirit prays through us.

I began to understand this as a young adult and have prayed in the Spirit many times, often with deep conviction, usually regarding something I'm agonizing over. The scripture says we pray with "groanings too deep for words." What a blessing! When we don't know what to pray, we can pray in tongues, knowing the Holy Spirit is interceding for us. And that gives us confidence that God hears and understands us and will answer that prayer. I thank God continually for gifting me with my prayer language, for it enables me to say things to God in prayer that I would not know how to say in my own words.

THE POWER OF PRAYING IN TONGUES

One of the most practical uses of the gift of praying in tongues was shared by Oral Roberts. He was already a well-known evangelist with a huge healing ministry when he bought several hundred acres of farmland in an undeveloped part of Tulsa, Oklahoma. He felt he should build a university, but he was not an academician, and he knew it would cost millions of dollars. He began to walk the land and pray in tongues, and then the Lord gave him the interpretation of his own prayer language. In time Roberts got the answers he was seeking and discerned what steps to take to open what came to be called Oral Roberts University, now one of the foremost Christian universities in the world.[9]

Mark Rutland, who was the third president of Oral Roberts University, told me he heard Roberts tell that story at a United Methodist ministers' meeting in Georgia. Roberts told the ministers to go into their prayer closets and pray in English and in tongues; then they would begin to understand what they were saying and interpret their own prayer language. Rutland says Roberts' words made a huge impression on him.

A self-described "uptight Methodist minister," Rutland tells how, after attending Methodist seminary and pastoring a few years, he was depressed and suicidal. He had battled depression since junior high. But it got worse, partly because of the pressures of ministry. His marriage also was hanging on by a thread. Rutland tried to take his life twice, making the second attempt in 1975. That time, the gun miraculously jammed after he pulled the trigger.

During that time, Rutland was associate pastor of a large Methodist church in the Atlanta area. The pastor was an on-fire Charismatic, and Rutland, a cessationist, resented having to attend a Charismatic conference called Power for Ministry Today. The speaker headlining the conference was Ralph Wilkerson, pastor of Melodyland Christian Center in Anaheim, California, a church that had become a center for Charismatic renewal.

What happened at that conference changed Rutland's life. First, a close friend who was anti-Charismatic received the Baptism of the Holy Spirit. Instantly he had a deaf ear healed, and he forgave his father, whom he hadn't spoken to in ten years. Then someone gave a word of prophecy to Rutland, who had never heard of such a thing. The word was: "'I'm going to do a great thing,' says the Lord. 'And it begins now in this room.'"

With that, Rutland fell facedown on the floor and began to weep uncontrollably. Others in the room were also weeping. Wilkerson saw Rutland weeping and approached him to ask if he wanted to receive the Baptism of the Holy Spirit. Rutland tried to say he didn't believe in Spirit baptism but instead heard himself saying, "Yes, I need this badly."

Wilkerson placed three fingers on Rutland's forehead, and Rutland describes what happened next: "He said, 'All right, son, receive the Holy Spirit.' And my whole world changed on December 5, 1975, in a hotel ballroom. Everything I had never believed in happened. I had never been in a meeting where anybody spoke in tongues. I did not have any idea what it was supposed to sound like. I had even preached against it. 'God have mercy on me,' I moaned.

"And Wilkerson said, 'OK, open your mouth and praise the Lord.' And I thought he wanted me to say, 'Praise the Lord.' So I opened my mouth for the second time in a matter of minutes, and I realized that I wasn't speaking English. It was like I was listening to somebody else. My first thought was that I was having the nervous breakdown that I'd been expecting for six years. And my second thought was, 'This is worse than a nervous breakdown! This is the end of my career in the Methodist Church.'"

Instead of a nervous breakdown, Rutland felt the depression lift, and he's never been suicidal again. "I think sometimes when we talk about the Baptism of the Holy Spirit, we make it sound as if there's absolute, immediate victory in every part of your life," Rutland says. "And that was not true for me. I did still struggle occasionally with depression. But I would say that since then, in the last twenty years, it's not just at a manageable level; it's at a negligible level. It was like a bell chiming in the distance that gradually got fainter and fainter, and now I can hardly hear it and only on occasion."

Within months of experiencing Spirit baptism, Rutland, who described himself as an "overeducated Methodist PhD," was on the Charismatic preaching circuit. Later he became a missionary, served as the pastor of several large churches in need of a turnaround, and presided as the president of Southeastern University in Lakeland, Florida, and later Oral Roberts University in Tulsa.

A second incredible Holy Spirit miracle happened a year or so later in the mountains of Mexico, where Rutland and three other Methodist ministers went on a mission trip. He also invited his father-in-law, a university professor who didn't believe in God.

Rutland had worked to learn three Spanish phrases: *Dios es amor* (God is love); *Cristo te ama* (Jesus loves you), and *Yo también* (Me too). In various churches, he'd say those phrases after a missionary translated for him. That's all he knew, but the people loved it and would applaud.

At one church the translator didn't show up, so someone suggested Rutland say the phrases he knew and sit down. He said the phrases, expecting nothing unusual to happen. But suddenly he kept preaching in Spanish, even though he hadn't learned the language. It was a miracle. His father-in-law stood and shouted questions to him in English because he didn't understand what was happening. Rutland gave an altar call and translated it into English, and his father-in-law was the first one at the altar. When he returned home, his father-in-law joined a Pentecostal church, which he attended until he died.

Rutland told me he'd never heard of anyone else being able to speak a

A New Song Through the Power of the Spirit

If you allow the Holy Spirit to fill you, it is hard to imagine the Holy Spirit of the living God living in you and not manifesting Himself in many ways. And that is what happens. You are the same person, but you now have different likes and dislikes. You have a strength of character, stronger than you had before. You have a living desire to please your Father, the One whose Spirit is living in you. He wants to be manifest in and through you.

That's what my book *A New Song* was about. I called it that because I'm a singer. And when I received the Baptism in the Holy Spirit, George Otis [founder of the Voice of Hope Radio Network] was trying to help me receive a prayer language. But I was too mental a person. I was trying to make it happen. He said, "Just thank God. Do you believe He's filled you with His Spirit like you asked Him to?"

"Yes, but..."

"Well, thank Him," said Otis, "but not in English."

"Well, how am I supposed to do that?" I asked.

He said, "Sing it."

I'm a singer, so I just offered my voice. And I was just singing in tongues and rejoicing and covered in goose bumps. When I stopped, I asked, "Can I do this when I'm driving?"

He said, "Yes, of course." So all the way home I sang in the Spirit.

Since I'm a singer, I received my prayer language by singing it. And when I titled my book, I remembered Psalm 144:9, where David says, "I will sing a new song unto You, O God." The Lord gave me a new song by the power of His Spirit.[10]

—PAT BOONE, SINGER AND AUTHOR

language he had never learned. But Vinson Synan, a Pentecostal scholar and historian, told him that speaking in tongues is called *glossalalia*, but learning a language supernaturally as Rutland did is called *xenolalia*. And as incredible as it may sound, Rutland continues to speak Spanish to this day. Even though the word *xenolalia* is not widely known, this is a biblical experience. Acts 2:5–12 says on the Day of Pentecost, there were people from every nation under heaven in Jerusalem, and they were confounded because they heard the Galileans speaking in their native languages.[11]

Recently I read an even more amazing story about how the Holy Spirit empowered a missionary to speak to a lonely teen named Nyo Chaw from Myanmar (Burma), who immigrated to Minnesota and got involved in the youth group of Solid Rock Assembly of God in Worthington. Raised a Buddhist, Chaw attended a youth camp and accepted Christ. But he was troubled because he learned his father had died back in Myanmar.

A friend in the youth group invited the teen to his home, and the friend's father asked to pray for him. He felt he should pray in tongues, and the young man from Myanmar broke into tears. What happened? The young man told his friend that the prayer in tongues was in perfect Karen, his native language, and it told him that God loved him as a father. He told his friends he could understand everything being prayed in tongues.

The news service of the Assemblies of God, which reported that story, said the young man has continued to grow as a Christian. What's more, the testimony has been an encouragement for those who may wonder if tongues is an actual language.[12]

FOUR TRUTHS ABOUT TONGUES

In his excellent book *The Beauty of Spiritual Language*, Hayford states four important truths about the gift of tongues.

1. Speaking in tongues is neither unbiblical nor outdated. Although not all Christians believe the same thing about the Baptism of the Holy Spirit and its accompanying evidence of speaking in "other tongues," nothing in New Testament Scripture restricts or confines speaking in tongues to being only a first-century exercise.

As we've seen, the benefits of receiving a supernatural prayer language are profound. When we do not have the words to express our need, we can use our prayer language—a language understood by the Spirit, who speaks through us to the Father, and understood by the Father, who empowers the Spirit to work in our lives to give us victory.

2. Speaking in tongues is not a transcendental experience. There is really nothing weird about praying in a language we have never learned. As Hayford puts it: "The ways of God in dealing with His redeemed children may be supernatural in the source of His operations, but they are not weird in their ways of working. To speak in tongues is not to resign the control of one's mind or indulge one's emotions to a point of extraction. The exercise of spiritual language does involve a conscious choice to allow God's assistance to transcend our own linguistic limits, but it does not surrender to any order of a mystical, trancelike trip beyond oneself."

3. Speaking in tongues is not a status symbol. There have been some abuses of tongues, including those who act is if they are spiritually superior to those who have never spoken in tongues.

The Bible doesn't tell us tongues are to be used to impress other believers with the spiritual maturity of the one who speaks. The Bible tells us, "Now, brothers, if I come to you speaking in tongues, what shall I profit you, unless I speak to you by some revelation or knowledge or prophesying or doctrine?"[13] In another place the apostle Paul says, "So tongues are for a sign, not to believers, but to unbelievers."[14]

4. Speaking in tongues is not a substitute for spiritual growth. Using our prayer language and speaking in tongues will not cause us to grow spiritually even if we do it seven days a week and twenty-four hours a day. Hayford tells us what will cause us to grow spiritually:

> As beautiful as an ongoing experience in the use of spiritual language can be at prayer, and as perfectly scriptural and desirable as it can be demonstrated to be, by itself, speaking with tongues holds no particular merit. Growth in the Christian life requires

feeding on God's Word, walking in the disciplines of His Son, and fellowshipping with His family—the church.[15]

The Baptism of the Holy Spirit is available to all believers, not a select few. Just as we receive new life in the Son of God by a definite act of personal faith, so we receive supernatural power in the Spirit of God by an act of conscious faith. Bible scholar John Rea created a simple acrostic, "READY," that can serve as an aid in remembering various important steps in receiving the Baptism in the Holy Spirit.

R—Repent. Those who seek to be baptized in the Spirit should first of all repent of any and all sin and accept Jesus Christ as their Savior.

E—Expect. Because the Holy Spirit is appropriated by faith,[16] those seeking the Baptism in the Spirit must have an expectant attitude, believing God will fulfill His promise to them.

A—Ask. Candidates for this baptism should come to Jesus in prayer, asking and expecting Him to pour out the Spirit upon them.

D—Drink. Jesus gave us this great invitation: "If anyone is thirsty, let him come to Me and drink."[17]

Y—Yield. Those seeking to be baptized and filled with the Spirit must be willing to yield control of every part of their being to Him.[18]

The Holy Spirit gives us the power to live the overcoming life. I, for one, need all the power I can get to live for Christ. We all do! But His power in my life has helped me step confidently into the destiny God has for me. I do not have to wonder every moment of the day if I am really going to make it or fear that right around the corner is the big temptation that will be too hard for me to withstand.

God's power has taken away the fear of failure and replaced it with "power, and love, and self-control."[19] He can do the same for you.

LIVING IT OUT

Read Acts 2:1–4:

> When the day of Pentecost had come, they were all together in one place. Suddenly a sound like a mighty rushing wind came from heaven, and it filled the whole house where they were sitting. There appeared to them tongues as of fire, being distributed and resting on each of them, and they were all filled with the Holy Spirit and began to speak in other tongues, as the Spirit enabled them to speak.

Think about it:

1. If you have received the Baptism in the Holy Spirit, write about the experience and name some things it has empowered you to do. (If you are still seeking the baptism, please see appendix B for some steps you can take to position yourself to receive this important gift.)

2. Describe your experience with speaking in tongues, whether you have received a prayer language as a result of being baptized in the Spirit or have seen others exercise this gift.

3. Romans 8:26 tells us the Holy Spirit prays through us when we don't know what to pray. Name some ways the Holy Spirit has aided or guided you in your life.

4. Read 1 Corinthians 14:13: "Let him who speaks in an unknown tongue pray that he may interpret." How does this verse influence your view of Oral Roberts' method of praying in tongues and then interpreting his own prayer language?

Chapter 4

EXPECT GOD TO SPEAK *TO* YOU AND *THROUGH* YOU

THERE ARE MANY ways God leads us by His Holy Spirit, and one is through the gift of prophecy, where the Spirit shows us something that will happen or gives us direction or a warning. I want to begin this chapter with two powerful stories that demonstrate the Holy Spirit is alive and well and speaks into the events of our lives.

I can take no credit for these stories. I didn't even know the people involved initially. But I can verify these accounts are true, and I believe in this gift. In *God and Donald Trump*, I wrote about several prophetic words that said a businessman from New York would one day be president—and those words were given nearly a decade before Trump ran.

The secular community and even many in the church can't fathom the idea that God would reveal future events to men and women today. But God still speaks to His prophets, and I felt those prophecies needed to be documented for history. Plus, many noticed a similarity between Trump's emergence on the political scene and how God raised up and used leaders such as Cyrus in the Old Testament.

Prophecy is among the most misunderstood spiritual gifts but one of the most worthwhile. In the Old Testament the prophet represented God and spoke for God to the people. Mike Bickle, founder of the International House of Prayer, writes that Old Testament prophets "were commissioned to speak 'God's very words,' which carried absolute, divine authority."[1] And they'd better not get it wrong because the penalty was death. False prophecy was and is judged harshly by the Lord.

In the New Testament, Bickle says, only the twelve apostles carried the same authority as the Old Testament prophets to speak the very words of God. Bickle draws his insights from the writings of Wayne Grudem, a well-respected theologian and general editor of the *ESV Study Bible.* Grudem argues that all prophecy since the twelve apostles was and is "a very human—and sometimes partially mistaken—report of something the Holy Spirit brought to someone's mind."[2]

Thus Bickle poses these questions: "Can people today speak 'God's very words' occasionally? Can prophecy be 100 percent accurate? Is all prophecy...a mixed-up combination of divine inspiration and the human spirit?" He believes most prophecies today have some degree of mixture in them and that some prophetic utterances "ring more true" than others. And no contemporary prophecy should be treated the way we treat Scripture.[3]

Over the years, I've reported on many prophetic people and those who claim to be prophets. One of the significant honors of my life was knowing Oral Roberts, whom I discussed in chapter 3. In my home growing up, we saw his ministry on television and always spoke of him in almost reverential tones. When we named the great evangelists of the day, they were Oral Roberts and Billy Graham, and always in that order.

I was invited to a leaders' meeting at Oral Roberts University (ORU) in 1981 when Oral Roberts was still president of ORU. He hosted a banquet on the top floor of what was then called the City of Faith. After the meal we stood next to our seats for a time of worship. President Roberts moved around the room, laying hands on and praying for everyone as we worshipped. I was nervous as he approached me, wondering what he'd say. He laid hands on me and whispered in my ear, "Never doubt the gift that's within you."

That word has come to mind many times, and I believe it was a prophetic word—as short as it was—to me. I was still in my twenties. *Charisma* magazine was beginning to be known nationally, but I was operating beyond my league, as we were gaining a national audience and covering the Christian community. I came from a family that believed small was better than big and preferred the status quo over taking a risk. As a result, an inbred uncertainty hounded almost every decision I made.

Jamie Buckingham, who was Roberts' good friend, is the one who introduced me to this great man of God. But he also had a prophetic word for me when I first got to know him in 1977. Someone had asked him to pitch a project to me—one many young journalists would have jumped at. But I knew it wasn't God's will for my life, so I said thanks, but no thanks.

Buckingham said he had hoped I'd say no, and then asked how he could get involved with my fledgling magazine. I needed a mentor at that point in my life, and Buckingham was that and more—he was a friend, a spiritual leader, and a confidant, and his wit and wisdom were guiding lights to me. I recently found a copy of his book *Look Out, World—I'm Me!* and enjoyed rereading many of his insights.

Buckingham was one of the most spiritual men I knew, yet he was down-to-earth. He had keen insight, saw through the hype of many ministries, and loved to poke a pin into the prideful balloons of buffoons that make a laughingstock of all those who call themselves Pentecostal. He was also the most open person I knew. He lived a life that was vulnerable and transparent. He was a great man in my eyes, even though I saw his weaknesses as well as his strengths.

But when I met him, I didn't think too much of myself. If anything, I was timid and overwhelmed by the challenges of starting *Charisma*. I didn't need a pin in my balloon; I needed an encouraging word. And here's where he gave what sounds like secular advice, but I believe it was a word prompted by the Holy Spirit. He asked me one day over lunch what I would do if I knew I could not fail. The key was "knew you could not fail." I never allowed myself to dream in those terms, and his word that day changed the course of my life.

In his book *Where Eagles Soar*, Buckingham wrote:

> Most of us dream dreams, however, then put them aside as impossible. Yet God never puts a desire in our heart, or beckons us to walk on water, unless He intends for us to step out on

faith and at least make the attempt. Whether we achieve or not is almost immaterial; the passing of the test lies in whether we try, in whether we're willing to be obedient to the inner call to greatness—the onward call to spiritual adventure.[4]

Unfortunately most Christians never learn this. Or after one attempt, they give up. They never learn that there is a price to be paid. I'm grateful for people like Buckingham that God put in my life to give me a "word spoken in due season."[5]

I'm telling these stories to increase your faith and to let you know that I believe this not only because it's scriptural but because I've experienced it. And you can too. The Holy Spirit will give you the right word at the right time. Some seem to have an unusual giftedness. But prophecy is a gift any of us can exercise. I wasn't taught that growing up. Even though my family was Pentecostal, they stayed away from people who called themselves prophets and apostles. Maybe that's because of the extremes and the abuses back in that era. But let me ask you: Did you refuse to get married because of the awful things people say and do in marriage? Of course not. As the old country preacher said, chew the fish and spit out the bones.

The examples I've shared thus far are dramatic. I've found that sincere believers touched by the Holy Spirit seem to long for this. Prophetic words aren't given often in most churches—even in Pentecostal churches. There are some ministries whose leaders seem to have this gift, and I've seen people flock to those services hoping to "get a word." Most never receive one, and I suppose it is possible to seek the gift instead of the giver—the Holy Spirit Himself. Yet this pursuit also shows a spiritual hunger, a deep desire to hear from God.

I seem to remember the prophetic words I received when I was just starting out, probably because, like the simple word from Oral Roberts, they made a big impact on me at that time.

A few years before that prophecy from Oral Roberts, Doug Wead, one of my early mentors, gave me a word that has affected me ever since. Wead became a frequent TV commentator and wrote multiple best sellers, often about US presidents or their families. He worked to get

George H. W. Bush elected in 1988 and as a result was given a position in his White House. During the Bush administration, I received invitations to several meetings with President Bush, always as a result of my friendship with Wead.

Like me, Wead grew up in a Pentecostal family. When I first met him in my teens, he was already making a name for himself as a speaker. I remember hearing him preach once on the gift of prophecy. He seemed to give the words effortlessly, and I remember being amazed. He later wrote a short book on the subject.

Then, in 1977, my wife and I visited Wead's family, and he took a picture of our family. When he mailed it to us, I found on the back an inscription:

> To Steve Strang, America's young publishing giant who will pioneer in fields unknown to his religious publishing peers, indeed, not only the religious world or even the publishing world will contain him (and you heard it here first 2/2/78).

Wead was my first significant professional/spiritual mentor. I looked up to him, and he encouraged me even when I was in college. While it seems like hyperbole looking back, considering I was barely twenty-six years old and just starting out, that inscription was prophetic. It was also encouraging. I was tempted to quit in that era, and I wonder if I didn't keep going just to try to live up to his expectations. Remember that you can speak life into those who admire and respect you and maybe change their lives as Wead changed mine.

I've given examples of words given in private settings. Some ministers are known for giving amazing words of knowledge in a more public setting. That may not be your gift (nor is it mine), but each of us can hear from the Holy Spirit.

Bickle says everyone who is born again can function in simple prophecy, whose purpose is to edify, exhort, and comfort people.[6] "It is the will of God for everyone who loves Jesus to prophesy," he says. "This really is the inheritance of every born-again believer."[7]

If you are seeking to grow in this area, Bickle says a simple way to receive more prophetic impressions is to ask the Holy Spirit, "What are You saying or doing at this time that You want me to participate in?" He says that as he goes throughout his day, whether to staff meetings, ministry times, fellowship times, family times, recreational events, meals, or study times, he likes to pause and ask the Holy Spirit, "Are You wanting to say anything *to* me or *through* me?"

He advises not to limit the Holy Spirit by asking questions like this only in spiritual contexts or for large things. The Holy Spirit is involved in both big and small matters, work and play, school and social events, and so on. There's never a wrong time to ask the Holy Spirit, "Is there anything You want to say *to* me or *through* me in this situation?"

Once you receive an impression, says Bickle, you must act on it. You must give expression to it, verbalize it. And then you must be grateful for the small things as you "cultivate a lifestyle of watching and waiting." Be faithful in little things, he says. "It takes humility to walk with God on His terms of being faithful and grateful in the days of smallness."[8]

As you grow in this area, the Lord may begin to use you in more public settings. Until you are mature in the area of prophecy, Bickle recommends submitting what you feel the Spirit is saying to you to your pastor or ministry leader for their approval before sharing it publicly. Many words are not intended to be shared publicly. But when God does choose to manifest His power through a prophetic person in a public ministry setting, it gives us the opportunity for spiritual growth.

I remember a personal example of this. In 1990 at a conference in Texas, a prophet named Paul Cain called me out of a huge crowd and gave me a prophetic word that shook me due to its accuracy. Cain started his ministry in what's called the healing movement and had some notoriety in Pentecostal circles. He was up in years then and widely respected. Sadly, compromise in his life created a scandal two decades later. He supposedly repented, but his reputation was so tarnished that I considered not telling this story. However, his word was so accurate and so unexpected when he gave it that I use it as an illustration here.

In front of a huge crowd while I stood nervously listening, he said he saw me at age fourteen, looking through *Venetian* blinds at a *lake*, and he saw the number *722*. He said I was God's maverick. And yes, during that period, I was a maverick and for a few years ran from the call of God on my life. But Cain said I had a great work to do. In 1980 I didn't understand. Today I can look back and see God's hand.

When I was fourteen, I lived in Lakeland, Florida, at 722 Venetian Avenue. How could he have known that?

Yet the most significant prophecy of my life came thirty years later.

God Connections Are Part of Spirit-Led Living

Someone once called me a "practical Pentecostal." I'm a pretty level-headed guy. I try to be led by the Spirit. I pray about all major decisions, and I seek wise counsel. I don't look for prophecies, yet they sometimes come in unusual ways. And though I appreciate them, the prophetic words are rarely dramatic.

But one day the Lord caused something unexpected to happen. I saw up close and personal that God does reveal to prophets what will happen, and it can make a huge difference. In my case the prophet was an unassuming accountant from New Jersey named Hubie Synn. I hope this story inspires faith that God still uses the gift of prophecy to accomplish His will.

One day one of my staff members said he met a man who had a word for me and asked if it was OK for him to give it to me. Something felt different about this—maybe how polite the request was. So I said yes and gave my staffer my personal email address, and soon I received an encouraging but general word from the prophet. Later I met him, and we are friends to this day, and it was out of this relationship that God performed a miracle—maybe the biggest in the history of Charisma Media.

First, a little background. Synn had a prophetic word more than a year earlier for one of his accounting clients: David Tyree, then an NFL player for the New York Giants who is a Spirit-led Christian. Later I discovered we had a mutual friend in Kimberly Daniels, a pastor in Jacksonville, Florida, whom I've known for twenty years and who told me about the prophecy Synn gave Tyree.

I'm not much of a football fan, but that year—2008—the New England Patriots were undefeated and greatly favored to beat the New York Giants. Daniels is a huge football fan, and she got excited when she heard about the prophetic word that God was going to bring Tyree out of obscurity into the spotlight and give him a platform so he would be known as a wide receiver rather than simply a special-teams player.

In this case Synn is spiritually sensitive, and as he got to know his new client, he found Tyree and his wife had been praying about how he could share the gospel. Yes, Tyree loved football, but that wasn't his greatest passion.

So in his unassuming way Synn said what he felt the Lord wanted him to say. Later he couldn't remember the exact words, but he wanted to encourage him that the Lord had heard the Tyrees' prayers. The word was, in essence, "God is going to bring you out of obscurity into the spotlight and give you a platform, and your name will go before you. You will be known as a wide receiver. I am about to highlight your skills as a wide receiver. I know about your desire to share your faith, and I am going to give you a platform to do that."

This is an important point. God was more interested in answering Tyree's prayer than in who won the Super Bowl. But He did it in a way that brought glory to Himself and set several things in motion.

At the time, I knew none of this. I just heard that a prophet had said Tyree was going to do something extraordinary. I was planning to watch the game anyway, so I was interested.

Synn also gathered with family and friends to watch the game. The Giants were the underdogs. When the fourth quarter arrived, the Patriots were four points ahead and the Giants looked tired. Still, Synn was confident something would happen.

To get the story right—and to share the drama and excitement—I'll let Hubie Synn tell the story, as he did in his book *The Tales of a Wandering Prophet.*

> With eleven minutes left in the game, David lined up as a receiver
> and ran a route that put him open in the end zone. Giants

quarterback Eli Manning zipped a pass to him, and David's catch gave the Giants the lead, 10–7. We all celebrated, but I noticed something: the flickering in my heart didn't change. Catching the go-ahead touchdown was a good moment, but not *the* moment.

Synn told his wife he felt something else was going to happen. Then he watched as New England took back the lead with two minutes, forty-two seconds left in the game. Things were looking dim for the Giants, but Synn sensed God had something more in store. He and his family remained glued to their TV, and as the game clock wound down to a minute, fifteen seconds, the Giants were somehow still alive. He recalls:

The next play was third down and five, and the Giants' offensive line looked out of breath. As soon as the ball was snapped, the Patriots poured through. One lineman grabbed hold of Eli's shoulder, another the back of his jersey, and it appeared to be a sure sack. The pocket collapsed entirely, and for a moment, Eli was almost invisible among the tumult of jerseys. Then, with a defender still grasping his jersey, Eli managed to slip into the open field and buy one more second. Far in the backfield, he squared up and tossed the ball thirty-two yards into the middle of the field.

"It's to David! It's to David!" I said as the ball sailed through the air.

Sure enough, David was the intended receiver. He leaped high and grabbed the ball out of the air with both hands. Rodney Harrison, New England's star defender, hit the ball out of David's hands while he was in the air, and it looked as if it would fall incomplete. But instead of falling to the ground, the ball fell on David's helmet, and David's right hand pinned it there. Rodney tackled him, furiously trying to whack the ball loose, but David managed to put both hands on the ball and hold it against his helmet.[9]

It might have been the most historic catch in NFL history. The Lord knew it would happen and that it would be an answer to David Tyree's prayer and give him the platform he desired. And it was documented that the prophecy was spoken before the game!

The whole nation was talking about "the catch." We even did a short *Charisma* article about the prophetic aspect of this historic play. Journalistically speaking, it's usually difficult to report this conclusively on a prophetic word. Rarely does a prophetic word come to pass so quickly, nor is one documented so well. We were thrilled to have this example to encourage the readers of *Charisma*.

As incredible as that prophecy was, a couple of years later Synn had another prophetic word that God has used in ways I could never have

"God, You Did It!"

In 2008, when my accountant Hubie Synn, a man with an incredible prophetic gift, told me God was about to highlight my skills as a wide receiver, bring me out of obscurity, and give me a platform to share my faith, I didn't know what to expect. I was a special teams player for the New York Giants, but like all other special teams players, I was in obscurity as an individual player. I loved the Lord and believed He had more ahead for me. But I never dreamed what would happen that year at the Super Bowl.

Before the game, I had received several prophetic words, including the one from Hubie. All those words gave confidence to my heart. The Bible says that things will be confirmed by two or three witnesses. God used many more than two or three to confirm what was about to happen at Super Bowl XLII. I heard these words and believed them. But I never could have imagined in my greatest dreams what God was actually about to do.

After what became known as "the catch," I could not help but hold my head down to my chest and say, "God, You did it!" I looked into the television set and gave a shout out to my mother in heaven. Then it was time to celebrate the miracle: We had finished our course on the road to victory. The curse of "almost and not enough" was broken. We did not die hard, and I know that what happened was only because of the intervention of God. I took great joy in saying, "God did it! God did it! God did it!"

The biggest thing about what happened on that field in Glendale, Arizona, is the platform God has given me to be a positive role model....I've gone from the Giants player no one recognized to a guy who can't have a quiet, anonymous dinner at a restaurant anymore. That's a good thing, if I can share what God has done through me.[10]

—DAVID TYREE, FORMER NFL WIDE RECEIVER

imagined. It was a word he gave a complete stranger in an airport early one morning while he was waiting for a flight.

THE STORY BEHIND THE STORY

The stranger turned out to be Jonathan Cahn, now a well-known best-selling author. At the time, Cahn had never published a book but had finished the first draft of what was later published as *The Harbinger*. A Messianic rabbi from New Jersey, Cahn had been praying as he waited for his flight in Charlotte, North Carolina. He was asking the Lord what to do because friends were giving him conflicting advice on publishing his book. With a busy schedule and on his way to a speaking engagement, he decided to spend the travel time praying about what to do regarding publishing his book.

Meanwhile, in the same airport, Synn was flying to visit his sister, who was dying. He was irritated by the bad weather and the flight delays. So when the Lord impressed on him to speak to a man with a black beard whom Synn took to be an Orthodox Jew, he wasn't happy about it, as the man seemed unlikely to want a prophetic word from a Christian.

After initially resisting the prompting, Synn finally asked the man, "What's the good word?" Cahn had been reading his Bible and praying when he looked up and saw Synn, who is of Korean, Mexican, and American Indian descent, and assumed he was a secular businessman. Thinking Synn was witnessing to him, he answered, "God loves you." Suddenly, Synn knew he should give the word that Cahn had a message for the nation and world and that it would impact both believers and nonbelievers.

Unknown to Synn, his act of obedience in the airport had an added layer of prophetic significance. It mirrored the opening scene of Cahn's written but then unpublished book, *The Harbinger*, in which a stranger, who turns out to be a prophet, sits to the left of the main character, Nouriel. The prophet strikes up a conversation with Nouriel in a public place to give him a prophetic word, which ultimately leads Nouriel to publish a book warning the nation of judgment and calling its people to repentance and salvation.

Needless to say, this prophecy had Cahn's attention. The two men sat together on the plane, and Cahn asked questions and took copious notes.

A few weeks later I got an email in which Synn told me he gave Cahn a word just as Cahn was praying about what direction to go concerning publishing his manuscript. He said after receiving the word, Cahn decided not to make any moves until he could discern how God was leading.

Synn went on to say in the email that he felt led to contact me: "I mentioned your name to Jonathan (I hope you don't mind), and he was excited about it. Maybe this can be a blessing for both of you. Jonathan wrote down the word he got, and some of it was something about being monumental. He will write a few books. Steve, I feel something is up with this, so pray about it."

I get calls and emails about potential books all the time. Industry insiders know most aren't worth publishing. However, due to my respect for Synn and maybe the prompting of the Holy Spirit, I replied, "You're not real clear on what the book is about…but we'd like to see it. Can you email it to me?"

Less than a year later, *The Harbinger* was released. It hit the *New York Times* best-seller list the first week and was on the list for 102 weeks. But more important than the remarkable publishing success were the countless lives touched, seeing God's hand at work, and launching Cahn's ministry to a level of prominence it never had before.

I tell you this story to increase your faith and because it is 100 percent provable. So far I've shared prophecies that affected me personally and prophecies that affected the audience we reach through our publishing company. Now I'd like to share an example of prophecy that affected a nation.

A Prophecy About an American President

Kim Clement, a South African who moved to the United States in the early 1980s, had an incredible gift of prophecy. Though not well-known outside Pentecostal-Charismatic circles, he was well respected as a prophetic minister. He was a frequent guest on TBN and spoke at large conferences and churches. Being a musician, he would often accompany himself on a keyboard as he ministered and spoke prophetically.

In 2007 he spoke at Bethel Church in Redding, California, and said, "Trump shall become a trumpet."[11] Even more startling, that same year he said at a service in Scottsdale, Arizona: "Listen to the word of the Lord. God says, I will put at your helm for two terms a president that will pray, but he will not be a praying president when he starts."[12]

That prophecy has been viewed more than 1.6 million times on YouTube yet has been virtually ignored by the media. Other than the reference to the trumpet, there is no specific mention of Donald Trump. Only in hindsight have people latched on to this video as a prophecy about Trump and passed it around.

I first met Kim Clement in the late 1990s, so I knew his story. He had been trained to be a classical pianist and later played in a rock band. Nearly overdosing on heroin led him to become a Christian in 1974. Gradually, as he grew in his faith and ministry, he developed a reputation as a seer, a prophet. As I mentioned, in Charismatic worship services, he would often accompany himself on the keyboard and sing his prophecies. (Unless you were raised a Pentecostal, this form of worship may seem odd.) A sort of mystic, Clement would often shake his long dark hair as he spoke or sang.

This resulted in a heavy, almost mystical atmosphere in the services, and most people in the room seemed to believe God really was speaking through Clement.

In Scottsdale in 2007 Clement also prophesied: "There will be a praying president, not a religious one. For I will fool the people, says the Lord. I will fool the people. Yes, I will, God says. The one that is chosen shall go in and they shall say, 'He has hot blood.' For the Spirit of God says, yes, he may have hot blood, but he will bring the walls of protection on this country in a greater way, and the economy of this country shall change rapidly, says the Lord of hosts."[13]

Again, only in hindsight can we notice what he said about Trump having "hot blood" or building walls of protection or helping the economy boom. But most interestingly is that he said, "Listen to the word of the Lord. God says, I will put at your helm *for two terms* a president that will pray, but he will not be a praying president when he starts."

Seven years later, on February 22, 2014, more than a year before Trump announced he would run for president, Clement prophesied that God had allowed a veil to be put on this nation, "for in darkness, faith grows." He went on to say God found a man after His own heart like King David, who would be singled out for the presidency of the United States. Clement continued: "I have searched for a man...who would stand in the Oval Office and pray for the restoration of the fortunes of Zion [Israel]....

"Watch how I will change everything, for there shall be those who are in justice, and there are those who are in a strong position (I am just hearing this now) in the highest court in the land. The highest court in the land. The Supreme Court. Two shall step down. For the embarrassment of what shall take place. But I wish to place in the highest court in the land, righteousness. And they shall attempt to put others in to reach their endeavors. But God says, 'Hear me tonight. Hear me today. I have this whole thing planned out, according to My will.'"[14]

For many conservative Christians who believe their nation is deteriorating before their eyes, such words bring hope. Even if they don't know whether to believe them, they want to.

In the same meeting, Clement shared a recent vision he had in which he saw a group of people, and a man emerged from among them that he sensed God had singled out for the presidency of the United States: "And the Spirit of God said, 'This man will throttle the enemies of Israel. This man will throttle the enemies of the West. And there are highly embarrassing moments that are about to occur for many, many politicians in this nation. There will be a shaking amongst, there will be a shaking amongst the Democrats in the upcoming elections, but unsettling for the Republicans.'"

Then he asked rhetorically, "Why is God doing this? For God said, 'I am dissatisfied with what emerges from both parties.'"

"And then there is a nation He showed me, He took me, itching for a new kind of war with America. They will shout, 'Impeach, impeach,' they say. But nay. This nation shall come very suddenly, but it shall not come in the time of President Obama. It shall come when this new one arises. My David, that I have set aside for this nation….They will shout, 'Impeach, impeach!' but this will not happen.

"God says, 'Once you recognize the man that I have raised up, pray. For the enemy will do everything in its power to put a witch in the White House. For Jezebel has chased away the prophets and even Elijah. Now I have said, "Go back." For this shall be dismantled so that there will be no more corruption in the White House,' says the Spirit."[15]

Clement said more, and not all of it has come to pass. But to me it's interesting that between these two prophecies, he touched on most of the significant issues at stake during Trump's presidency, and he uttered specific words about Trump that have taken place.

In case you are wondering, Clement suffered a stroke in 2015 and passed away in November 2016, the same month Trump was elected. So there is no way someone could have recorded him saying these things after they played out during Trump's presidency and post-dated it to look as if he said them in advance. Both prophetic words were given before Trump had even announced he was running for office.

When Clement shared those words, Donald Trump was a reality TV star and well-known real estate billionaire. I knew only what I saw in the media. How could this be true? At the time, George W. Bush was still president. Yet around 2014 I began hearing others talking about these prophecies.

Seldom did prophets in Pentecostal-Charismatic circles prophecy about politics. Their prophecies were usually about an upcoming revival to sweep the world or about a blessing a believer was going to receive.

This was so interesting to me, I wrote a book called *God and Donald Trump*, even though I was no fan of Donald Trump early on. (I didn't even like his TV show *The Apprentice*.) Before the election, I became a big supporter of Trump because I was terrified of where his opponent, Hillary Clinton, would take the country. I also wrote the book because few outside Charismatic circles seemed to know Trump's election was prophesied. Some of the same prophets said he'd be elected twice. When Biden took office in 2021, there were some who sneered at the inaccurate prophecies. But the same critics were silent when I wrote about the accurate prophecies in 2016.

As a Spirit-led Christian, I believe in prophecy, healings, and signs and wonders. As a journalist, I've learned to be careful and say *I believe* someone is healed or *it's my opinion* that God still speaks today, and to document healings and prophetic words when they come to pass. (Many prophetic utterances are given in some sort of spiritual code. Yet Clement gave actual names and dates.)

This is not a political book, and my aim in sharing this isn't political. It is to dive into how God speaks today and how He answers prayer. One of my friends, who is a respected prayer leader, told me that after the 2016 election "millions were praying God would send us a leader to turn things around, but we didn't have anyone in mind," to explain in a humorous way that he believed Trump's presidency was an answer to prayer.

I wanted to share that last story because it's an example of how the gift of prophecy works on a broader scale. Prophecy has a purpose beyond personal ministry.

Mike Bickle agrees. He believes the church is to function as a "corporate prophet to the nation" and that there are seven dimensions of prophecy that go beyond simply being "something that Charismatics do." He believes prophetic ministry is a function of the worldwide church to proclaim the fulfillment of end-time events and speak forth revelatory messages in a broad and multidimensional way. "Prophetic ministry is not just something the church does, but something it *is* by its very nature," he writes.

Bickle defines the seven dimensions of the prophetic church as

1. the revelation of the testimony of God's heart,[16]

2. the proclamation of end-time prophecy,[17]

3. the preservation and proclamation of the Word of God as His prophetic standard on the earth,[18]

4. the reception of prophetic direction (awakening the purpose of God in the present—what He wants to do in us and through us now),[19]

5. prophetic dreams and visions and the power of God,[20]

6. the prophetic outcry against social injustice, and

7. the prophetic call to holiness.

Like Bickle, my prayer is that God will use this book to stir up the prophetic gift in your life so "God will work mightily in our generation to help the church live up to and express its prophetic nature and calling among the nations of the earth."[21]

LIVING IT OUT

Read 1 Corinthians 14:1:

> Follow after love and desire spiritual gifts, but especially that you may prophesy.

Think about it:

1. Why do you think Paul emphasizes prophecy over the other spiritual gifts in 1 Corinthians 14:1?

2. Have you struggled to believe that God speaks in the way discussed in this chapter or to believe prophetic words you have heard about? Why do you think Paul exhorted us not to despise prophetic utterances in 1 Thessalonians 5:20?

3. Mike Bickle describes seven dimensions of the prophetic church. How do you see this generation helping the church live up to and express its prophetic nature and calling?

4. We've seen that the Holy Spirit gives the gift of prophecy to His people to encourage and exhort them. How is the Spirit speaking prophetically in your church to comfort and encourage God's people? How are you proclaiming God's Word through both your words and actions?

Chapter 5

DISCOVER HOW THE GIFTS
OF THE SPIRIT WORK

THE EARLIEST MENTION in Scripture of the gifts of the Spirit is when Isaiah prophecies of the Messiah: "The Spirit of the LORD shall rest upon him, the Spirit of wisdom and understanding, the Spirit of counsel and might, the Spirit of knowledge and of the fear of the LORD. He shall delight in the fear of the LORD, and he shall not judge by what his eyes see, nor reprove by what his ears hear."[1]

The reason we receive these gifts, all embodied in Jesus, is so the body of Christ will function with diverse gifts, each "according to the grace that is given to us," as Paul tells us, "if prophecy, according to the proportion of faith; if service, in serving; he who teaches, in teaching; he who exhorts, in exhortation; he who gives, with generosity; he who rules, with diligence; he who shows mercy, with cheerfulness."[2]

Most Evangelicals would agree that the gifts of the Spirit are unique skills and abilities given by the Holy Spirit to faithful followers of Christ to serve God and benefit His people, the church. However, many seemingly sincere Christians twist their beliefs into pretzels to say these gifts ended with the death of the last apostle.

Many commentaries have been written on the gifts, if you are motivated to look. There are four distinct lists in the Bible, and there is both significant overlap and differences among them. One commentator wrote: "This suggests that none of the lists, taken either individually or together, is intended to be comprehensive. Rather each is suggestive of the diversity of ways God endows Christians for spiritual service."[3]

A commentary would provide a bulleted list of the gifts, but this is no commentary. I want to show the gifts of the Spirit in action.

Early in my career I got to know Derek Prince, probably the most respected Charismatic teacher of his day. He was well known for the way he could make deep scriptural truths understandable to average people. He describes the nine gifts of the Spirit listed in 1 Corinthians 12:8–10 as "manifestations" of the Spirit. Many use this term because the Holy Spirit is invisible, but when these gifts operate, they allow us to see, hear, feel, and sense Him.

Prince explains that these nine gifts—the word of wisdom, the word of knowledge, faith, gifts of healings, the working of miracles, prophecy, the discerning of spirits, various kinds of tongues, and the interpretation of tongues—all have a practical purpose and are used as tools of ministry. They are supernatural, meaning they are not produced by natural ability. "If a certain gift regularly manifests itself through a certain person," says Prince, "we may say that the person has that gift."[4] He goes on to emphasize that the gifts are given by God's grace. We receive them by faith; we cannot earn them.[5]

We've already discussed the gifts of prophecy and tongues. In this chapter I want to address the other gifts listed in 1 Corinthians 12.

WORD OF KNOWLEDGE

Prince explains that a word of knowledge gives the facts about a situation, whereas a word of wisdom tells how God wants to deal with it. According to the *FireBible*, a word of knowledge is "a statement inspired by the Holy Spirit that reveals knowledge about people, circumstances or Biblical truth that likely would not have been known or understood apart from God. Its aim is usually to provide guidance, to help confirm a decision or to expose something that is important for a person's spiritual development."[6]

I remember seeing this in action when I attended one of Kathryn Kuhlman's crusades in Lakeland, Florida, in 1975. I wrote about the experience in *Florida Magazine,* the Sunday magazine of the *Sentinel*

Star (now called *Orlando Sentinel*), where I worked at the time. It was an objective article, even citing some of her critics. But it was friendly, not hostile. I rode to the crusade in a bus with other attendees, and I wrote what I saw and heard. My article may have been one of the last ones written about her before she died, almost exactly ten months after this article was published.

Kathryn Kuhlman was well known for "calling out" miracles with a word of knowledge, but I'd never personally seen her do it before attending that crusade. My article described what I saw:

> Then, suddenly, she pointed toward the back of the arena. "Someone with varicose veins has just been healed." Before that person can respond she says an ear has been healed, then that bursitis has been healed. Christians call this a "Word of Knowledge"—one of seven New Testament gifts given by the Holy Spirit. The apostle Paul said this gift gives knowledge to a person about something that has just happened. The announcements of healing in this manner continue off and on for an hour.[7]

As I read that all these years later, I can't help but think that was a different era in journalism. At the time, I considered the newspaper to be very liberal and secular. But in today's climate, I doubt an editor would even assign the story, let alone let me describe gifts of the Spirit. (A few months after I wrote about Kuhlman, I started *Charisma* and published a revised version of the article as the cover story of our second issue.)

Even though we don't often read about words of knowledge, there are other examples. One of the most incredible accounts I've heard came from Reinhard Bonnke, the German evangelist who declared, "Africa shall be saved," and whose ministry reached an estimated seventy-nine million before his death in late 2019. I had the privilege of getting to know Bonnke well after he moved his ministry to Orlando, Florida, in the early 2000s. In his book *Evangelism by Fire*, he explains that we don't always have to know what God is doing when we're given a word of knowledge. We are simply to deliver the message and let the Holy Spirit do the rest.

To illustrate the point, Bonnke told an amazing story. He and his brother had grown up in the same household with godly parents, but while Bonnke had chosen to follow Jesus, his brother had not. Instead, his brother had chosen the path of financial success and had an amazing career.

Many years passed, and there was little communication between the brothers. Unknown to Reinhard Bonnke, his brother's wife had left him, and his best friend had died of cancer. His life had become meaningless to him. Then he had a vivid dream one night that he was walking on a bridge high in the air. He slipped and started falling.

Bonnke's brother woke up drenched in sweat. Shaken by the dream, he got down on his knees and said, "Lord, You know that I do not even know that You exist, but my brother Reinhard is Your servant. Give me a sign through him that You are alive."

Meanwhile, Bonnke was six thousand miles away in South Africa. He didn't know anything about his brother's problems or, as he would later learn, that he was considering taking his own life. But early one morning he too had a terrible dream. He saw his brother walking on a bridge high in the air. It was foggy, and the bridge had no railings, so Bonnke feared his brother might slip and fall off. His brother continued walking into the fog. In the dream, Bonnke desperately called out his brother's name. Then he heard his brother's voice crying out from the bottomless depths below the bridge.

Bonnke also woke up drenched in sweat. He asked the Lord the meaning of the dream and sensed God telling him that his brother was on the bridge to eternity and he was to warn him. Bonnke put his reservations aside and immediately wrote his brother a letter, telling him of the dream. He pleaded with his brother to receive Jesus Christ as his personal Savior.

A few days before Christmas that year, Bonnke received a letter from his brother in reply. He had accepted Christ and knew that his sins were forgiven. Bonnke said: "When I received that letter, I could not control my emotions, and I just wept for joy. How wonderful the Holy Spirit is! How effective are His gifts! They are God's powerful weapons."[8]

My friend Sid Roth also experienced this gift when he ministered in

Ukraine. Once a Jewish stockbroker, in the early 1970s he came to believe Jesus was the Jewish Messiah. In the years since then he's become a leader in the burgeoning Messianic Jewish movement and today hosts a popular TV program called *It's Supernatural!*

One of Roth's friends, Jonathan Bernis, who later became head of Jewish Voice, had held large rallies in Ukraine and found Jews there were open to the gospel. He invited Roth to go with him to Russia to host Jewish music festivals. Roth went a step further and said he would go and give lectures on the supernatural. Roth and Bernis did a lot of promotion, even hanging a banner next to an advertisement for an upcoming KISS concert. They played up that Roth had studied the paranormal for many years. He said his lecture was one night only, and he predicted people who came would be healed.

As soon as the lecture started, Roth began hearing the Lord tell him that people were being healed. "The minute I started speaking, I had words of knowledge. Now, *that* I had framework for, but what I didn't have the framework for was talking before large numbers of Jewish people," he told me on my podcast. His audience did not know he was a believer in Jesus; they just knew he was giving a lecture on the supernatural.

Roth knew he had to be careful not to let his unsaved audience think he was the one doing the healing. God will not share His glory with anyone. All these thoughts flooded his mind, but he decided to take the chance anyway. When he asked for anyone whose pain or other symptoms were totally gone to stand up, he said as many as 60–70 percent of his Jewish audience instantly stood up, saying they'd been healed.[9]

THE GIFT OF FAITH

What about the other gifts? One of the most powerful is the gift of faith. The Bible says every believer is given a "measure of faith."[10] The writer of Hebrews tells us, "Faith is the substance of things hoped for, the evidence of things not seen."[11] And Jesus told us that if we have faith as tiny as a

Supernatural Encouragement

My friend Rafael invited me to preach in his church in Humacao, Puerto Rico. It was Pentecost Sunday, so I brought a message about the Holy Spirit's power. Then I asked God to use me in a supernatural way because I figure we shouldn't talk about the Spirit's gifts if we're not willing to demonstrate them.

After I finished my sermon, I noticed a young man sitting in the fourth row. I'd never met him, but I could sense God's love for him. I pointed to him and began to give a word of prophecy about how God wanted to use him. I then prophesied over other people and prayed for many others, and then I left Humacao.

Recently I returned to Puerto Rico to speak at a men's retreat. Guess who showed up? The young man to whom I gave the prophecy came to the event. His name is John, and I learned that he had never visited the church in Humacao until the day I met him there. Because John felt God speaking to him in such a very personal way that Sunday, he has been attending that church ever since—and he has been growing spiritually. One simple word of supernatural encouragement changed John's life.[12]

—J. Lee Grady, Senior Contributing Editor, *Charisma*;
Founder, The Mordecai Project

mustard seed, we can speak to mountains and they will be removed and cast into the sea.[13] This type of faith is available to all believers.

But the gift of faith is something more. It's not saving faith but an extraordinary faith to see the impossible done. Without realizing it, I believe God gave me faith to believe *Charisma* magazine—and all the things we've done since its founding—into existence.

I can remember once lying flat on my face, praying for a financial miracle at an important time, and what I prayed for came to pass. Another time I fasted for forty days during a time when I needed to hear from God. It wasn't easy, but I was desperate for an answer, and I believe the answer came. Although not everyone operates in the gift of faith, as each of us walks in the Spirit, we can believe and be inspired by the ministries of faith leaders such as Kenneth Copeland or by the many books on faith such as *The Believer's Authority* by Kenneth E. Hagin.

WHAT KENNETH COPELAND TAUGHT ME

To walk in the Spirit, we must walk in faith. One of the primary experts on faith is Kenneth Copeland, whom I have known since I interviewed him for *Charisma* in 1979. I was twenty-eight. At the time, he was teaching on the radio and leading Victory Campaigns and making a name for himself. I'd been influenced by him, and I thought an interview would be an interesting story for the readers of my new magazine.

That interview made such an impact on me, I dug back into our archives to remind myself what Copeland shared. Remember, faith is listed as both a gift and fruit of the Spirit. That tells me it's really important. Plus, without faith it's impossible to please God.

Through that interview I learned that faith is not some passive concept but something each believer can "use." As I wrote in my article, "Kenneth Copeland leaned over, looked me straight in the eyes and said, 'A man can use faith the way a mechanic uses a wrench, or a carpenter uses a hammer. Faith can be controlled just like fear can be controlled. You can turn it off, or turn it on.' Although I've had a few problems turning fear on and off, it was hard to deny Copeland's claim."

I wanted to know how someone could turn faith on. "Isn't faith something that falls from heaven like tongues on the Day of Pentecost?" I asked.

> "Oh no," Copeland said. "What most believers don't realize is that they can use the faith God gave them. In fact, a man is handicapped if he doesn't know how to use his faith. Usually we think of the handicapped as people who can't use their limbs or mind. But the greatest disadvantage is someone who can't use his faith."

"Why is faith so important?" I asked. Because, Copeland said, "we're saved by faith, we're righteous by faith, and Romans 14:23 says whatever is not of faith is sin. A man should do everything by faith."

Everything? What about getting up in the morning? For Copeland, he even got up by faith, never setting an alarm. I'd never heard this. What about getting a job or what you eat. "The Bible says to eat by faith," he said, reaching for his Bible. "Romans 14:23 is talking about eating when it says that anything not of faith is sin. A man should do everything by faith."

How do you learn to turn on your faith? Copeland's plan is simple:

1. Develop faith in God's Word; accept it as the final authority.

2. Meditate on the Word of God. Thinking about what the Bible says feeds faith into your spirit. As you feed on the Word, your faith and God's faith become one, and your capacity for faith grows.

3. Act on the Word of God. If the Bible says to do something, do it, much as you'd act on the word of a doctor or lawyer. As you read and study the Word, ask questions, such as, How does this apply to me?

First John 4:4 became one of Copeland's foundational faith verses: "Ye are of God, little children, and have overcome them: because greater is he that is in you, than he that is in the world."[14]

As Copeland meditated on that verse, realizing God was talking to him through it, he told himself, "I'm of God; God is my heritage; God is my source; I have overcome Satan. It's not that I will overcome, but I am victorious right now."

Although he had committed the verse to memory long before, he read it over and over, wrote it on a note card, and carried it around with him. As he thought about the verse, the Holy Spirit showed him how it related to other truths he had studied in the Word and to situations in his life.

One day as he was meditating on 1 John 4:4, Copeland came to a life-changing realization as he read, "Greater is He that is within you."

"I had been putting my faith in the God in heaven, but I was ignoring the God inside me. One day I felt my prayers weren't getting to the ceiling.

But then I realized 'greater is He who is *within* me.' But it doesn't matter if the prayers don't get above my nose. God is inside me." As part of acting on the Word of God, decide to live by faith. The Bible says, "The just shall live by his faith."[15] It's a matter of the will.

The result of all this, Copeland was quick to point out, is that miracles begin to happen. The promises in the Word of God begin to become reality in one's life, and you experience blessings such as peace of mind, financial increase, and good health. All these things result from having a positive, active faith.[16]

That interview was more than four decades ago. A lot has happened since then, and Copeland's ministry has become huge. But the fact is

Playing by the Spirit

I am from a singing, evangelistic family. I considered my father a musical genius, and my mother was an amazing musician as well. I grew up traveling and singing and surrounded by music in our Pentecostal denomination. As a little girl, I could pick out tunes on the piano. I learned to read a little bit of music from my daddy and a woman at church, but instead of being formally trained, I mostly picked up chording and other helpful tools from my parents and other gifted people I knew.

I received the Baptism of the Holy Spirit when I was six years old, and after that the anointing on my life became very strong. I could play things easily but couldn't tell you how I did it. As I grew, the anointing and musical ability became much stronger, and I knew it was only by the Holy Spirit that I was able to do these things.

One Sunday I was playing at my church in Florida and noticed my hands reflected on the glossy black finish of the baby grand. I saw myself playing some beautiful chords that were enhanced by notes not usually played in that chord. I remember thinking, "Wow, that's so cool!" Then I heard the Holy Spirit say, "I could do so much more if you would just get out of the way," and I heard Him whistle the tune the scarecrow sang in *The Wizard of Oz*, "If I Only Had a Brain." I smiled and thought, "You want me to be brainless?" He then proceeded to tell me He didn't need my gifts, my talents, or the knowledge I had gathered about music. He just needed my hands on the keyboard, a willing spirit, and my ears attuned to hear. With that He could play the music of heaven.

—REBECCA MCINNIS, WORSHIP LEADER

that God's Word is true. The truth of what Copeland was teaching then is still true today and will be true a thousand years from now. You must believe it, just as you must believe the other promises of God as you walk in the Spirit.

THE GIFTS OF HEALINGS

Another spiritual gift is the gifts of healings. These gifts (plural) are given to the church to restore healing in a miraculous manner. Every believer may not operate in this gift, but it's for the church as a whole.

In the last chapter of her book *I Believe in Miracles*, Kathryn Kuhlman shared what she believed to be the key to healing. Her quest to know this truth started with her heartbreak over some of the practices among faith healers she encountered early in her ministry. Often if people received prayer and weren't healed, they were told they didn't have enough faith, and Kuhlman said the looks of despair on those people's faces haunted her. She remembers sobbing and asking God why some were healed and others were not. She knew God was a healer because she had seen people healed with her own eyes, but one question plagued her: *What was the key?*

She knew God could do anything, but there were those who were bringing reproach to the cause of Christ "through ignorance and lack of spiritual knowledge." But what was the answer?

Kuhlman said the answer came one night during a series of services. A woman in the audience stood up and asked Kuhlman if she could share a testimony of something that happened in the previous night's service.

"As you were preaching on the Holy Ghost," she said, "telling us that in Him lay the Resurrection power, I felt the power of God flow through my body. Although not a word had been spoken regarding the healing of the sick, I knew instantly and definitely that my body had been healed. So sure was I of this, that I went to the doctor today and had my healing verified."

So that was it. It was the Holy Spirit. Kuhlman understood that night there was no need to have healing lines or exhortations to "have faith" as many healing evangelists did in that day.

> That was the beginning of this healing ministry which God has given to me; strange to some because of the fact that hundreds have been healed just sitting quietly in the audience, without any demonstration whatsoever, and even without admonition. This is because the presence of the Holy Spirit has been in such abundance that by His Presence alone, sick bodies are healed, even as people wait on the outside of the building for the doors to open.

She went on to share her understanding of the Holy Spirit's role in healing, which seems fitting to include in this book.

> If you can once grasp the concept of the Holy Trinity, many things which may have once puzzled you become clear....God the Father planned and purposed the creation and the redemption of man, and is the "Big Boss." God the Son provided and purchased at Calvary what God the Father had planned in eternity. He made possible the realization of God's eternal plan. All that we receive from the Father must come through Jesus Christ the Son, and that is why at the heart of our faith is a Person—the very Son of the very God....But the Holy Spirit is the power of the Trinity. It was His power which raised Jesus from the dead. It is that same Resurrection power that flows through our physical bodies today, healing and sanctifying.[17]

THE WORKING OF MIRACLES

The gift of miracles is the gift to display signs and wonders that give credibility to God's Word and the gospel message and overcome the work of Satan.

The gifts of healing and miracles often are almost interchangeable. If I'm sick and pray for healing, and then am healed, I give glory to God. But sometimes a healing is so enormous it can be explained only as a miracle.

Heidi Baker, who has ministered powerfully all over the world, has based her outreach in Mozambique, and in her book *Birthing the Miraculous*, she shares a powerful story of how she lived in the slums and worked with the poorest of the poor in that nation.

Because so many were sick and some were blind, she prayed for the gift of healing for many years and eventually received the Lord's promise that the blind would see. For a year she prayed for every blind person she could find, but no one gained their sight. Then one day she was in a dark little mud-hut church in central Mozambique, laying hands on an old blind lady. Suddenly the woman said she could see.

The amazing thing is that the old woman was called Mama Aida. That's what people in Mozambique call Heidi Baker, as Aida is the Portuguese version of the name Heidi.

Not only that, but within a short time two more blind women named Aida were healed! In three days, three women who went by "Mama Aida" received their sight.[18]

To me, that three women all with the same name as Baker would be healed of blindness in three days takes this beyond healing and puts it in the category of miracles. God's power was on full display, and many came to the saving knowledge of the gospel through this amazing demonstration of His power.

DISCERNING OF SPIRITS

There's one more gift listed in 1 Corinthians 12 that I want to discuss in this chapter. It's the discerning of spirits. Sometimes this gift is called discernment. It is the special ability given by the Holy Spirit to know whether a person claiming a word or action is from God is, in truth, from God or operating under satanic influence. In other words, it's when the Holy Spirit reveals that a problem or situation is caused by evil spirits that must be cast out or otherwise dealt with. Jesus did this when confronted with people who were tormented by demons. In Matthew 17:21, His disciples couldn't minister to a demoniac, and Jesus said that type of demon came out only with fasting and prayer.

We can find an account of the discerning of spirits in operation in Acts 5:1–11, when Ananias and Sapphira were lying about giving the church all the proceeds from the sale of their property, and in Acts 16:16–18, when Paul knew the origin of the spirit operating in a slave girl.

People filled with demonic spirits act in certain ways. Paul describes them in Galatians 5:16–21, 1 Timothy 6:3–5, and 2 Timothy 3:1–13. The Holy Spirit's gift of discernment empowers you to recognize right from wrong, truth from lies, and the work of the Spirit from the work of false spirits.[19]

The gifts of the Spirit aren't reserved for a select few who are "super anointed." If we are filled with the Holy Spirit and being led by Him, the gifts should manifest in our lives. In fact, Paul tells us to "follow the way of love and eagerly desire gifts of the Spirit."[20]

God wants His gifts flowing through you; all He needs is your availability. If you will surrender to Him, He will jump-start His power in your life.

LIVING IT OUT

Read 1 Corinthians 12:8–10:

> To one is given by the Spirit the word of wisdom, to another the word of knowledge by the same Spirit, to another faith by the same Spirit, to another gifts of healings by the same Spirit, to another the working of miracles, to another prophecy, to another discerning of spirits, to another various kinds of tongues, and to another the interpretation of tongues.

Think about it:

1. There are many gifts but one Spirit. What gifts has the Spirit stirred up in your life?

2. Read 1 John 4:4. What does "greater is he that is in you" mean to you? How does knowing the Holy Spirit is within you influence how you live and respond to the Word of God? Do you believe living by faith is a matter of the will? Why or why not?

3. Kathryn Kuhlman said the power that raised Jesus from the dead flows through our physical bodies today, healing and sanctifying. Describe a time when you prayed for healing for yourself or someone else. How does what you've read in this chapter give you faith to believe God still heals?

4. Which spiritual gifts would you like the Holy Spirit to give you more of? Why do you desire these gifts? Write a prayer asking Him to give you these gifts to minister to others for His glory.

Chapter 6

PREPARE FOR SOMETHING
GREATER IN YOUR LIFE

WE MUST COMMIT to doing only what the Spirit leads us to do if we are going to truly be Spirit led. Without Him, anything we do is what the Bible calls a work of the flesh.[1] Instead of creating a problem by doing things in our own effort and then asking the Spirit to get us out of the mess we've made, we must wait upon Him and follow His leading.

Dietrich Bonhoeffer, the German theologian and anti-Nazi dissident, put it this way: "The Holy Spirit is the living God, not some inert concept. The church community has to trust the Holy Spirit in every decision and believe strongly that the Spirit continues to be present in the community and at work in it. The Spirit will not permit our community to grope about to darkness, if only we are willing to take the Holy Spirit seriously."[2]

The Holy Spirit is very sensitive. He can be grieved, quenched, and resisted. He will not force His way into our lives, and many people never invite Him in. But if history tells us anything, it is that He is more than willing to touch those who seek more of His power.

WHAT HAPPENED AT AZUSA STREET

After the Holy Spirit was poured out on the Day of Pentecost, immediately signs and wonders began happening—the sick were healed, the dead were raised, the demon-possessed were set free. So many people began believing the disciples' message, the Jewish leaders tried to snuff out this new movement. So the new believers fled, and as they did, they took the gospel with them, eventually spreading it around the world.

Yet if you study church history, you'll see a pattern of ups and downs. The move of the Spirit seemed to ebb and flow. The Protestant Reformation Martin Luther led was an outbreak of the Holy Spirit to come against the established church, which had become corrupt. As Protestantism spread across Europe to France, those who embraced it were called Huguenots. Stories are told of people getting excited and falling to the floor, as if in a trance. Later, during the first Great Awakening, records report the same thing happening. It sounds like what we sometimes see in Pentecostalism.[3]

In the late 1800s a holiness movement began emphasizing purity, zeal, and devotion to Christ. People began praying for a new Baptism in the Holy Spirit. At Bethel Bible College in Topeka, Kansas, a handful of students of a Holiness preacher named Charles Parham prayed on New Year's Eve in 1900 to receive this Baptism in the Holy Spirit. First, a young woman named Agnes Ozman began to speak in an unknown tongue. Soon other students did. When Parham heard this, he believed it confirmed his theory of tongues being the initial evidence of the Baptism in the Holy Spirit.

Parham began going around the country preaching about Spirit baptism, and in the summer of 1905 he took his teaching on a Baptism in the Holy Spirit evidenced by speaking in tongues to Houston, where a young Black preacher named William Seymour heard the message and believed.[4]

Seymour began leading prayer meetings at 216 Bonnie Brae Street in Los Angeles that attracted so many people the house's foundation collapsed. The group was forced to move to a vacant former livery stable at 312 Azusa Street, which gave one of the twentieth century's most influential revivals its name.[5]

Someone prophesied that what happened at the Bonnie Brae meetings would go around the world, and it has. These events marked the birth of the Pentecostal movement, which has become one of the fastest-growing religious movements in history.[6]

Sadly, because many Christians in that era believed the miraculous gifts of the Holy Spirit died with the apostles in the first century, they weren't open to this new outpouring. (This is called cessationism.) So when the Baptism of the Holy Spirit was poured out at Azusa Street, Christians struggled to know what to call it. Most settled on the term Pentecostal, referring to the Day of Pentecost (the Greek word for *fifty days after Passover*).

Most of the church rejected this new Pentecostal movement.[7] To some, the term Pentecostal became a put-down.[8] That may be because early Pentecostals tended to be poor and uneducated and were looked down on by more upper-class denominations that rejected the worship style and theology of this new sect that quickly spawned new denominations such as the Assemblies of God. The Church of God (Cleveland, Tennessee) and the Church of God in Christ were both formed before the Azusa Street Revival of 1906, but when leaders received the Baptism in the Holy Spirit, the denominations quickly became known as Pentecostal.

I know because I've reported on these groups many times in *Charisma* magazine. Interestingly the Pentecostal movement has grown (much of it outside the United States) to more than 644 million. The upper-class mainline denominations that looked down on Pentecostals have all decreased in size over the decades, and many of them are so liberal today they are part of what I call the upside-down world.

As Pentecostals slowly moved up the socioeconomic and education ladders, they wanted to use more widely respected terms such as "full gospel."[9] Yet that term put off a lot of believers, who felt it implied those who may not believe in the work, power, and gifts of the Holy Spirit believed only part of the gospel, not the "full gospel."

Some Pentecostals have used the term Spirit-filled, including the late Jack Hayford, who was the general editor of the *Spirit-Filled Life Bible*. Yet that term also drew its critics, who made the point that all believers have the Holy Spirit living inside them.[10]

Over the years, we've used the term Spirit-led. The first issue of *Charisma* in 1975 was called "the magazine on Spirit-led living." Later, during the heyday of the magazine industry, we published a popular magazine called *SpiritLed Woman*. And now it's part of the title of this book.

As a journalist, I've always enjoyed how words develop, so bear with me before we delve into what the Bible says about the Holy Spirit. Let's look at the history of the name Charismatic.

When the Baptism of the Holy Spirit was poured out in 1967 on some Roman Catholic university students (and quickly spread around the world), people began calling them Catholic Pentecostals. In early 1969, Paulist Press, a respected Catholic publisher, published a book by that title.

But some Catholics were uncomfortable with the term Pentecostal because many in the movement during that era were known to be legalistic. I've told how my family were early Pentecostals, and I remember all the dos and don'ts: Don't go to movies because that is worldly entertainment. Don't go dancing because it's sensual. Don't wear makeup because holiness is about simplicity and humility. I knew one Pentecostal family that wouldn't let their kids read the comics on Sunday because it was the Lord's Day.

Most of these restrictions have since fallen by the wayside, but at the time, Catholics who never had these types of Holiness rules felt awkward being associated with them. This even though, theologically, they suddenly realized the New Testament gifts of the Spirit were for today. So the Catholics came up with their own term for this move of the Spirit: the Charismatic renewal. The movement was a renewal of the *charismata* (the Greek word for *gifts of the Spirit*); thus these new tongues-talkers were called Catholic Charismatics.

MY STORY

It wasn't long before a new generation of Pentecostals picked up the term, wanting to seem modern while still identifying with this amazing move of the Spirit. They also wanted to distance themselves from their parents and grandparents. However well-meaning they were, these older believers held to standards of holiness that we now see as legalistic, which caused many to reject the good parts of Pentecostalism.

I know. I was one of those people. As a teenager eager to move beyond the confines of my narrow Pentecostal background, I rejected much of my Pentecostal upbringing. I had been touched by the Lord but was running from Him. To me, surrendering to God meant ending up in some forlorn mission field, and I didn't want that for my life. Plus, I was influenced by the rebellious hippie culture, and as I was coming of age, I wanted to experience what had always been forbidden in my Pentecostal home: a liberal lifestyle. As uncomfortable as I might have been, I made it my goal to join a fraternity and be like the other college kids.

When I broke my foot running across campus, I had a lot of time to think while it was healing. I was unhappy and afraid I was getting far from God. So I called out to the Lord and prayed that if He was real to give me power to live for Him. I didn't want the up-and-down spiritual existence I'd had, where I'd repent of my behavior, then repeat it and repent all over again.

I can show you exactly where I was at the University of Florida when

A Catholic Encounters the Holy Spirit

Fifty years ago, in 1973, my story was published in a book called *Clap Your Hands! A Young Catholic Encounters Christ*. I never intended to write a book, yet it became a blockbuster, selling over a quarter million copies. It all happened because a major speaker at a Christian convention had to cancel his appearance at the last minute, and I was asked to fill in and share my story. A publisher was present, who then asked me to write a book. And as it happened, my experience converged with thousands of Catholics who found themselves caught up in the Catholic Charismatic movement that had exploded on the scene in the late 1960s.

Two important events led me to that moment. First, I came to know Jesus as my Savior. Although I grew up in a Roman Catholic family, spent twelve years in Catholic school, and was a faithful Mass attender, I never read or even opened a Bible. I knew "church" and all the rituals and rules, but I never realized I could know Jesus in an experiential way.

When I discovered that Christianity is not a set of rules but a dynamic, personal relationship with Jesus, I put my trust in Him, believing His finished work on the cross is what saves me, not good works. I prayed a simple prayer, repenting of my sins, and pledged to follow Him. My life has never been the same!

I finally surrendered to God and was forever changed. The Lord touched me and set me on fire during my second year of college. This was in the early 1970s, just when the Jesus movement was exploding around the country.

At the same time, I got to know Charismatic Lutherans and Episcopalians in Gainesville, Florida, who were also excited about the Lord and freshly baptized in the Holy Spirit. They didn't identify with the Pentecostal legalism I knew as a youth. And in my opinion they were more full of the Spirit than some of the grumpy, legalistic Pentecostals I knew.

Much like the Spirit-led Catholics, these people called themselves Charismatics. (A few years later when I started a little magazine, I chose the name *Charisma*. The gifts [*charismata*] and power of the Holy Spirit

---

Second, I experienced what we read about in Acts 2, when on the Day of Pentecost, the believers were filled with the Holy Spirit and began speaking in a supernatural language. When I was shown this from Scripture, I wanted the same experience for myself.

Late one night when I was with two of my former Lost Souls band members, who had also come to know Jesus, I prayed in faith, claiming the promise to be baptized in the Holy Spirit. As thanksgiving erupted from within, I felt the joy of the Lord surging through me, and the more profuse my praise, the more intense became my desire to magnify my God.

I grew impatient with the inadequacy of the English language to fully express all that I was feeling; then, at just the right moment, new words began to flow from my heart. I could not restrain my tongue as a new language somersaulted from my mouth.

Jesus touched me that night, and oh, the joy that filled my soul! All the uncertainty in my life—the doubts that went along with faith in God—were erased. I would never feel God was distant or nonexistent again. I walked home in the wee hours of the morning as if floating on a cloud. Looking up at the early-morning sky, I grinned, drunk with joy just like those in that first-century Pentecost outpouring.

—LARRY TOMCZAK, BEST-SELLING AUTHOR AND CULTURAL COMMENTATOR

were so great and wonderful, millions were experiencing this power, and so was I.)

A few students banded together to form a prayer group. One of the student centers allowed us to meet there on Tuesday nights. We'd often sit cross-legged in a circle in the center. Someone would play a guitar, and we'd pray for one another and worship with upstretched arms. Often we'd pray for a healing if someone was sick. We'd lay hands on one another and pray for the power of the Holy Spirit.

During this era, riots against the war in Vietnam were common. Student unrest was particularly high one Tuesday when we had our meeting. We huddled in the student center and prayed the best we knew how. We even rebuked Satan, following what we'd been taught by older Charismatic Christians. The situation was frightening. We felt almost helpless. Tear gas was being used on the rioters, and we worried some would blow our way. But I believe our prayers that day shifted something in the spiritual realm, because as far as I know, during my time as a student there, the University of Florida never again had an anti-war rally.

In our simple way we were experiencing the power of the Holy Spirit and learning to walk in the Spirit. Several of those students went on to full-time ministry.

At first, the long-established Pentecostal denominations, such as the Assemblies of God and Church of God, were called "classical Pentecostals," but gradually, Pentecostals began using the term Charismatic. The Pentecostal Fellowship of North America reorganized in 1994 as the Pentecostal/Charismatic Churches of North America. Today in *Charisma*, we use both terms together and sometimes interchangeably.

In 2022 the Pennsylvania marketing firm Infinity Concepts did a scientific survey of a thousand evangelical Christians to see how many were Charismatic or Pentecostal, and I was surprised to learn that the group can't seem to agree on what to call themselves. (Only 18 percent of respondents who fit the definition of a Pentecostal/Charismatic would use those terms to describe themselves.)[11] This book isn't about terms but about the power and work of the Holy Spirit, which you learn not so much in books but through personal experience.

I've shared all this history because it shows a pattern of people who were hungry for more of the Spirit, and when they came together in unity and prayed for more of Him, they were touched in a mighty way.

A GATEWAY TO THE SUPERNATURAL

To understand more deeply what all this means, I look to a man whom I considered an expert in the things of the Spirit, both theologically and experientially: Derek Prince. In his important book *Foundational Truths*, he explains that God intends the Baptism in the Holy Spirit to produce many great results in the believer's life. He points to Hebrews 6:4–5, which speaks of believers who "have become partakers of the Holy Spirit, and have tasted the good word of God and the powers of the age to come."[12]

Prince says these verses "indicate that those who have been made partakers of the Holy Spirit have tasted the powers of the age to come. The Baptism in the Holy Spirit gives the believer a foretaste of an altogether new kind of power—a supernatural power that belongs, in its fullness, to the next age."[13]

Prince explains that this is the reason Paul describes the seal of the Holy Spirit as the guarantee of our inheritance.

> In Him you also trusted, after you heard the word of truth, the gospel of your salvation; in whom also, having believed, you were sealed with the Holy Spirit of promise, who is the guarantee of our inheritance until the redemption of the purchased possession, to the praise of His glory.[14]

Prince teaches that an alternate translation of the word *guarantee* is "down payment," and the Lord gives us—through His Holy Spirit—a "down payment" of heavenly power and glory, a foretaste of the next age. He explains, "This down payment sets us aside as His purchased property, not to be offered to any other purchaser. It is His guarantee, too, that at the appointed time He will return with the balance of payment and take us to His home, to be with Him forever. That is why Paul calls it 'the guarantee of our inheritance until the redemption of the purchased possession.'"[15]

Prince writes that when we are Spirit baptized, we gain new understanding of what Jesus meant when He said God is Spirit and those who worship Him must worship Him in spirit and truth.[16] We are no longer satisfied with man-made worship, writes Prince, because we've been in the heavenly land and glimpsed its glories and God's holiness. No matter where circumstances may take us, we now worship on holy ground. We worship in Spirit—the Holy Spirit—and in truth.

What is true in our worship as Spirit-filled Christians is equally true in every other aspect of our experience. The Baptism in the Spirit serves as a gateway to a new kind of supernatural life. The supernatural has become natural.

Few understand the supernatural life better than my friend Sid Roth. He believes a great revival of the glory of God's presence is coming. He loves to wax eloquent about this on his *It's Supernatural!* TV broadcast, one of the most-watched Christian programs in the country. I interviewed him for this book because I believe he's onto something. Where others try to downplay the supernatural, he has embraced it so completely it's part of his ministry name.

Roth explained that he feels called to the Jew first, and the supernatural is a key component of that outreach. "The Bible tells us in Corinthians that the Jew requires a sign. Hence, I operate in the supernatural," he said. "I teach Christians that the supernatural or miracles are signs that can be used to reach the Jew to be a catalyst to reach the world. That's what makes me tick. That's the purpose of my life. That's my passion. Everything I do revolves around that. And I decided that many years ago."[17]

Like me, Roth encourages praying in tongues because when we pray this way, we can have confidence we're praying for what God wants in heaven to be done on earth. And we can pray in perfect faith (without which it is impossible to please God). Everything we pray in tongues is heaven's will for our future, our families, our ministries, and our health.

Roth believes American cities will be ablaze with the glory of the

Lord—not the glory of the devil, as happened during the riots in 2020. He sees the best yet to come and believes that as we draw closer to the end-time, each believer is being commissioned to live in what he calls global glory. So he tells Christians we can't afford to get depressed by what we see. If we do, we will become prey for the devil. And we'll be telling God He's not big enough to solve our problems.

"I see the best season in the history of the world—the pandemic of God's glory—about ready to hit at a high level. And so many things are going on right now, you'd have to be dead not to realize....Yes, the devil was up to something; the devil wants to abort all these things. But God is ready to abort what the devil is doing. And I'm a part of it, and you're a part of it," he said.

"You are called; you are commissioned; you are chosen," he continued. "I'd rather be chosen for this generation than any generation in history. This is the wrap-up. I'm not saying Jesus is coming today....I am saying Jesus is coming soon—sooner than He ever was before. And I'm saying that you and I are going to live in the global glory."[18]

Meanwhile, the culture has brainwashed an entire generation through the media, the educational system, entertainment, and even business. In many ways believers have lost the culture wars. The American church is like ancient Israel, which turned away from God. We are in what Roth calls an "Isaiah 60 moment"—a time of deep, thick darkness. And what is going to overcome this? It's what God showed Moses—His glory.

I interviewed Roth after the release of Jonathan Cahn's explosive book *The Return of the Gods*, which he believes is Cahn's best book ever. As we spoke, he told me he also believes that in response to the paganism reemerging in Western civilization, God is using Cahn's book to usher in this period of His glory and presence.

"The next move of God's Spirit is where our hope is," Roth told me. "A synonym for *glory* is *goodness*; a synonym for *glory* is *presence*....It's starting to erupt now but in a very minor fashion—but it's going to grow and grow."

It's like in the story in Ezekiel 47 about the water in the temple. The water level started at the ankles and went up to the knees, then to the hips, and then so high you could only swim.[19]

Roth's conviction about the coming of God's glory is one Jonathan Cahn seems to share. In a recent interview he told Roth: "There is glory that can come, but we have a job to do. God's people have to be courageous. You know, I was once on Capitol Hill to speak to the leaders of Congress, and I was led to say, 'Listen, we will not bow our knee to Baal. We will only bow our knee to one God, the God of Abraham, Isaac, and Jacob, and Him alone.' We have to have that spirit if we're going to see the power of God. Be bold, because this is our hour."[20]

"This is America's greatest hour," Roth added. "Do you know why? Because as the prophet Isaiah said in Isaiah 60, in deep darkness, the glory, or the manifest presence, or the goodness of God, will fill the whole earth."[21]

Roth bubbled with excitement as he recalled Cahn's words confirming his vision of coming glory. "This is what you're going to be covering in *Charisma* and in your publishing house," he told me. "This is what I'm going to be covering on my programs. We will literally have prophets whose words do not fall to the ground. I believe [God will raise up] better prophets than even Samuel."[22]

That's pretty amazing coming from Roth, who has seen the advent of the Messianic movement, the Jesus movement, and the Charismatic movement. He has witnessed some pretty amazing manifestations of the Holy Spirit's presence, yet he believes Jesus' statement in John 14:12: "Truly, truly I say to you, he who believes in Me will do the works that I do also. And he will do greater works than these, because I am going to My Father."

THE LAST GREAT MOVE OF GOD

Roth reminded me that there have been many prophecies about the last great move of God's Spirit, and what they describe is the manifest glory of God. He points in particular to one from healing evangelist Smith Wigglesworth, who in 1947 said he saw the end-time move of God's Spirit.

During the next few decades there will be two distinct moves of the Holy Spirit across the church in Great Britain. The first move will affect every church that is open to receive it, and will be characterized by the restoration of the baptism and gifts of the Holy Spirit.

The second move of the Holy Spirit will result in people leaving historic churches and planting new churches. In the duration of each of these moves, the people who are involved will say, "This is a great revival." But the Lord says, "No, neither is this the great revival but both are steps towards it."

When the new church phase is on the wane, there will be evidence in the churches of something that has not been seen before: a coming together of those with an emphasis on the word and those with an emphasis on the Spirit.

When the word and the Spirit come together, there will be the biggest move of the Holy Spirit that the nations, and indeed, the world have ever seen. It will mark the beginning of a revival that will eclipse anything that has been witnessed within these shores, even the Wesleyan and Welsh revivals of former years.

The outpouring of God's Spirit will flow over from the United Kingdom to mainland Europe, and from there, will begin a missionary move to the ends of the earth.[23]

Roth said that during his ministry, Wigglesworth had seen every miracle Jesus performed multiple times. So Roth finds it significant that Wigglesworth said the glory he saw would eclipse anything he had ever witnessed.

Similar but less known is a prophecy Wigglesworth gave Pentecostal evangelist Lester Sumrall in 1939:

> I see a healing revival coming right after World War II. It'll be so easy to get people healed. I see it! I see it! I won't be here for it, but you will....I see another one. I see people of all different denominations being filled with the Holy Ghost....I see another move of God. I see auditoriums full of people, coming with notebooks. There will be a wave of teaching on faith and healing....

After that, after the third wave...I see the last-day revival that's going to usher in the precious fruit of the earth. It will be the greatest revival this world has ever seen! It's going to be a wave of the gifts of the Spirit.[24]

Roth explained to me that the difference between the glory and the anointing is that when God's glory shows up, it does all the work. When you're operating in an anointing, you lay hands on people; when the glory is manifest, no man gets the glory, only God. Roth said he believes that as the glory of God covers the earth, we will see such miracles as dead people coming to life.

"That's coming soon, very soon," he said. "The glory of God will change the face of Christianity. It will be the great divider." By that he means everyone will have to choose whether to go with God or against Him. Roth then said, "And it's going to be very dangerous for a Christian that is in sin."[25]

I've written about Roth's testimony, and I know he says he was "a radical for the devil." Then as a Jew he encountered Jesus as his Messiah and suddenly was radical for Jesus. As one of the first Messianic believers during the hippie era, Roth attracted the attention of Kathryn Kuhlman, who invited him to be on her national television program to tell his story. You can watch it, as I did, on YouTube.[26]

When the Soviet Union opened in the early 1990s, he was one of the first who began holding outreaches for the huge numbers of Jews who lived there. Thousands responded to the gospel with public professions of faith. The numbers were so staggering some of Roth's Messianic friends said the response was impossible, to which he replied: "Well, I agree that it's impossible. But in the presence of God, guess what? All things are possible!"[27]

This is what Roth calls "living in the glory." Moses saw the glory of God, and the glory caused him to live one hundred twenty years!

Roth believes this glory has already descended to Earth, and it's going to do nothing but get stronger and stronger until it reaches a level the world has never seen. First Corinthians corroborates this: "Eye has not seen, nor ear heard, nor has it entered into the heart of man the things which God has prepared for those who love Him."[28]

To me, Roth is an example of someone empowered by the Holy Spirit to live in this upside-down world. He's not just surviving. He's not discouraged by what he sees happening around him. He's energized by the promise of seeing God's glory manifest on the earth. Roth's ministry has long focused on experiencing God, but he believes everything he has done thus far has been in preparation for the coming release of God's glory.

"I believe that there's going to be a major paradigm shift even in my ministry, and I don't know what it is because I've never experienced the glory 24/7," he told me. "I believe that if you desire to, you'll live a lot longer in the glory. Every prayer you've ever uttered is going to be instantly fulfilled. We won't need 'meditating on the Word' type of teaching, where you really believe and believe and work up your faith. Our faith is going to be instant. And I'm going to see it in my lifetime. I know that no one has ever seen what is coming. It's what Wigglesworth said: a thousand times greater."

How do we wrap our minds around something a thousand times greater? It goes back to John 14:12. Jesus said that we will do the same works He did—*and even greater works*. Roth admits, "This might be blasphemous to some people, but it's what I believe: The coming move of God will make Pentecost look like nothing. It's a second Pentecost, and that's not just a good theme for a conference. It will be the end-time outpouring to welcome in the King."

Roth is convinced this is so close it will happen in his lifetime. "I'm going to see it," he said. "I'm going to walk in it. I'm going to be part of it. And I'm going to mentor these young Jewish believers to fulfill their destiny."[29]

What Roth describes seems wonderful beyond words to me. In our fallen world it almost seems impossible that we would experience God's manifest presence. Yet we believe it will happen, just as we believe in heaven. And we can get a glimpse of it on earth, in much the same way a godly marriage gives us a glimpse of the relationship between Jesus and His bride, the church.

Years ago a friend told me he believed people flocked to Benny Hinn's healing crusades because they knew they'd see miracles and feel an anointing they rarely, if ever, experienced in their own churches. This is what people long for. We want to feel and experience God's presence. It's something beyond words, and it's why some people shake or fall or exhibit other behaviors as they are overcome with the power and presence of the Holy Spirit. It's also why Pentecostals have been called Holy Rollers and why in the Book of Acts the believers were thought to be drunk on the Day of Pentecost.

I'm a reserved person, but I've experienced some dramatic responses to the power of the Holy Spirit. Sometimes I've resisted it because I wanted people around me to think I was dignified or because I'm sensitive to the criticism of Pentecostals and Charismatics that our worship experience is all emotionalism.

Let me ask, What is wrong with emotionalism? Our emotions are part of what makes us human. We're happy or sad, sometimes depressed. Sometimes we're overcome with feelings of love or excitement. Look at how people react when their favorite team scores or wins. They get crazy. We call them fans. Yet if church folk get a fraction of that excited, they are called fanatics. It's common sense that we feel love for family or grief when a loved one dies; those are emotions we understand and don't question. Yet if we get excited about God or the Holy Spirit and how He empowers us, then some people call that emotionalism, and somehow it's bad.

In 1976, Karl Strader, my former pastor, addressed this criticism that Spirit-led Christians are "emotional" in the third issue of *Charisma* magazine, writing: "The supernatural phenomena of the Holy Spirit excites people like nothing else....[When I've talked to non-Charismatics about this, I've asked:] Since when did God become unemotional? Have you ever watched a thunderstorm?

"The church of Jesus Christ was born in a tremendously emotional atmosphere. Fire, wind, noise! The scene is described in the Book of Acts, chapter 2. The heart is where the very seat of our emotional make-up is located. And that's where the Spirit of God enters—into our hearts! [I believe] this world is the quietest place Christians will ever live. It's going to be noisy in heaven!"[30]

Of course, it would be deplorable indeed if a person had nothing but emotion in a so-called experience with God. But on the other hand, it's impossible to have God in our hearts without experiencing some emotion, whether it's demonstrated outwardly or not.

Deep worship, singing in tongues, and moaning under the anointing of the Holy Spirit are all part of the worship style we associate with Pentecostals. Interesting to me is that the Pentecostal style of uplifted hands and the more worshipful music that came out of the Charismatic movement have been adopted by many churches that probably don't consider themselves Charismatic. This shows me they are open to the Holy Spirit and long for more of God. The good news is that those who seek more of Him will find Him if they search with all their hearts.[31]

This desire for more of God is part of how the Holy Spirit draws us to God and leads us to a place where we can overcome condemnation, guilt, and shame. As we will see in the next chapter, the power of the Holy Spirit delivers us from the snares of the enemy and helps us overcome the immoral culture we live in.

Living It Out

Read John 14:12:

> Truly, truly I say to you, he who believes in Me will do the works that I do also. And he will do greater works than these, because I am going to My Father.

Think about it:

1. We've seen that the Holy Spirit is very sensitive and can be grieved, quenched, and resisted. Considering this, how are you inviting Him into your life?

2. Sid Roth says Smith Wigglesworth had seen every miracle Jesus did multiple times. But he prophesied that the coming glory of God would eclipse all he had seen. List some miracles of salvation, healing, or deliverance you have witnessed. How did seeing those miracles affect your faith?

3. As amazing as it sounds, the Lord promised we would do greater works—signs, wonders, and miracles—than Jesus did! But we must be willing, surrendered vessels because the Holy Spirit's power flows through humble people. What do you think needs to happen to release the Holy Spirit to do greater works in your life and your church?

4. As wonderful as past revivals are, each generation needs a new move of God. What do you see happening spiritually in our time? Are you drawn to learn about historic moves of God? What can you do to spark revival?

Chapter 7

LET THE HOLY SPIRIT HELP
YOU OVERCOME SIN

ONE OF MY favorite chapters in the Bible is Romans 8, which could be called "Life in the Spirit," the subject of this book. Yet before the apostle Paul deals with life in the Spirit, he must deal in chapter 7 with the problem of indwelling sin and the war between our sinful natures and the righteousness God calls us to. Romans 7 reminds us that even though we as believers may delight in the law of God, another law wars against the law of our minds and brings us into captivity to the law of sin.

"O wretched man that I am," Paul writes. "Who will deliver me from the body of this death?"[1] Paul adds that his mind wants to serve the law of God, but his "flesh," what he calls the sinful nature tied to our humanity, wants to serve the law of sin.

The answer, says Paul in the first verse of chapter 8, is "for those who are in Christ Jesus, who walk not according to the flesh but according to the Spirit." He is telling us that life in the Spirit sets us free from the law of sin and death. The Spirit-led life is a life free of sin and one in which we follow the Holy Spirit in a personal way.

Paul goes on to say: "For the law of the Spirit of life in Christ Jesus has set me free from the law of sin and death."[2] This "is the life-regulating and life-motivating power of the Holy Spirit at work within the lives of Christians," the commentary in the *FireBible* reads. "The Holy Spirit comes into the lives of those who accept Christ's forgiveness and yield themselves to him, freeing them from the power of sin and from its end result of spiritual death....They find a new power working within them, which enables them to overcome sin and temptation and to fulfill God's purposes for their lives."[3]

John Lindell, pastor of James River Church in Springfield, Missouri, put it this way:

> In Romans 8 we see that the Spirit works powerfully in us. God's Spirit is not just at work in you when you are doing overtly spiritual things—when you are reading your Bible, fasting, praying, or worshipping. The Spirit is at work in you continually—even while you sleep! ...And what is this work that so preoccupies the Spirit all day every day? To help you, to strengthen you, to bring you along...*to change you.* Ultimately, to conform you to the image of Christ Himself until everything in you and about you is shaped in the likeness of Jesus.

Lindell goes on to say:

> While Romans 8 describes the limitless promise of life in the Spirit, Paul also contrasts it with another path—life in the flesh.... Either we will go the way of the flesh, which is hostile to God's law, or we will submit to the Spirit, who shapes our lives in a manner that is pleasing to God. There is no middle ground.

In an upside-down world where things thought unthinkable a decade ago, such as gender fluidity, are now in the news, even believers are bombarded as never before. Paul wrote his letter to the Romans almost two thousand years ago, long before modern media. But technology has made it easier to be assailed by temptation and to rationalize it.

No one is immune. We are all sinners. Even a couple of godly women I know had abortions years ago. Yet there is now "no condemnation" because the Holy Spirit forgives and makes all things new.

But as Lindell puts it, if a person is saved, he no longer lives in the realm of the flesh, which Lindell says is code for "a life that is disconnected from the source." If you're walking in the flesh, says Lindell, your priorities are not the things of God. But when you walk in the Spirit, you care more about what God thinks about your life than what anybody else thinks. God is your first love, so you don't want to do anything that will grieve the Holy Spirit. You want to become all that God says you are and to have everything He has for you.

This doesn't mean you'll always get it right, Lindell says, but your "default settings are changed." Pleasing God is your new normal. And "if there's a tie in your life, God wins it." As a pastor, his greatest concern about people living in a world as crazy as ours is that it can appear as if God loses most ties. By this he means we live in such a way that we regularly choose things that don't build our faith instead of choosing the things of God.

He says this is not a new kind of legalism; rather, it's choosing to live the kind of life where we put God first. He says this is how we train for life in the Spirit.

> Life in the Spirit doesn't mean we don't attend to the world around us or aren't present for the people God has placed in our lives. It is quite the opposite: when we are delivered from the tyranny of the flesh and its disordered desires, we attend to the world around us *better*; we are *more* present for the people we love and who love us—not less![4]

I had an opportunity to make this point on national news. When I was on a media tour for my book *God and Donald Trump*, I was interviewed by Alisyn Camerota on CNN the week Donald Trump was said to have had an affair years ago with a porn star named Stormy Daniels. The charges came to nothing, and the lawyer who brought the suit, Michael Avenatti, is now in prison for theft and defrauding former clients.

The media had no interest in me or my book but wanted to cover anything that made Donald Trump look bad. Their theme that week (which happened to be Passion week) was that evangelical Christians who embraced Trump (partly because he supported values the Democrats didn't) would finally turn their backs on him after this revelation.

I had no personal knowledge of the situation other than what I read in the news. Yet in that interview, I said if the allegations that he had an affair with a porn star were true, then no born-again Christian approved of it. But we are all sinners who are forgiven, and besides, the charges were from long ago, and I believe Donald Trump has changed. Camerota asked me how he'd changed. On live national television, I said, "Because I believe that he accepted Christ."

I went on to say that everyone who has accepted Christ has been forgiven of at least one thing they'd be embarrassed to have reported on the front page of the newspaper. That was my way of saying even I'd done some things I wouldn't want splashed all over the news media.

Camerota was trying to say "gotcha" regarding Trump, but I was able to share that the entire essence of the gospel is that Christ forgives sin. A lot of people saw that interview, and I hope what I said made them think. This core truth of Christianity is not discussed on secular media very often.

Yet forgiveness is not a one-and-done. We must walk in the Spirit day by day, and we have a sinful nature plus the habits, resentments, unforgiveness, and addictions we pick up along the way. When we don't resist those desires, Paul says we're setting our minds "on the things of the flesh, but those who live according to the Spirit, the things of the Spirit.

"To be carnally minded is death," Paul continues, "for the carnal mind is hostile toward God, for it is not subject to the law of God, nor indeed can it be, and those who are in the flesh cannot please God." However, he's writing to believers in Rome (and to you and me these thousands of years later) who are not in the flesh but in the Spirit, and he reminds us that "to be spiritually minded is life and peace."[5] Isn't that what we want even in this upside-down world?

TWO TYPES OF PEOPLE

I agree with the editors of the *FireBible* when they say, "Paul describes two types of people: those who follow the pull of selfish desires that come from their rebellious natures and those who live by the guidance and power of the Holy Spirit." They explain that the corrupt desires of sinful human nature include "immoral behavior, selfish ambition, jealousy, hatred, drunkenness, outbursts of anger and any other attitudes or choices of behavior that do not please God."[6]

Does this seem old-fashioned and square in the modern world, where any type of dress or behavior is considered OK if it doesn't hurt anyone?

As a child, I remember how strict and legalistic my church was. Not only was there no drinking or smoking but also no makeup, jewelry, or pants for women, and no card games, dancing, movies, or other forms of what they called "worldly entertainment."

I can remember feeling so inadequate. No matter how much I followed the dos and don'ts, I knew I'd violated something, sometimes by accident but usually on purpose. Sincere Christians flooded the altars at the end of every sermon to beg God for forgiveness for whatever was done the week before. Thank God these people (including a young Steve Strang) were sincere, but we had little confidence in who we are in Christ and, in my opinion, an over-reliance on rules and regulations to make us right before God.

Paul writes, "For if you live according to the flesh, you will die, but if through the Spirit you put to death the deeds of the body, you will live."[7] The good news is that the Holy Spirit lives within true children of God in order to lead them to think, speak, and act according to the principles, standards, and examples found in God's Word. He leads mainly by inner promptings, such as urges, motivations, and inspirations within one's spirit. These inner promptings help us follow and accomplish God's purposes and overcome our sinful nature, and they are always in agreement with God's written Word. Through them, the Holy Spirit guides us in our daily lives, giving us direction.

These inner promptings are also opposed to sinful desires and keep us sensitive to the dangers of sin, Christ's standard of right and wrong, and the reality that God will judge evil. They encourage believers to remain devoted to Christ, warning us not to fall into temptation or drift away from personal faith in Him. Yet they become weaker if they are repeatedly resisted and disobeyed, and rejecting them entirely results in spiritual death.

The Holy Spirit "will absolutely make us feel uncomfortable when we sin (in particular, if we persist in willful, unrepentant sin)," notes respected Bible teacher Michael L. Brown. "...He makes us feel uneasy; He brings a word of loving rebuke; He puts us under holy pressure—all because He loves us so much! It's like the rough gravel on the side of the highway that tells you you're getting off the road. It gets your attention— both with the sound and with the feel—waking you up to the potential danger of an imminent crash. That gravel can save your life."[8] We call that conviction from the Holy Spirit.[9] (Read his testimony in chapter 1.)

It's easy for any believer to allow little things to creep in and not rely on the Holy Spirit to convict of sin. This can be especially challenging for those who equate living in the Spirit with the legalism that marked early Pentecostalism because of its roots in the Holiness movement. Some of the dress, entertainment, and lifestyle rules are important only in church circles. And when there is a genuine failure, often it's played up and used by secular people to make all Pentecostal preachers seem hypocritical like the fictional Elmer Gantry. I believe this is due in part to a sort of spiritual cancel culture, which has seen some large ministries have their reputations tarnished by what were small indiscretions in light of what's now acceptable in this upside-down world.

This is not to minimize the importance of living right and the serious- ness of sin. But even the most committed Christians stumble. The press loves to play that up and ignore the good the person or ministry has done. When this happens, it discourages other Christians in the same way watching someone prominent get canceled by the culture makes others afraid the same thing will happen to them.

We must keep things in perspective. God is a God of grace. As someone said, He's the God of the second chance. A church billboard near where I live says in huge letters: "God is not mad at you." Yet many of us feel that way. Some have become discouraged and left the faith because they didn't live up to someone else's standards or, in a moment of weakness when they were under stress, failed to do what they knew was right.

Whenever there's a failing, whether in a family, a church, a ministry, or even a nation, there is hurt and disappointment. Sometimes it brings disrepute to the cause of Christ. But it's like the old preachers used to say: "Everyone sins. Some are brought to light, and others aren't."

Satan is always pulling us toward our lusts, carnal desires, and old habits or addictions. But through the power of the Holy Spirit, we can overcome them. Being a Christian, even a Spirit-led Christian, doesn't make us perfect. The Bible says "all have sinned and come short of the glory of God."[10] There are none that are good, no not one.[11] The question for us as believers isn't if we will get knocked down, but if when we get knocked down, we will get up and try again.

Sometimes when we are at low ebb, we don't feel like getting up and fighting. Yet the Holy Spirit can empower us to not quit and instead turn to Him. He is full of grace and will help us to keep pushing forward to attain the destiny we have in Him and try to make a difference in this upside-down world.

And let's face it. Each of us will be hurt, whether by divorce, a bad business deal, or any number of other disappointments. What do we do? We must ask the Holy Spirit to help us forgive and move on.

But even more than being hurt by others, we are more likely hurt by our own fears, weaknesses, or addictions. It's like evangelist Dwight L. Moody is quoted as saying: "I have had more trouble with myself than with any other man I have ever met."[12]

THE HOLY SPIRIT PROVIDES A WAY OUT

Many times, I've quoted Ephesians 6, which says we wrestle not against flesh and blood but against rulers and principalities and rulers in high places.[13] There are demonic spirits that oppress believers who give them a foothold in their lives. I believe most addictions and destructive behaviors are rooted in spiritual forces that counseling or psychiatry cannot overcome. However, the power of the Holy Spirit gives a way out—as many drug addicts have discovered through the ministry of Teen Challenge.

In 1958, there was a well-publicized trial in New York about several gang members who were accused of murder. It caught the attention of a young Pentecostal preacher from Pennsylvania named David Wilkerson. He traveled to New York and began preaching a message of miracles, renewal, God's love—and a power that could enable a person to get off and stay off drugs.

Drugs had the ability to gain a tremendous hold on the human body that could not be explained in physical terms alone, he found. The young people who stopped abusing drugs told Wilkerson there were two habits they had to kick to overcome drug addiction—the body habit, which they kicked in three days by quitting their drug use cold turkey, and the mind habit, which was far more entrenched.

In his best-selling book *The Cross and the Switchblade*, Wilkerson tells the story of one young addict named Joe, who came to their Teen Challenge center in Brooklyn to kick an addiction to pain killers he developed after a serious on-the-job injury. They put Joe in an upstairs room, where he stopped using pain killers cold turkey and went through intense withdrawal. For four days someone was with him 24/7, helping him through the shakes and cramps and lending prayer support.

Finally, after four days of intense pain, Joe was free. Everyone rejoiced. When he said he wanted to go home to see his parents, Wilkerson was dubious but allowed it. But Joe did not return. Later they discovered he'd been arrested for robbery and possession of narcotics.

Why had Joe failed? Someone suggested they ask the young drug addicts who had successfully stayed off drugs to see if there was an answer.

When Wilkerson asked Nicky Cruz, the young gang leader whose conversion is central to the story of *The Cross and the Switchblade*, Cruz told him that real freedom came for him when he received the Baptism in the Holy Spirit.[14]

The wonderful truth is that the Holy Spirit is no respecter of persons. His power is available to all of us to overcome habits or addictions, or to believe for miracles, finances, or even for the right spouse. The Holy Spirit is not a magic wand or a genie in a bottle. But He fills us with power to overcome whatever obstacle is keeping us from His will for our lives.

If you were in a dark room and couldn't see and needed only to flip a switch to get light, you'd do it, of course. Taking advantage of the power of the Spirit through faith is just as easy as turning on a light. Simply ask Him to show you what needs to change in your life and to reveal the path forward. He will direct you with those inner promptings; as He does, respond to His leading. Change rarely happens overnight, but over time you will find yourself progressively walking in greater and greater victory.

But there's more to the story about David Wilkerson and Teen Challenge that most don't know. John and Elizabeth Sherrill, who, with Wilkerson, wrote *The Cross and the Switchblade*, became my good friends. John Sherrill told me that a Catholic priest once visited Teen Challenge and asked Wilkerson what was the difference in their approach

A Promise Kept by the Power of the Spirit

My dad was an alcoholic and a high school dropout. His addiction was ruining his life. When he and my mother learned she was pregnant...it was a shock. They had been married seven years, but had not been able to have children.

My dad had tried to quit drinking many times, and he tried again when he learned they were expecting—without success. Everyone had given up hope in my father and his many broken promises.

Shortly after learning about the pregnancy, my parents were driving home from a Fourth of July celebration. My dad had been drinking and started having chest pains. Without saying a word, he began to slow down to lessen the impact. While clutching the steering wheel and sweating, he whispered a prayer, "God...spare my life to see my child. Save me, and if I ever take another drop of liquor as long as I live, I want you to poison me and let me drop dead."

Dad had never kept a promise to stay sober, but in His mercy, God looked past all the prior failures and broken promises and saved him, healed him, and delivered him from alcohol addiction. From that day forward, my dad never took another drink.[15]

—ALTON GARRISON,
FORMER ASSISTANT GENERAL SUPERINTENDENT, ASSEMBLIES OF GOD

SPIRIT-LED LIVING IN AN UPSIDE-DOWN WORLD

to helping people overcome addiction. What was this power Wilkerson spoke of? The priest was introduced to the Baptism in the Holy Spirit, which he knew nothing about, so in the middle of the book, the Sherrills took one chapter to explain it.

Five years later, some young Catholic collegians eager for more of God read *The Cross and the Switchblade* and were attracted to that chapter and wanted to have that glorious experience. At a weekend spiritual retreat in 1967 at Duquesne University in Pittsburgh, they prayed to receive the Holy Spirit, and several were baptized in the Holy Spirit and spoke in tongues. Soon participants shared their experience with other Catholics at Notre Dame University in Indiana, and that was the spark of what we now call the Catholic Charismatic Renewal, which is estimated to have touched millions worldwide.[16]

It was the Holy Spirit that touched off this enormous movement, not a book. But as a publisher, I'm fascinated with what a book can do. I'm certain neither David Wilkerson nor the Sherrills had a foreshadowing their simple testimony of changed lives in the streets of New York City would have such an impact.

I was coming of age when all this was happening and dealing with my own youthful issues as I've shared in this book. Thankfully, the wild oats I sowed did not include drug use.

As a young adult, I wanted to serve God but felt the pull of the world and battled things I couldn't seem to overcome. I heard the new Charismatics talking about deliverance, and one described a service led by Derek Prince, where demons were cast out. As the spirits manifested, the people would yell and sometimes vomit. But afterward, they would testify of being freed of things that had tormented them for a long time.

In college, I was eager to receive all God had for me, and I wanted to know there was nothing holding me back. So I asked a Charismatic prayer group leader who was known for deliverance ministry, to pray for me. There weren't any dramatic manifestations, but I knew the power of sin had been broken in my life. I know this story isn't too exciting, but I believe I experienced deliverance that day, and it was through the power of the Holy Spirit.

I will talk more about deliverance ministry in a later chapter, but for now I want to encourage you to believe the Holy Spirit will strengthen you to live different from the world. In this upside-down world, where there are so many vices that make people feel better in the short-term but are often addictive and sinful, we need His power His power to survive. Porn of every type is available with a few clicks on the internet. Once available only in magazines hidden behind a store counter, porn is now accessible to children, and few Christians speak up to blast it. In fact, many Christians and even some pastors are addicted to porn.[17]

Drinking, once taboo in Christian circles, is now acceptable by many Christians, and I have learned that a few Christians I know even drink in excess. Gambling and drug use aren't common among churchgoers, but are now socially acceptable, and as more and more Christians go the way of the world, I imagine it won't be long before we are facing that in the church too. And I haven't even mentioned all the unmarried Christians who live together these days.[18]

It may not be that doing some of these things will send you directly to hell as fire-and-brimstone preachers may have preached at one time. But seeking the pleasures of the world pulls us away from God. It takes our attention off pursuing God and serving Him and focuses it on satisfying our carnal desires. Sin is pleasurable for a season. And with so much carnality portrayed on TV and movies or played up in music, it's easy for Christians to slide back into their old ways or settle for a powerless Christianity full of compromise and half-truths.

But if that happens, it's an indicator we need more of Jesus and less of the world. We don't have to accept defeat. If we just reach out to Him, the Holy Spirit will free us from whatever binds us. Whom the Son sets free is free indeed.[19]

LIVING IT OUT

Read Romans 8:1, 5:

> There is therefore now no condemnation for those who are
> in Christ Jesus, who walk not according to the flesh, but
> according to the Spirit....For those who live according to the
> flesh set their minds on the things of the flesh, but those who
> live according to the Spirit, the things of the Spirit.

Think about it:

1. We must walk in the Spirit daily, but each of us has a sinful
   nature plus the habits, resentments, and addictions we pick
   up. What are some practical ways you can keep your mind
   focused on the things of the Spirit instead of the flesh?

2. The Holy Spirit comes into your life, and He frees you from
   the power of sin and spiritual death. Describe a time when
   the Holy Spirit helped you overcome sin or temptation or
   fulfill part of God's purpose for your life.

3. John Lindell wrote that you get to choose whether you will
   go the way of the flesh or submit to the Spirit. What aspect
   of "flesh" do you deal with, and how can you choose differ-
   ently the next time you are temped?

4. The story of Nicky Cruz is a powerful example of how the
   Holy Spirit can set us free from past sin. How has the Holy
   Spirit helped you to walk in freedom from not only the
   sin of your past but also the shame or condemnation you
   experienced?

Chapter 8

FULFILL EVERY BIT OF POTENTIAL
GOD HAS GIVEN YOU

NOT LONG AGO my friend Ben Inman of Nashville, Tennessee, told me about a secular motivational speaker named Grant Cardone, who wrote *The 10X Rule*. Cardone criticizes Americans who have a passive mentality. These people think the government will take care of them, or they believe a mediocre life is all they can expect. Instead, Cardone says to succeed, people must work ten times harder than anyone else and be ten times more passionate about life.

That made me wonder if attitudes about one's spiritual life are any different. Are we passive and indifferent and think a mediocre spiritual life is all we can hope for? If *The 10X Rule* helps secular people succeed in life, what would happen to believers if they experienced ten times more power—from the Holy Spirit?

After reading *The 10X Rule*, I told my friend that Christians needed a book to encourage them to believe for ten times more of the Holy Spirit's power. Christians need more power to have a more fulfilled life and overcome the spiritual attacks that come with life. But most are missing the real opportunity to experience God's power and are living spiritually mediocre lives instead. He agreed such as book was needed, and that was the seed of *Spirit-Led Living in an Upside-Down World*!

The Holy Spirit's power and presence can change everything in our lives. People are desperate to experience this power and to do so at a great level. But the culture discounts most things that have to do with being a Christian, and many lukewarm believers downplay the Holy Spirit's power as unimportant. Yet if a motivational speaker can win in life with his 10X rule, shouldn't those of us who have the Spirit's power be able to do even more?

The reality is, we can have ten times the faith for our ministry efforts and our lives can be ten times more effective for the kingdom. I'm not advocating that we contrive something and then claim our works of the flesh are spiritual. I'm talking about sincerely seeking God with our whole hearts, as Psalm 119 encourages us to do. I'm talking about not being satisfied with anything less than God's presence filling our lives and churches to overflowing, and then pouring out from us to a desperate world.

British revivalist Henry Varley once said: "The world has yet to see what God can do with a man fully consecrated to him. By God's help I aim to be that man."[1] I ask what any of us can do if we are fully empowered by the Holy Spirit. The last two thousand years of church history is full of men and women who have done great things for God through the power of the Holy Spirit, beginning with the apostles. But what about today? Who dares to believe God in new and fresh ways? Who will be fully led by the Holy Spirit? Who will move in His gifts and demonstrate His fruit so His presence is evident in our lives?

A Neglected Key to Living Boldly in the Spirit

I firmly believe one key to living more boldly in the power of the Spirit is something rarely discussed in Christian circles—setting goals. Businesspeople emphasize it, but to many sincere believers, goal-setting isn't spiritual. Yet if we are to have a dynamic life in the Spirit, we must include this important concept. It's as someone once said: If you want to see miraculous fruit in your life, you must have faith as if it depends on God and work as if it depends on you. Goals help us focus our efforts as we pursue God's vision for our lives.

Mark Batterson recognizes the significance of this topic, so much so that in his book *The Circle Maker*, he takes a break from telling people how to pray circles around their biggest dreams and greatest fears to spend a chapter discussing goal-setting. He begins by sharing the legendary story of John Goddard, who in 1940 at age fifteen made a list of 127 daunting goals—from milking a poisonous snake to climbing the world's major mountains to lighting a match with a .22-caliber rifle—and accomplished almost all of them. Batterson then shares his philosophy of dreaming with deadlines and the importance of visualization, or envisioning your desired future, before relating his own audacious goals, which almost put Goddard's to shame.

I discovered goal-setting when I was in my twenties and floundering to know how to best spend my life. My mentor Jamie Buckingham challenged me to ask myself what I would do if I knew I could not fail. He had a large, framed sign above his desk that read: "Attempt something so big that unless God intervenes it is bound to fail." That's the kind of life he lived. After two devastating moral failures that would have ruined most ministers, Buckingham sought the infilling of the Holy Spirit and pursued a new life of what he called "risky living."

That decision changed his future. He did not begin writing books until he was thirty-five years old—a time in life when many men are giving up on their dreams. Yet he wrote or cowrote more than forty-five books before his untimely death in 1992.

No matter what stage we are in—a young believer excited to pursue a new life in Christ, someone who has enjoyed a measure of success in following her dreams, or a longtime Christian who is tempted to coast—God wants us to move into risky living, or *faith living.*

We should believe God for new mountains to climb and new visions to pursue. That is how we grow and develop our faith and move from "glory to glory."[2] As Buckingham put it so well, each of us should "attempt something so big that without God it is bound to fail."

Many times as Buckingham and I sat over lunch, he would speak directly into my life. Here are the kinds of things he told me:

- When you have a clear vision, you can risk your own life.
- Know what your vision is worth.

- Great athletes train hard for a gold medal. People who run to win are willing to pay the price.

- The reason most people quit growing is that they are not willing to pay the price.

- Faith equals risk. The Bible says without faith (not "without spirituality" or "without Scripture memorization") it's impossible to please God.

- God has big plans for you. Don't take what God meant for you and ruin it with mediocre living.

- Ask yourself what you are willing to give up to get what you want.

Once we have let God birth a vision into our spirits and have determined to implement it no matter the cost, then we must decide how we are going to accomplish it. This is where goal-setting becomes a critical tool. In fact, over the years I have found this has been key in seeing God's vision unfold in my life.

The closest most people get to goal-setting is making a list of New Year's resolutions, which last only a short time. But goals are so much more. As Batterson points out, they are dreams *with a deadline.*

For those who know me well, such as the men in my men's group or those who work with me at Charisma Media, it has become something of a joke that (when appropriate) I will eventually work something about goal-setting into a conversation. If I'm asked to speak extemporaneously, I'll talk about setting and meeting goals. I do that because I know the topic well and I have found most people know little about it. They drift through life because no one has shown them how to move ahead purposefully.

Setting a goal is like focusing sunlight with a magnifying glass. When your life energy is shining on a pinpoint, you can start a fire. A goal poorly set is better than no goal because if you have a goal of any kind, you're at least going somewhere, even if the destination is not carefully mapped out. Writing down spiritual, family, professional, self-improvement, or fitness goals often will set in motion the habits necessary to achieve them. The mind moves in the direction of its dominant thoughts, and what you measure and monitor improves.

When Jamie Buckingham challenged me to think of what I would do if I knew I could not fail, I realized how small my dreams had been and how much I was limiting God. I made a decision to change. Now I consciously try not to limit God, even though I am sure His plans for my life go further than I imagine.

A few years ago I read a book by Jim Collins and Jerry Porras called *Built to Last*, in which they document that great companies have unattainable goals that propel their organizations to greatness even after the founders die. For example, not long after World War II, a small Japanese company set a goal of making the phrase "Made in Japan" synonymous with quality. At that time, "Made in Japan" meant only one thing: cheap. The name of that small company: Sony.

Another small company set this goal in the late 1970s: "A computer on every desk and in every home."[3] That company: Microsoft. If nonbelievers can be motivated by big goals (and achieve them), how much more should those of us led by the Spirit of God Himself?

Consider Oral Roberts' goal of combining the healing power of God with medicine. It was radical when first set; today prayer for healing is commonly accepted in churches around the world.

Or think about David Yonggi Cho's goal to lead the largest church in the world. Impossible? That vision came to pass when his Yoido Full Gospel Church in Seoul, Korea, grew to nearly eight hundred thousand members.[4]

I remember Lester Sumrall telling me when I was a guest on his television program in the 1970s about his goal of reaching one million souls with the gospel in his lifetime. Impossible? Seemingly. But it propelled him to get onto Christian television and work at a pace that would have tired ten average men. Although there's no way to verify it, I believe more than a million people will be in heaven because of his huge goal.

These great men of the past (each of whom I knew) had great goals. What about you and me?

MAKE A PLAN

Myles Munroe, a respected pastor who taught often on the power of purpose, believed God wants us to become people who have plans, which he described as documented imaginations. If we can document an imagination, we've developed a plan for action.

"If you are having real problems in your life, you probably don't have a piece of paper on which you have documented your plans for the next five years," he wrote. "You're just living from day to day in the absence of a concrete, documented plan. You've been dealing with the same issues and habits and struggles for years. You slide forward a little only to slide backward again. Whenever things get hard, you start reminiscing about 'the good old days' and fall back into habits you had conquered. Progress requires a plan of action. Ideas must be put down if they are to influence the way you live."[5]

It's so important to know how to set goals. Munroe pointed out that

The Power of Vision

When your thinking changes, it moves you almost without your knowing it. Vision has this magnetic, invisible pull that redirects our entire lives. It can apply to any area of our lives and any problem. For example, I learned over time that if my vision is to make down payments when buying something new, then I will make down payments on everything. But if my vision is to pay cash and remain debt-free, I will pay cash for things and remain debt-free. I used to make down payments on everything, but now I pay cash for everything, including our house and our cars. Our finances didn't really change, but our vision for how to use our money did.

Your outcome depends on how you see things. Jesus never saw lack, sickness, death, or calamity. He saw only solutions. He always knew what He would do—He had vision for every circumstance. We never read where Jesus became fearful or flustered about anything. Why? Because Jesus received direction from His Father through the power of the Holy Spirit and not from earthly circumstances.[6]

—BILL WINSTON, SENIOR PASTOR, LIVING WORD CHRISTIAN CENTER

they should be put down if they are to influence your actions. Are your goals written down? Do other people know about them? Does your spouse? Do your friends?

If you don't know where to begin, consider setting some life goals. Most people have an opinion about these things, but few actually have a plan.

Then, establish a personal mission statement. Many people, men in particular, go through a difficult midlife period that may rob them of their vision or make them feel as if what they have achieved is ephemeral. Patrick Morley, author of *The Man in the Mirror*, says midlife is like a lake.

"Early in our lives we run swift like a river, but shallow. As we put years behind us, though, we deepen. Then one day, we enter the opened jaws of midlife," Morley says. "Where once we felt direction and velocity, suddenly we find ourselves swirling about, sometimes aimlessly, or so it seems. Each of us, like a droplet of water, will take a different path through this part of the journey. For some of us it will only be slowdown. Others will feel forgotten and abandoned by the father of the river. Some, unable to see where the waters converge and once again grow strong, will despair."[7]

Morley's crisis started around age thirty-seven. He says it can occur well into your mid-fifties. (Remember, in our diverse culture there is no singular midlife experience anymore.) "You come to a point that you feel somehow imbalanced—like something is missing," he says, "like it's not enough. All the years of pressure deadlines have taken a toll. You have discovered a vacuum in your soul for meaning, beauty, and quiet."[8]

He recommends writing a life mission statement that includes four elements:

1. A life purpose: why you exist

2. A calling: what you do

3. A vision or mental picture of what you want to happen

4. A mission: how you will go about it

In his book *Second Wind for the Second Half*, Morley takes us full cycle through the birth of one vision, the implementing of that vision, the setting of goals to attain it, the commitment to a personal mission statement, and on to the birth of a new vision greater than the first.

"A new vision must spring up from a foundation of gratitude for what God has already done to use us and make us useful. The motivation cannot merely be wanderlust; not more for the sake of more. Rather, one chapter has closed and another beckons to be opened. A vision is a goal—a big one. Visions are not the work of today or tomorrow or even next month," Morley says. "Rather, a vision has a longer term."[9]

He reminds us that visions rarely turn out exactly as planned. The apostle Paul had the vision of going to Jerusalem and then on to Rome. He didn't consider that he would make those visits as a prisoner, but that's how it came about. Often, God must delay the fulfilling of a vision or desire until He has prepared us to be people who can handle it with grace and humility. It is not God's nature to give us greater visions and accomplishments if they will work to our destruction. Instead, God allows us to be hammered into the shape of a vessel that can gracefully contain the vision.

What God-inspired goals do you have for your life? Are you a scientist or doctor who can set a goal of finding a cure for a disease? Are you an entrepreneur who can pledge to give several million dollars to a credible mission organization? Are you a board member or pastor who can start a program for the poor in your city or network churches to meet the need?

What would you do if there were no boundaries on your imagination or budget?

If you haven't had big goals and dreams before now, I pray you will learn to set goals and give them deadlines. Keep in mind that when you stand before the Lord, He will hold you accountable for the talents, resources, and dreams He bestowed upon you. You stand to lose nothing by going for God's highest plan for you, and on that day when He says to you, "Well done, good and faithful servant," you will know that you attempted and accomplished much for your Savior.

Not only was Jamie Buckingham's challenge pivotal in my life, but it also set me on a quest, and I began reading every Christian book I could find on setting goals. One of the most influential was *The Fourth Dimension* by David Yonggi Cho, who came out of abject poverty after the Korean War to build the world's largest church. He was on the cover of *Charisma* in the 1970s. I visited him three times in Korea and once in Bermuda, where he loved to golf. I even published a couple of his books. For me, what stood out about him was that he did everything in the faith realm, which he called the fourth dimension.

I remember him encouraging people to stand in faith and let the vision God gave them incubate, almost like being pregnant with whatever you're believing God for. That's not something the Lord showed me, but I've found I can learn from those who walk in a realm of the Spirit I aspire to. I wish I did this perfectly. I don't, but there have been times I've believed against belief that something that didn't exist would become reality. It's like that passage in Romans that says against all hope Abraham believed he'd be the father of many nations. He was old, and so was his wife, but the Scripture says:

> And not being weak in faith, he did not consider his own body to
> be dead...he did not waver, but was strong in faith, giving glory
> to God....Therefore it was credited to him as righteousness.[10]

But don't miss what Paul says next: "Now the words 'it was credited to him' were not written for his sake only, but also for us, to whom it shall be credited if we believe in Him who raised Jesus our Lord from the dead."[11]

I find that so encouraging, and I hope you do too. In fact, I urge you make it your own. May the power of the Holy Spirit open your eyes to this truth and enable you to believe it "against all hope."

Cho was a man with a great vision. In *The Circle Maker*, Batterson writes that Cho impacted him also: "Very few people have dreamed bigger dreams or prayed harder prayers." He went on to say: "Scripture says that without a vision, people perish. The opposite is true as well. With a vision, people prosper. The future is always created twice. The first creation happens in your mind as you envision the future; the second creation happens when you literally flesh it out."[12]

Setting Spirit-Inspired Goals

One of the most successful businessmen I have met was Dan Arnold of Rockford, Illinois, who at age twenty-six founded a retail chain that expanded to forty-two gas stations and thirty-two truck stops in the Midwest and Texas. Before he died unexpectedly in 2015 at age fifty-eight, he had more than one thousand employees and a host of accomplishments.

He wrote an article I published about setting not "big, hairy, audacious goals" as a secular person might, but "God-inspired faith goals."

I want to go beyond that and suggest we set Spirit-inspired goals for our Spirit-led lives. After all, the apostle Paul was a great goal-setter, and he's the one who almost single-handedly brought Christianity to the Gentile world. Arnold pointed out that when you read Paul's letters, you see a pattern of him setting a goal and then articulating clear direction for achieving it.

For example, Paul states his goal to "become all things to all men, that I might by all means save some."[13] (Now, that's a God-sized goal!) Then, Arnold noted, he directed all his efforts into accomplishing that goal, saying: "Everyone who strives for the prize exercises self-control in all things. Now they do it to obtain a corruptible crown, but we an incorruptible one. So, therefore, I run, not with uncertainty."[14]

When Paul made this Holy Spirit–inspired faith goal, Christianity was a brand-new religion, and the world was pagan. But God helped Paul reach the Gentile world with the gospel message, which until then had been given only to the Jews. Isn't that inspiring? Shouldn't you do the same? Remember, "According to your faith, let it be done to you."[15]

As you set Spirit-inspired goals, consider these principles modeled after those Arnold articulated:

1. **Spirit-inspired goals must be routed into our callings and assignments.**

Remember Your word to Your servant, on which You have caused me to hope.[16]

We can call on the Lord to provide wherever He leads us and bless what He has put into our hearts, but we shouldn't expect Him to respond to self-appointed works and self-promotion. As Arnold said, our goals "must be rooted in what God has inspired in our hearts according to His will for us." Let us recall what the Lord has said about how He wants to use us, dust those words off, and pray them back to Him full of faith.

2. Spirit-inspired goals must be full of faith.

But a man may say, "You have faith and I have works." Show me your faith without your works, and I will show you my faith by my works.[17]

Our goals must require amazing faith—"if you can believe God for little, add some zeros to it and believe God for *much*," Arnold wrote. Our work is to trust God: "Jesus answered them, 'This is the work of God, that you believe in Him whom He has sent.'"[18] People with Spirit-inspired goals believe God to do "exceeding abundantly above all that we ask or think, according to the power that works in us."[19] In other words, don't be timid. "God can handle whatever you believe Him for," Arnold said, "so go for it. *Big*."

3. Spirit-inspired goals must be held in persistent trust in God's ability.

I say to you, though he will not rise and give him anything because he is his friend, yet because of his persistence he will rise and give him as much as he needs.[20]

We need to write our goals, and we should persistently declare our goals in prayer or whenever we feel the need to express confidence and remind ourselves what outcome we are anticipating.

4. Spirit-inspired goals must dare the impossible.

But Jesus looked at them and said, "With men this is impossible, but with God all things are possible."[21]

If we look at our own ability or what those around us have accomplished, we will never set God-sized goals that take faith to achieve, Arnold said. Spirit-inspired goals "require God, and with Him, the impossible goal becomes possible. In fact, with God all things are possible. What we lack in potential, God makes up in power, and without God's power our human potential is just potential. Think and pray about what your goals should be with the end in mind—the end being that day when you stand before Jesus."[22]

I hope I'm making this clear: We must rely totally on God, but we must work as if it's up to us. That's where goal-setting becomes useful. And it's a discipline we must practice all our lives to help us achieve our potential.

For Batterson (and me), the purpose of goals is to accomplish the vision God has given you. "The simple act of imagining doesn't just remap your mind; it forms a map," he writes in *The Circle Maker*. "That is the purpose of goal setting. If dreams are the destination, goals are the GPS that gets you there."

He goes on to share a helpful list of ten steps to goal setting that can both encourage you and help you start making your own goals.

1. Start with prayer.

2. Check your motives.

3. Think in categories.

4. Be specific (or it's not measurable).

5. Write it down.

6. Include others.

7. Celebrate along the way.

8. Dream big.

9. Think long.

10. Pray hard.

Notice he starts and ends with prayer!

Batterson has built a great church and influenced millions through his books, so he speaks with authority. He writes that "when you live by faith, it often feels like you are risking your reputation. You're not. You're risking God's reputation. It's not your faith that is on the line. It's His faithfulness. Why? Because God is the one who made the promise, and He is the only one who can keep it. The battle doesn't belong to you; it belongs to God. And because the battle doesn't belong to you, neither does the glory. God answers prayer to bring glory to His name."

Then, tying goal-setting into the theme of his book, he reminds us that "drawing prayer circles isn't about proving yourself to God; it's about giving God an opportunity to prove Himself to you."[23]

But what happens if you know this and then sort of forget, or simply let the enemy get you sidetracked by discouragement, sin, or laziness?

ONE FINAL GOAL YOU MUST HAVE

I believe the Holy Spirit's power will help us lead amazing, fruitful lives even in an upside-down world. But a life God stops using is a very sad life indeed. So we must focus not only on achieving goals but on being used by God and being a friend of Jesus. Jesus said He would be with us to the end and that He would never leave us nor forsake us.[24] So be sure to tag this onto one of your Spirit-inspired goals: "And my main goal is to know *You* and the power of Your resurrection and to become Your friend, Jesus."

LIVING IT OUT

Read Matthew 19:26:

> But Jesus looked at them and said, "With men this is impossible, but with God all things are possible."

Think about it:

1. British revivalist Henry Varley once said: "The world has yet to see what God can do with a man fully consecrated to him. By God's help I aim to be that man." What changes do you need to make to be the kind of Christian Varley aspired to be?

2. Jamie Buckingham had a sign above his desk that read: "Attempt something so big that unless God intervenes it is bound to fail." What God-sized dreams would you attempt if you knew you could not fail?

3. Patrick Morley recommends writing a life mission statement that includes four elements: a life purpose (why you exist), a calling (what you do), a vision (mental picture of what you want to happen), and a mission (how you will go about it). Take time to write your life mission.

4. Mark Batterson outlines ten steps to goal-setting. Review his list and then, using your responses to the previous questions, list some goals that can only be accomplished with the power of the Holy Spirit.

Chapter 9

WALK IN DELIVERANCE BY THE POWER OF THE SPIRIT

A RECENT SURVEY FOUND that more Americans believe in Satan than in God.[1] I don't encourage anyone to be more concerned about what the devil is doing than how God is moving in the earth. But the reality is that even among Christians there is a level of satanic activity that must be dealt with if we are to live a Spirit-led life. In his book *Free in Christ*, Pablo Bottari, an internationally recognized authority on the ministry of deliverance, makes the point that the process of casting out demons (often called deliverance) is an important part of what God does in the life of an individual and consequently in the church.

Most Christians seem to overlook the ministry of deliverance, but Jesus integrated it with the believer's call to evangelism in the Great Commission found in Mark's Gospel. Not only did He say, "Go into all the world, and preach the gospel," but He said, "In My name they will cast out demons."[2] (Jesus also mentions baptism and speaking in new tongues, which we focus on elsewhere in the book.)

Other than talking about the movie *The Exorcist*, few Christians focus on ministering deliverance, even in Charismatic and Pentecostal circles. A story about a Baptist preacher who experienced deliverance shows how important this ministry is. James Robison was a firebrand, known as "the Southern Baptists' angry young man." A Texas preacher, he railed against sin from the pulpit and developed one of the country's most successful ministries. Men like Jerry Falwell and Jimmy Draper (at one time the president of the Southern Baptist Convention) were Robison's friends and colleagues. By some estimates, by the early 1980s Robison had already preached to twelve million people and seen a million people saved under his ministry. But Robison was going through personal torment.

He was dissatisfied with the lack of permanent life changes he saw in the people to whom he preached. Even worse, he was frustrated by his own inability to live a truly Christlike life. He began overeating and gaining weight, and his mind became more plagued by lustful thoughts. As he preached, he would make inappropriate eye contact with women in the audience. He began to sense that demonic spirits were taunting him, and he would often sit on the platform of a church afraid to look up for fear of sinning in his heart.

Robison realized that much of his so-called righteous anger was really just meanness. The rage against sin that attracted so many had less to do with the Holy Spirit and more to do with Robison's own inner battles.

He was not experiencing the joy, peace, and freedom he saw modeled in the New Testament, and he didn't know anyone who was. He began a quest for freedom that brought him into contact with a church layman who was known to have a deliverance ministry, meaning he prayed for people to be free of the harassment and control of demons.

After an evangelistic crusade Robison was conducting, he invited the layman to his hotel room, and there they talked about the Word of God. Then the man looked at Robison, began to cry, and said, "I have been listening to you and praying for you for six years. I feel so sorry for you. I have cast demons out of prisoners, convicts, murderers, witches, drug addicts, and Hell's Angels, but I believe you are the most demonized [oppressed] person I have ever seen. You are so tormented I do not know how you have kept your sanity."

Robison wanted to run from the room as pride welled up in him, but he knew the man was right. He asked the man to pray for him, and he did, praying scripture after scripture and rebuking Satan.

Then the man stopped abruptly and said, "It is all over. All the traffic in your head is going to stop. All that noise is going to be silent." Though Robison felt nothing, he was hopeful and a little intrigued.

Two days later, when he arrived home, Robison woke up with

scriptures he had never memorized flowing from his mouth. He felt different than he had in years. He grabbed his wife and said, "It's gone—it's gone!" She said, "What is gone?" Robison answered, "The claw in my brain is gone. I have been set free."

Robison says that was the day he was set free of demonic torment. That experience almost forty years ago changed his life. Members of his staff said it was like working for another person. Robison began to focus on God's love, a subject he said he had neglected.

He apologized for his divisive and abrasive behavior in the ministry. He began to pray for people to be delivered at the altar at his evangelistic meetings. Thousands flocked to his meetings, even though he was criticized from many angles by people who thought (rightfully so) that he had "gone Charismatic."

From that day to this, Robison's ministry has thrived. Better yet, he has the joy, peace and freedom he sought. He is a respected, mature Christian with keen insights into deliverance and tearing down enemy strongholds.[3]

WEAPONS NOT OF THIS WORLD

Deliverance is not readily understood. Start a conversation about confronting demons, and some people will roll their eyes, saying you have gone too far out on a limb.

Some will accuse you of looking for a demon under every rock. Others will tell you how they were scarred by a horrible experience when, desperate for answers, they submitted to deliverance ministry, only to have people encourage them to "vomit up" demons and do all sorts of strange things during a grueling "deliverance" session.

Others will say they are experts in the deliverance field. Some Christians believe that raising the decibel level of their prayers will chase away more demons. They have a great desire to yell at the enemy, but they lack understanding of spiritual authority. They might scream at demons all day long with no results.

I have seen and heard much in the area of deliverance. While I know deliverance is sometimes handled poorly or even arrogantly, I do believe there is an aspect of spiritual warfare to many human problems.

Paul clearly states this: "For the weapons of our warfare are not carnal, but mighty through God to the pulling down of strongholds, casting down imaginations and every high thing that exalts itself against the knowledge of God, bringing every thought into captivity to the obedience of Christ."[4]

There are Christians who do not want to believe they can have demonic problems. I personally believe a problem that will not go away after prayer, positive confession, fasting, strong-willed determination, or medical treatment must have a demonic basis that needs to be dealt with spiritually. Problems that are hard to deal with, such as rage, drug addiction, and even sexual addictions or alcoholism, have, I believe, spiritual problems at their root. There may be strongholds in the mind and soul ties that must be dealt with along with the sinful habit or behavior that is being acted out.

Let me give an important disclaimer. Some very odd behaviors are caused by some physical conditions that can be treated with medicine. I believe you should consult a doctor to rule this out as a possible cure. If the problem continues, then it may be spiritual in nature, and deliverance may help.

On this point, you may agree or disagree with me. You may feel that deliverance is not central to the gospel or is a ministry that ended in Bible times. But if you look at the ministry of Jesus, the subject of deliverance is unavoidable. You bump into it again and again throughout the Gospels. I firmly believe that His ministry is the same today as it was then—to save, heal, deliver, and preach the gospel of the kingdom. To subtract deliverance from that equation, I believe, is to diminish the gospel.

Jesus certainly understands the need to extend deliverance to those who were "bound." Many verses show us His response to the needs of the people who came to Him for help. Matthew 4:24 tells us the sick came to Him from many miles away: "And they brought to Him all sick people who were taken with various diseases and tormented with pain, those who were possessed with demons, those who had seizures, and those who had paralysis, and He healed them."

Jesus said plainly in the Great Commission, "These signs will accompany those who believe: In My name they will cast out demons; they will speak with new tongues...they will lay hands on the sick, and they will recover."[5] And He instructed His disciples to "heal the sick, cleanse the lepers, raise the dead, and cast out demons. Freely you have received, freely give."[6] In Luke 10:17, the seventy-two disciples are astonished that "even the demons are subject to us through Your name." In Luke 4:36, the people see deliverance as a sign of great authority: "They were all amazed and said among themselves, 'What a word this is! For with authority and power He commands the unclean spirits, and they come out.'"

Try to imagine the Gospels without deliverance, and you will see just how many times our Lord confronted demons and set people free. I firmly believe that it would be foolish, considering what we see in the Gospels, to exclude demonic activity entirely from the twenty-first century experience.

VICTORY HAS BEEN WON

Jesus won our redemption on Calvary. He took away the shame of our sin long before we were born. But we must appropriate that wholeness into our lives. We must take authority over Satan and renounce all control he might claim over us. This can often be done with a "self-deliverance," or taking our rightful authority over Satan in our own lives. I do this when I feel I am facing a problem that is demonically energized. If that does not work, there are ministries trained in deliverance that can help.

Some habits are rooted in the physical side of our being, and breaking the habit becomes a matter of taking practical steps to change behaviors, much like a smoker quitting cigarettes would do. These steps include

- substituting a healthy activity for the unhealthy one, and
- enlisting the support and encouragement of others, who spur you on to the desired outcome.

Bad habits often have other problems at their root, including strongholds in the mind or soul. James Robison makes the point well that strongholds are not demons. If they were, we could cast them out. A stronghold

Set Free by the Power of the Holy Spirit

I was baptized at the highest level of witches and warlocks, and appointed to be a gatekeeper of the demonic world by the devil himself. But everything changed one night in October 1999.

I was sitting on my bed and felt depressed for the first time. I didn't realize I was in the middle of a spiritual tug-of-war, but as I sat on my bed that night, I told Jesus: "I will never serve You. Christians are weak. I have more power than they do." After I said those words, I started falling into what I describe as an anesthesia sleep, and I was passing away. The last words I said were, "If You're bigger than my daddy the devil, show me tonight, or leave me alone."

As my spirit left my body, I was on a train hell-bound, filled with people. Eventually, I ended up in one of the tunnels in hell, and the devil showed up and said, "Why are you leaving me? I loved you like a son. I gave you powers. Now you break my heart because I have to destroy you because you will tell the world about my kingdom."

When he went to grab me, the wooden cross of Calvary showed up. As he made contact with the cross, he fell to the ground like a feather. I ran deeper into another portal in hell, thinking I was escaping, but the devil showed up

is like a beachhead from which Satan tries to attack us. Another way to see it is as a dungeon that contains unhealthy thought patterns. At the center of any stronghold is an idea that runs contrary to the nature and character of God. That idea may be

- fear,
- insecurity,
- lust,
- greed, or
- pride.

Any number of "faithless" thoughts like these can form the center chamber of a stronghold. Sometimes what appears to be a sexual problem is really a stronghold of insecurity or fear.

again. I showed him the marks on my body, the scars of the initiation the night I sold my soul to him. He laughed and said, "I'm going to destroy you, and they will pronounce you dead on the earth." When he went to grab me, the cross showed up again, and when he made contact with it, he again fell to the ground like a feather.

Suddenly, I was pushed back into my body. It felt like I was in ICU receiving an electrical shock, but I was alone at home. That night I knew Jesus Christ was bigger than the devil. And I gave my life to Jesus Christ that night.

A year-and-a-half later, I decided to be baptized. When they dipped me backward, I was blown away because I saw the hands of Jesus Christ go into the pool and rip from my body every demonic ceremony I'd participated in from age eight to thirty-five. He made me clean and set me free. That was my first deliverance. My second deliverance took place during discipleship class. The teacher asked me to read Isaiah 53, and halfway through the reading, the Holy Spirit came upon me, and I began to weep, but it wasn't normal weeping. It was the weeping of a broken little boy. That day I got my inner healing.

I now bear the mark of Jesus Christ. By His grace I will finish my race and make my King proud He chose me.

—JOHN RAMIREZ, EVANGELIST AND DELIVERANCE MINISTER

Then there is an inner wall of reasoning and human logic. This is built when we try to fight a stronghold on human terms with arguments, intellect, and analysis. The inner wall can become a barrier to getting rid of the stronghold because no matter how much we think about it, or will it away, it will not budge. As the Bible says, "Not by might nor by power, but by My Spirit, says the LORD of hosts."[7] Strongholds are supernaturally built and must be torn down by supernatural means.

An outer wall of pride also keeps us from victory. This pride sometimes leads to fear that others will find out about our problem. Perhaps this wall is built when we grow fond of the pet sin we have, or brag about it—the kind of thinking the Bible calls a "high thing that exalts itself against the knowledge of God."[8] If we are to be free, we cannot fear what others will think. We must be willing to throw down our pride and admit who we really are—to ourselves and to others. We cannot fawn over or make excuses for our particular area of weakness.

FREE INDEED

Is deliverance a cure-all? It might appear so at times because the change is so radical. But deliverance does not negate the need for "working out our own salvation with fear and trembling,"[9] renewing the mind, and changing behaviors. While I believe deliverance is a spiritual reality (and I can testify to achieving great spiritual victories as a result of breaking spiritual strongholds), it isn't the panacea to all spiritual problems. Remember that Jesus said those demons can come back—and bring their friends.[10]

For example, I believe in divine healing. I know people who have been miraculously healed, and I believe I have been healed of various ailments over the years, including back problems and a battle with prostate cancer in 2013. But is everyone who is prayed for healed? No. Just because some people are not healed, it doesn't change the fact that others are healed—*instantly and totally*. In the same way, some people continue fighting the same battles even after deliverance, but perhaps in varying degrees. Others, however, are delivered and set free—instantly and totally.

Deliverance is a real part of the gospel package, but it is only one part, neither something to be feared nor a magic bullet.

DELIVERANCE TODAY

Deliverance can take many forms. For example, I believe that when some people go to the altar for salvation, they are delivered. Sometimes it is messy, with crying and all the manifestations of a significant emotional experience. At other times it happens quietly and privately, as with James Robison.

There are three requirements for people to be set free.

1. The person must want to be set free. Deliverance depends on a person's free will, but people do not always want to be delivered. Unless a person is willing to surrender to the Lord, God will not unleash His power over that person's life.

2. The person must be hungry for more of God. If a person is not hungering for a change, then that means he is satisfied with things as they are. Until people long to get rid of bondages that seem to hang on no matter how they try to overcome them, they are not ready for deliverance.

We must cry out to God and say, "Lord, I need You. I am not satisfied with what I have. I want more of You and more of Your presence. Please come and satisfy my hunger—fill me with Yourself and take all that is not of You out of my life."

If there is no other message you get from this book than this one, it is that you must hunger for more of God if you are to live a Spirit-led life.

3. The person ministering deliverance must be able to take authority over the enemy. John Eckhardt, founder and presiding apostle of IMPACT Network Global, has a large church in a rough area of Chicago. Every week there are many salvations, and when someone goes forward to accept Christ, they receive prayer, and then are taken to a side room and ministered deliverance. It isn't a question of "if" they need it; the assumption is that whatever lifestyle they came out of, they must be set free.

Many churches have discipleship programs for new believers or new members that deal with deliverance. Church of the Highlands, an influential church in Alabama, has Freedom groups and a Freedom curriculum. Lake Mary Church in Florida, pastored by Shaddy Soliman, has a similar program. They have a twelve-week group that focuses on establishing biblical foundations for new believers (and even mature believers who are new to the church and want to participate). This leads to Victory Day, where people receive deliverance and the Baptism of the Holy Spirit. The resulting testimonies of people being set free are amazing.

Did anyone pray for you to receive deliverance? Do you feel maybe there are what the Bible call spiritual "strongholds" in your life that should be dealt with?[11] If so, here are some things you need to know about this important topic.

Eckhardt wrote *The Deliverance and Spiritual Warfare Manual.* In it he explains that each believer who has the power of the Holy Spirit has the authority in the spiritual realm to engage the enemy and set people free.

Eckhardt says there are two important revelations every believer needs:

1) an understanding of power and 2) an understanding of authority.[12] He says authority and power are used by faith, not feelings, and it is important to find a church that teaches on power and authority based on the Word of God, and to study these subjects on your own. Doing this will give you confidence to minister deliverance.

Eckhardt says it is also important that our sins are forgiven when engaging the enemy. He cites 1 John 1:9, that if we confess our sins, He is faithful and just to forgive us, and to cleanse us from all unrighteousness, and warns not to engage the enemy with unconfessed sin in our lives. Instead, access the power of the blood of Jesus to cleanse all sin. We must operate in righteousness, Eckhardt says.[13]

Another authority on deliverance and spiritual warfare is John Ramirez, who once was a high-ranking satanic priest in New York City. He testifies to even selling his soul to the devil in a blood-soaked ritual. That's before God intervened in a powerful way through a miraculous dream, revealing Himself to Ramirez and snatching him from the grip of hell. (Read his powerful testimony in this chapter.)

In his book *Fire Prayers*, Ramirez explains the authority believers have over Satan: "The name of Jesus establishes the authority of the One who sits at the Father's right hand. In His name, we fight from the third heaven in all authority and victory. The devil is under our feet, in the second and first heavens and underground. We don't engage the enemy in our own names. We engage in Jesus' name—the highest name of all.[14]

"It is sad to say that many churches have removed the Word of God and the name of Jesus from their language, teaching, and preaching. How can God's people be victorious without them? They are the weapons God gave us to reach the promised land of our purpose and destiny."

Ramirez goes on to say, "Unfortunately many churches have also removed the blood of Jesus from their versions of the gospel. But without Jesus' blood, there is no gospel. The blood of Jesus represents the finished work of the cross and the destruction of the devil's kingdom.

"Revelation 12:11 reminds us that our believing brothers and sisters 'overcame and conquered {the accuser} because of the blood of the Lamb and because of the word of their testimony, for they did not love their life and renounce their faith even when faced with death' [AMP]. If we want to be equipped for every battle, we need to always remember the blood of the Lamb. Without it our faith is empty."[15]

If God can save someone like John Ramirez and set him free from the occult, he can deliver you too. Deliverance is not spooky, weird, or bad. Deliverance is the gift of God. It enables you to get rid of sin and bondage that may have been gripping your life for years. It moves you from spiritual death to spiritual life, and could be a solution to the sinful-nature struggles you are dealing with.

Do you want to be set free from that thing keeping you from being the person you know God wants you to be? Are you hungry—starving—for more of God? Then allow His work of deliverance to take place in your life. Become the new person God wants you to be.

God really does want to meet you face to face in a glorious encounter of power. He will quench your inner thirst and remove any barriers to an intimate relationship with Him. The power of His Spirit will break off any bondages or hindrances keeping you from reaching your destiny in Christ.

LIVING IT OUT

Read Revelation 12:11:

> They overcame him by the blood of the Lamb and by the word
> of their testimony, and they loved not their lives unto the death.

Think about it:

1. Think about James Robison's story of being set free of
   demonic oppression. That experience years ago changed
   his life. How does this motivate you to pray for yourself or
   others to be set free from sin or bondage?

2. Has the idea of deliverance seemed spooky to you? Has
   someone prayed for you to be set free from things that
   seemed to hang on no matter how you tried to overcome
   them? Search your heart and write what the Holy Spirit is
   bringing to light about different areas of your heart.

3. John Ramirez reminds us that the name of Jesus gives us
   authority in the spiritual realm. How has understanding
   your spiritual authority made a difference in your life and
   in how you pray for others?

4. The one message I hope you get from this book is that you
   must hunger for more of God to live a Spirit-led life. If you
   agree, pray this prayer: "Lord, I need You. I want more of
   You. Please satisfy my hunger—fill me with Yourself and
   take all that is not of You out of my life. Amen."

Chapter 10

EXPERIENCE VICTORY OVER PROBLEMS AND TRIALS

MANY GOOD THINGS come to you when you serve God and live by His Spirit: joy, health, purpose, forgiveness, and miracles, just to name a few. But the Spirit-led life is filled not only with peaks but also with valleys, and there are many powerful, Spirit-filled Christians who persevered despite having to endure terrible circumstances.

Any book about walking in the Spirit must grapple with the difficulties we may face in life. I call these trials, a topic the Book of James tackles head-on. There are many types of challenges in life, but I'll focus on three:

1. Some hardships are a result of this fallen, upside-down world. When the Antichrist comes and terrible things begin to happen, there's not much we can do except persevere and rely on the Holy Spirit to guide us. Much of the craziness we see in the world today is due to the fact we are nearing the end-time, as I explain in a later chapter.

2. Some challenges are tests from God. The apostle Peter knew adversity could be a good thing. He wrote that we may have to "suffer various trials, in order that the genuineness of your faith, which is more precious than gold that perishes, though it is tried by fire, may be found to result in praise, glory, and honor at the revelation of Jesus Christ."[1]

143

3. Some trials, however, are a result of our own bad decisions or our fallen, sinful nature. Going through a horrible divorce may be a trial brought on by a choice to marry the wrong person. Being fired may be a terrible trial, but you may have brought it on yourself by not being a reliable employee. If you've let bad habits and addictions control your life, changing your behavior can sure feel like a trial. But these are all hardships of our own making.

If you are going through a test or trial, I hope this chapter will at least help you understand what is happening spiritually. When we're facing hardship, it's easy for our emotions to get the best of us. We can easily find ourselves discouraged, depressed, or even in despair. But it doesn't have to be that way. I've made this point elsewhere, but it bears repeating: When you're living in the power of the Holy Spirit, you're not facing life on your own. You're not limited to what you can accomplish in your own strength. No matter what kind of trial you may be going through—whether it's a financial, relational, or health crisis, or even something else—you can tap into His strength to keep pressing forward until you see victory.

Robert Schuller, founder of the Crystal Cathedral in Southern California, famously wrote a book titled *Tough Times Never Last, But Tough People Do!* I believe trials never last, but overcomers do, which is an important key to living in the Spirit. Consider these spiritual giants whose lives still inspire us though they lived through terrible afflictions:

- John Wesley had such a terrible marriage that when his wife died, he didn't attend her funeral.

- Eric Liddell, made famous by the Oscar-winning movie *Chariots of Fire*, died of brain cancer during World War II in a Japanese prison camp occupied by China.

- Amy Semple McPherson, who founded the Church of the Foursquare Gospel, had a failed marriage and was embroiled in a well-publicized scandal.

- Oral Roberts, the best-known of the healing evangelists of the 1940s and 1950s, endured unimaginable tragedy when his daughter died in a plane crash and his oldest son committed suicide.

Aren't stories like these why people ask, If God is so good, why does He let bad things happen to good people?

CAN A GOOD GOD ALLOW BAD THINGS TO HAPPEN?

Bill Johnson, senior pastor of Bethel Church in Redding, California, was asked questions like this when his wife, Beni, passed away in 2022 after a long battle with cancer. The message he preached the first Sunday after Beni Johnson's death was so moving that videos of it went viral. After greeting his congregation, he said:

> The backslider in heart will always judge God by what He didn't do. But those who run with tenderness for who He is will always define Him by what He has said, by what He has promised, by what He's done. And to be as honest as I know how to be, I have seen too much of His kindness to think anything other than that He is absolutely good, always good.
>
> We don't get to choose stuff like, "I don't want to experience any pain." That's not an option we get as we do life. In fact, let's be really honest; He says things like, "Rejoice always; pray without ceasing; in everything give thanks." Those verses are completely useless unless you're going to experience loss and disappointment. I mean, nobody needs to be taught to rejoice if everything works the way you want it to work. It's pointless.

He went on to explain to his congregants that there is an aspect of the Lord's presence that we can only find in the shadow of death. He said,

"It's only in darkness of soul, in the trial of not knowing what's going on, doing everything you know to do and having things not work out like you think they should."

Johnson said he looks at trials as special opportunities to do what he calls "growing down." By that, he means growing childlike. "It's a simplicity of childlikeness that just says, You know what, He knows what's happening and I don't. And I'm going to trust Him. I don't want my why to come between me and God."[2]

A few months after he preached this message, we asked him to write an article in *Charisma* magazine on the subject. Here's some of what he wrote:

> Beni died after a long battle with cancer. For the last fifteen months or so, I was by her side day after day. Cancer is a disease that we see healed regularly. And while she is now forever with Jesus, perfectly well, never to die again, those of us who remain are still facing pain, confusion and tremendous loss.

An Infusion of Hope by the Power of the Spirit

In 2019, after experiencing what I thought was a digestive disorder, I was diagnosed with aggressive, stage 3 ovarian cancer. The situation was so serious, my doctor said I would need immediate surgery followed by six months of chemotherapy. Receiving that diagnosis was, of course, devastating. I immediately thought about my children and grandchildren and all the milestones I might not be around to see.

But having spent over forty years in ministry with my husband, Larry, teaching people to lay hold of God's promises, I knew I couldn't park there. So I made a conscious decision to shift my focus. I determined that although I had cancer, cancer was not going to have me! I was not turning over my identity and destiny to become a victim of the big C. I was determined to be a *victor*. Saturating my soul with God's promises of healing became my number one priority. Over many years the Holy Spirit had implanted His promises deep within my soul, and in my hour of need, I declared them to myself. The Holy Spirit brought the Word up out of my heart to counterattack the realities of cancer and help me see myself healthy in my future.

That doesn't mean I didn't have low days. The first time I wasn't able to accompany Larry to film our TV program, I felt an overwhelming sadness that

Pretending all is well when it isn't doesn't help. I must anchor my soul to who He is and what He has promised. Otherwise, I will spend my days wandering without a sense of purpose, never settling into why I am alive. Who He is remains the foundation of my life.

He went on to write:

You might say, "But she wasn't healed!" That's true. But my experience, or the lack thereof, can never be allowed to redefine who He is or what He has promised. His Word stands supreme over my experience.

Besides, no matter the situation, the lack is never on His end of the equation. I learned the beauty of this many years ago when my dad died. I had questions, pain, confusion and an overall struggle with my faith. Then I realized that if I captured this moment, with all its pain and confusion, I could give Jesus

I was missing out on our life. All the negative emotions I had been keeping at bay flooded in, and my heart was so heavy all I could do was whisper, "Lord, please help me." But with my simple heart's cry, the Holy Spirit became so real to me. His peace filled my heart, mind, and body, and then I suddenly realized the heavy burden had lifted off me. Instead of a chemotherapy infusion, I felt an infusion of peace, hope, faith, strength, confidence, victory, and joy by the power of the Holy Spirit!

I didn't get to circumvent the struggle. I didn't return to the doctor and discover the cancer had miraculously disappeared. I underwent surgery and endured months of chemotherapy. All the while, I held on to God's promises of healing, praying over a hundred healing verses each day. Larry and I did absolutely everything we needed to in the physical realm, and then we looked forward with the eye of faith, which is a fruit of the Spirit—and we saw our victory.

Today, I am happy to say I am healed and cancer-free—whole, healthy, and doing fantastic! If you are still in your season of trial, hang on. For every problem, our God has a promise. For every challenge, He has a triumph, and your victory is already in the works. God has a way through. As Romans 8:28 says, He is working *all* things together for our good!

—Tiz Huch, Co-pastor, New Beginnings Church

a priceless gift. There is no pain in eternity. Neither is there confusion or regret, and He wipes all tears away. That means if I can give Him praise in the middle of this mystery, I will have given Him something I will never have a chance to give Him in heaven.

It's true that I will be a worshipper forever. Throughout eternity, I will bow before the Lamb of God and declare His greatness. But I only have the chance to give Him praise in the midst of pain in this life.

As for how this affects his faith, he wrote:

> Real faith does not deny the existence of a problem. Instead, real faith denies the problem a place of influence. The difficulties in life have no right to redefine us or direct us. And of greater importance is not allowing our challenges to redefine God or His Word. Each gives us opportunities to encounter His presence, grace and renewed purpose for our lives.[3]

When speaking to his congregation that Sunday after his wife's passing, Johnson said God "gives the peace that passes understanding, which means I have to give up my right to understand in order to enjoy the peace that He has purposed to give me." He said that even if God answered all the whys, it wouldn't take away our pain. What we need in times of trial and sorrow aren't answers; we need the Lord's presence. This is the power of the Comforter, the Holy Spirit.[4]

In *Charisma* he wrote that there are two types of mourning. One leads you into hardness of heart and disbelief. The other leads you to God and gives you hope. He wrote:

> Those who mourn with hope will always end up in surrender to the Father, yielding to the working of the Holy Spirit, being healed by the Comforter Himself. Here's a key verse: "I do not want you to be ignorant, brethren, concerning those who have fallen asleep; *lest you sorrow as others who have no hope.*"[5]

Sorrow without hope has no legitimate conclusion. No closure. Sorrow with hope always takes us into life, into greater expressions of God and His will for our lives. In other words, sorrow and mourning are not the end. They are the hallway that takes us from one room to another.

Johnson says we undermine hope when we focus on what God isn't doing. He recommends we feed our souls on what God is doing; then we'll find strength. As for how he answers people who ask him why God did or didn't heal or otherwise bring the outcome they were seeking, his answer is simple:

> He doesn't work for me. I work for Him. He does not owe me an explanation for anything. All I need to know is what He would have me do next. For me, that is the beauty of embracing mystery. The lifestyle of miracles is not only the normal Christian life; it is the sacred responsibility of the believer.[6]

Johnson's example profoundly teaches us that a Spirit-led life isn't exempt from problems. Instead, it's a life of hope that is sheltered and strengthened in God's presence during the storm.

Every person has trials, even if they aren't as life-altering as those I've mentioned. It may be the disappointment of raising your kids in church and instilling the right values but seeing them get sucked into the world's culture and drift from the Lord.

Or maybe you're a young person with vision and faith who is seeing your career go nowhere and wondering what the answer is. Or perhaps you've had success in life, but things have gone wrong financially or you've experienced setbacks you can't seem to understand.

Or maybe you're on fire for God and want to grow but can't find a church to nurture your faith. You instead go from conference to conference and don't know why God doesn't answer your prayer to get plugged into a healthy, Spirit-led community.

A few years ago, I walked with a close friend through a trial. His son was born with Down syndrome and on top of that, he was severely autistic. The boy would pound his own eyes (as some autistic children do) until the he was in danger of going blind. The situation was so severe he required surgery to save his sight. While being prepared for surgery, he was given the wrong medicine in the wrong dosage and died. Way too often faith and marriage commitments go out the window when a family experiences this kind of tragedy and the loss of a child. That horrendous ordeal could have crushed their faith, but they came through the trial as strong believers.

Sadly, not everyone overcomes the trials and cares of life. Instead, they become discouraged. Bitterness often creeps in and just makes a bad situation worse.

They may have experienced the power of the Holy Spirit in the past but begin to feel God has forgotten them and that relying on the Holy Spirit doesn't really bring results. Or if they haven't faced a tragedy, it's the disappointments, addictive behaviors, or poor decisions that pull them down.

STRENGTH TO OVERCOME

If these struggles sound familiar, you are not alone. I have met many Christians who sincerely want to live overcoming lives, but they feel helpless and alone, often because they are disconnected from a life-enhancing community of believers. Maybe they have never really been strengthened and established in the Christian faith. So they toss to and fro, as the Bible puts it, never really experiencing the fullness of Spirit-led living.[7]

Others they just feel a malaise, to use the word Jimmy Carter made famous. They seem to have lost their purpose or become cynical, doubting God can use them to accomplish something lasting and meaningful in this life. Their lament is the same as that of the prophet Habakkuk: "O LORD, I have heard the report of You, and was afraid; O LORD, revive Your work in the midst of the years! In the midst of these years make them known; in wrath remember mercy."[8]

Still others hear sermons or read books about God's power to deliver us from sin and make our lives work, but those kinds of breakthroughs always seem to happen to someone else. They feel empty, inept, and powerless to experience the victorious life they know God wants them to have. Alone, discouraged, and weak, they pretend to be fine and hope no one notices.

People want to know the will of God. They want to know their purpose, but often they are clueless: Where do I turn? Who can help? How can this change? They feel as the disciples must have felt in the upper room after Jesus' death. They had no idea the power they were about to receive; they only knew they had none at that moment.

King David is one of my favorite Bible characters. He wrote most of the psalms and tells us the following:

- "Be strong, and He will strengthen your heart, all you who wait for the LORD."[9]

- "Let Your lovingkindness, O LORD, be on us, just as we hope in You."[10]

- "My soul, wait silently for God, for my hope is from Him. He only is my rock and my salvation; He is my refuge; I will not be moved."[11]

But David also wrote Psalm 69, where he cried out to God in great distress. And while David was a man after God's own heart, he was also a violent man, and he's most famous for taking another man's wife and sending her loyal husband to certain death in battle. As a result, David lost an infant son, even though he travailed and begged God to spare the child's life.

There are a lot of bad things that happen to good people. But James 1:2 says, "Count it all joy when you fall into various trials."[12] The word translated "joy" in this verse means a "calm delight."[13] That's what we're supposed to have when we're going through trials. And notice it's not if, but *when* we go through trials.

Why are we supposed to have a calm delight as we face hardship? The next verse explains: "Knowing that the trying of your faith develops patience."[14] *Knowing* means you have a conscious awareness of what's taking place. You know and understand. What do you know? That your faith is being tested, proven, and examined. You also know the reason for the testing is to produce patience, which can also mean endurance.

The purpose of the trial is to prove you. It tests your character to see whether it is good or not-so-good. The implication is that when you are surrounded by temptation, you either fall into it or you don't, and your character is strengthened by the encounter.

Remember what Paul wrote to the church in Corinth: "No temptation has taken you except what is common to man. God is faithful, and He will not permit you to be tempted above what you can endure, but will with the temptation also make a way to escape, that you may be able to bear it."[15]

James says, "Blessed is the man who endures temptation, for when he is tried, he will receive the crown of life, which the Lord has promised to those who love Him."[16] How do we endure these trials and temptations? As my friend Evan Trinkle puts it, we must develop desperation for and utter dependence on the Holy Spirit.

What practical steps can we take to draw closer to the Holy Spirit? The most important is to make a daily habit of spending time in the Word and prayer, which is not only talking to God and telling Him your problems but also listening.

Joe Suro, an associate pastor at my church in Sanford, Florida, preached recently on Christ being described as the "Wonderful Counselor" in Isaiah 9, the passage prophesying the coming Messiah.[17] When you think of a counselor, you think of someone who provides wisdom, advice, and a listening ear.

Suro explained that "Christ's position as our Wonderful Counselor means we can trust Him to listen to our problems and guide us in the right direction. We can be sure He is listening because He told us to pray to Him about our worries. And His love is so wide and deep (and wonderful) that we cannot fully understand it."[18]

We all need this "counseling" from God. His counsel is beyond human reason or advice. He helps us in a supernatural way that will comfort, heal, protect, guide, and refresh. Each of us needs this divine counsel each day to make right decisions.

"OK," you might be saying. "That sounds great and makes a good sermon, but often I don't know how to hear God when I need Him to show up and when I'm dealing with trials. How can I hear Him amid the distractions of life?"

The answer is in Psalm 91:1–2, which says, "He who dwells in the shelter of the Most High shall abide under the shadow of the Almighty. I will say of the LORD, 'He is my refuge and my fortress, my God in whom I trust.'"

The key is to "dwell," or rest, in the secret place, which is the presence of God. Resting brings us to a place of vulnerability and submission. We cannot fight in our own ability when we're resting and dwelling in God. God wants us in this position so He can be our strength when we have none. He wants us to cling to Him and allow Him to uphold us in times of hardship, confusion, and pain.

We may not understand what's happening when a trial hits our lives, but we must trust that God Almighty wants to use it to bring something good. We must cling to Him in faith, even when it seems our faith has failed. We must continue walking with the Holy Spirit through prayer, worship, and studying the Word, even when it's hard and the urge to quit is too much. This is what it means to abide in Him.

In his message, Suro said: "There are moments in life when you do not know what to do or say, and it's in these moments that we need to just dwell and remain in Him. It's not about getting over it but getting through it. [It's knowing], 'Even though I walk through the valley of the shadow of death, I will fear no evil; for You are with me.'"[19]

LIVING IT OUT

Read Psalm 91:1–2:

> He who dwells in the shelter of the Most High shall abide
> under the shadow of the Almighty. I will say of the LORD, "He
> is my refuge and my fortress, my God in whom I trust."

Think about it:

1. One key to overcoming trials is to dwell, or rest, in the secret
   place, which is the presence of God, because this brings
   us to a place of vulnerability and submission. What does
   dwelling in the presence of God look like in your daily life?

2. What did Bill Johnson mean when he made the following
   statements? And how does each apply to your life?

   - "There is an aspect of the Lord's presence that we can
     only find in the shadow of death."
   - "Trials are special opportunities to 'grow down.'"
   - "Peace that passes understanding is the peace we get
     when we give up our right to understand why."

3. What is the power of dwelling, or resting, in the secret
   place (God's presence), as Psalm 91:1–2 instructs?

4. Describe a time when you walked "through the valley of
   the shadow of death." Looking back, in what ways was the
   Holy Spirit walking with you? What good did God bring out
   of that trial?

Chapter 11

LET TRIALS PRODUCE THE
FRUIT OF THE SPIRIT

ACCORDING TO FUCHSIA Pickett, we bear the spiritual fruit Paul listed in Galatians 5 as we live in the Spirit, are led by the Spirit, and walk in the Spirit. It is the fruit of the Spirit in our lives (not spiritual gifts) that is the evidence of godly character and spiritual maturity. And while spiritual gifts can be given instantaneously, bearing spiritual fruit takes time.

In fact, Pickett says the development of spiritual fruit, or godly character, requires three things: *time, testing,* and *trials.* There is no other way to develop spiritual fruit in our lives besides through testing and afflictions. These are the opportunities God gives us to mature and develop godly character.

She wrote:

> We must remember that the development of godly fruit is nei-
> ther automatic nor instantaneous. Christlike character doesn't
> develop without diligence on the believer's part to yield continu-
> ally to the Holy Spirit in each situation he confronts in life.…
> Fruit will only be brought forth by much prayer, study of God's
> Word, and perseverance in life's difficulties.

James understood this when he wrote, "My brothers, take the prophets, who spoke in the name of the Lord, as an example of suffering and patience. Indeed we count them happy who endure. You have heard of the patience of Job and have seen the purpose of the Lord, that the Lord

155

is very gracious and merciful."[1] James teaches us that we develop maturity through a process of endurance and struggle.

Paul was able to declare, "For I have learned in whatever state I am to be content,"[2] because he had learned contentment in life's less-than-desirable circumstances. In that statement, he confirms that contentment is a learned virtue and must be developed. It is the same with all godly virtues and characteristics.

Pickett reminds us that "what we may think is a time of adversity and standstill could be God's time element of preparation in our lives for a task for which we are not yet ready. The manifestation...of godly character may be seen in a single act, but the development of each is the result of many testings and trials. The character we develop as we respond properly in our trials may well be the preventative of failure in the future."[3]

Sometimes trials are God's way of pruning us so we will bear more fruit. Other times they purify us and make us more Christlike. There are other reasons for trials, and in their book *Faith in the Night Seasons*, authors Chuck and Nancy Missler list several of them:

- to strengthen our faith and trust in Him[4]

- to produce all the fruit of the Spirit[5]

- to silence the enemy[6]

- to glorify Himself through us[7]

- to conform us more to His image[8]

- to enlarge our ministry[9]

- so that we might see and deal with our sin[10]

- and finally, to search our hearts to see if we love Him[11]

It all comes down to how we respond to the trial. Our response determines our entire spiritual future. Respond with doubt, giving up, or our own effort, and we only get deeper into trouble.

Bill Johnson, who I quoted in the previous chapter, points out that there is a difference between reacting and responding. Johnson says it's easy to live in reaction to whatever we're facing. But it's much more challenging to live in response to what God is doing and saying through those trying circumstances. "*Reaction* gives me a conclusion; *response* connects me to a process," he says.[12] If we yield ourselves to the process, the Holy Spirit uses our trials and suffering to accomplish God's highest will and purpose in our lives.

Trials are often personal, and we must hear from God to discern how He wants to use them in our lives, but what about the trials of this crazy, upside-down world? What do we do when we face persecution? As I've said, there have always been attempts to cancel Christianity, but in America, our freedoms are under greater assault than ever. We hear of Christian ministries having their credit card processing capacity blocked just because they oppose abortion or the gay agenda.[13] Christian bakers have been prosecuted for not designing cakes for gay weddings. The list goes on. It seems that more trials will come for just believing the Bible and trying to live for Jesus.

No one likes to struggle and endure hardship. Did you wake up this morning and ask God to send a massive problem your way? Of course not; they come when least expected. Remember what the apostle Paul said of his sufferings.

> Five times I received from the Jews forty lashes minus one. Three times I was beaten with rods; once I was stoned; three times I suffered shipwreck; a night and a day I have been in the deep; in journeys often, in perils of waters, in perils of robbers, in perils by my own countrymen, in perils by the Gentiles, in perils in the city, in perils in the wilderness, in perils in the sea, in perils among false brothers; in weariness and painfulness, in sleeplessness often, in hunger and thirst, in fastings often, and in cold and nakedness. Beside the external things, the care of all the churches pressures me daily. Who is weak, and I am not weak? Who is led into sin, and I am not distressed?[14]

Paul didn't wake up one day and ask for any of those challenges, and you likely won't either. When you go through a trial or struggle, what are your options? You can give up on your faith walk and stop honoring Jesus. But where is that going to get you? Right back where you started: miserable. Or you can press on in faith, knowing the Lord is with you. Jesus promised that He would never leave you, ever. Trust the One who is trustworthy.

Most of us have a preconceived notion of what a trial must look like. Without knowing it, we set parameters for God. We believe He can only bring us through the trial the way we think He should. But those notions may actually keep us from seeing what He wants to do in our lives. He wants to help us grow through the circumstance, not just provide us the provision we expect.

If you are looking for an answer, I believe the way out will show itself to you, but it may come in a way you're not expecting. It may be a word of encouragement or a tangible experience. Whatever it is, it will be

A Revival of Hope After Divorce

After twenty-one years of marriage and three children, I found out my husband was having an affair. I was Christmas shopping and heard the Spirit say, "Go to your husband's shop." He was a mechanic and working late that night. When I got to the shop, the other woman was there, and within a few days everything had been revealed. The grief was unreal, much like suffering through a death. After putting the kids to bed one night, I was kneeling by my bed, weeping. The Bible was on the bed and opened to Psalm 42. Through the tears, my eyes focused on verse 5: "Why are you cast down, O my soul?...Hope in God." I then found the same message in Psalm 42:11 and Psalm 43:5. I started to speak that word out loud, and hope began to rise in me. The Holy Spirit would regularly direct me to scriptures that would bring comfort and strength.

During the next six months, my husband returned home twice. The second time he returned, the suspicion was killing me; he kept certain texts private, answered some calls outside, and so on. I heard the Holy Spirit say, "Give him the benefit of the doubt." I did and was no longer stressing out but just trusting that all was well until one morning I heard the Holy Spirit say, "Look at his phone." I did and found that nothing had changed. During the time clear and bring hope so your countenance, attitude, emotions, and heart change, and you're strengthened.

Expectations will absolutely wreck us during our bouts with trials. It seems many of us almost demand that God respond the way we desire. When we think this way, we don't have the relationship right. Surrender first; then ask for patience and endurance.

Floyd Brown, the successful founder of the Western Journal, one of the nation's leading conservative news outlets, knows something about trials. We covered his story in *Charisma* magazine, and it's worth repeating here.

He grew up in a Pentecostal home. His grandfather was a pioneering missionary to Indonesia who in 1936 helped found the Indonesian Bethel Church, which today has many congregations and three million members in Indonesia, the nation with the world's largest Muslim population.

As a young adult, Brown worked for President Ronald Reagan and succeeded at nearly everything he did. He married his sweetheart and

my husband was back home, the Holy Spirit was giving him a final chance to change and protecting me from all that was going on. But when change was not the choice, the Lord showed me the marriage was over.

My husband was gone for good, though he would still come and see the children. The night before Father's Day, as I was wrapping gifts for my children to give him the next day, I was feeling very sorry for myself and crying on and off. My husband had a new, younger love and all kinds of things he had wanted. I asked, "What about me? And what about my children?" I then heard the Holy Spirit say, "Isaiah 54." I had no idea what Isaiah 54 said, but as I read that chapter, the first thing that stood out was, "The woman that was wooed and won in her youth and scorned in later years, I the LORD God will be your husband."[15] It went on to say my children would be taught by the Lord, have great peace, and take the nations!

In the twenty years I was married, we never owned a home, and our cars were always old and broken down. After the divorce, with one income and three children, I bought a great car. Not long after that, I purchased my own home. And I've never been lonely or wanting for anything. The Holy Spirit has proved Himself over and over. My "husband" is faithful and an amazing provider!

—NAME WITHHELD

started a family. But in the span of two years, their lives dramatically changed. First, in 2005, his wife, Mary Beth, was rear-ended in what appeared to be a minor fender bender. But the accident created problems that continue seventeen years later.

Then his son Patrick had an even more serious auto accident that forced him to finish high school at home and delay college for a year. Brown says he cried out for his son's healing, and God answered, but the trials didn't end. However, the miracles started.

His son was able to get the surgery he needed, and his pain went away within six months. Then Brown lost a high-paying job due to the downturn of 2008, but he began speaking at seminars on investments, his area of expertise. Around the same time, he began a small blog, which his son posted on a new social media platform called Facebook, and that was the start of the Western Journal.

But the trials continued. In 2012, Brown picked up a heavy box that triggered an old back injury, and he was suddenly flat on his back awaiting surgery. Lying still caused a pulmonary embolism, which kills two out of three people who get it. His miracle is that he lived.

"With each trial, my relationship with God was changing, growing, deepening. God was preparing me. He was walking with me. He was remaking me," Brown wrote in *Charisma*. "Each time I cried out to God, He was answering and providing. My dependence on Him was growing. He was building my faith with every answer."

By 2016, Brown says, the Western Journal had forty million followers on Facebook. This led to content from the company appearing eleven billion times in the Facebook news feed that year. Their website had more than one billion views in 2016 and became the fourth largest publisher on the Facebook platform in 2016. Then Donald Trump was elected.

Silicon Valley reacted with tech suppression of conservatives. New problems such as shadow banning and social media censorship followed— more trials, but Brown said God was faithful, and with each Big Tech attack, the Western Journal built workarounds and found alternate news distribution outlets.

But again, though the miracles didn't stop, neither did the trials. Two of Brown's greatest challenges were straight ahead.

In the spring of 2019, his wife, Mary Beth, went to the Mayo Clinic for a routine ultrasound, and it revealed a tumor on her adrenal gland—a very rare and difficult cancer to treat. Doctors gave her only five years to live.

Then before the tumor could be treated, during a service at their church, pastor Randy Vanesian, who did not know about her condition, interrupted his sermon and said God told him to pray for her. He went to where Mary Beth Brown was sitting and asked the entire church to pray for her. She said she felt an electrical charge course through her body, and miraculously, against all odds, she is completely cancer-free.

The story didn't end there. The family faced more challenges and saw more miracles, but Floyd Brown says the bottom line is this: All these trials have changed him. In his *Charisma* article, he wrote:

> Today, I have peace. I don't know what the future holds, but I know my loving Savior, Jesus, will be with me through it all. During these years of trouble, He has never left my side. Today, I hear His voice more than ever. I hear it when I read His Word and when I pray. When He gives me an assignment, I try to act on it immediately. The more I say yes to Him, the more peace and contentment I have.
>
> I live every day for Him, and my prayer for you is to hear Him too. Just listen; He still speaks today through His Holy Spirit, just as He has throughout history. He fills me up. He makes me happy. He is always there. My only regret is not releasing my life completely to Him earlier.

Brown says he can testify to the truth of James 1:3, which says the testing of our faith produces patience. While God doesn't promise we'll have only good times in life, He does promise to be with us through it all.[16]

As we saw previously, James tells us to "count it all joy" when we face hard times.[17] If that's the case, today's upside-down world gives us plenty of opportunities to choose joy! Remember, joy is a fruit of the Spirit. Not only that, but to exist in an upside-down world, where it seems most of the news is bad and there are forces taking away more and more of our rights and freedoms, we must find joy. In fact, it's as important to find joy in these perilous times as it would be if we were grieving after the death of a loved one or trying to believe God for a good outcome after receiving a horrible diagnosis.

THE HEALING POWER OF JOY

Best-selling author Dr. Don Colbert is a board-certified physician. And though it may be surprising to hear this from a medical doctor, he has some of the best teaching on joy. He says part of embracing joy is understanding how our brains work and how to control our thoughts and manage our feelings. That starts with remembering what the apostle Paul says in Philippians 4:4: "Rejoice in the Lord always. Again, I will say rejoice."

To put this into perspective, think about the world in which Paul lived. He was telling these early Christians to rejoice in the Lord while Nero was tarring and burning them in the streets of Rome and their family members were being imprisoned. Paul was in prison too, and he was writing his epistles with Luke's help. The Spirit of God was instructing Paul to tell the church to rejoice at its darkest time in history. If Paul and those early Christians were able to rejoice, or have joy, how much more should we!

Even with the world being upside down in so many ways, Colbert reminds us that no matter how bad things get, we can have joy, which is a state of being. Compare that to happiness, which is based on circumstances such as falling in love or getting a big raise.

Our brains control everything we do. We worry using our brains. And when we feel joy, it's the brain giving us that joyful feeling. As Colbert says, the same brain with which you worry or are depressed can shift to joy. That's pretty exciting. No matter what's happening around us, instead of worrying, we can have joy!

Colbert has a way to activate joy and happiness, and he shared his formula in a recent podcast: "For years, I've been prescribing ten belly laughs a day. Why? Because belly laughter activates joy. But you must activate your joy with happiness, and you activate it by smiling and laughing."

He noticed that many of his patients seemed to have what he calls a spirit of heaviness. They weren't necessarily depressed, but they were down. There was no joy in their faces, no smiles or laughter.

The reason might surprise you. Colbert says this may occur if our joy center wasn't filled when we were babies. You see, there's a joy center in the right orbital prefrontal cortex of the brain. And when it's developed, it regulates emotions and pain control, and even controls the immune system. That's why people full of joy and laughter usually have stronger immune systems.

This "joy center" begins to develop at three months of age. Babies begin to feel joy by being held close as they are breastfeeding or just by being held close to Mom or Dad. This is also when the visual areas of the brain start to develop, and the baby literally starts to look for eyes that are looking at them with joy. When they find eyes that are smiling, the baby starts to smile back. Have you ever smiled at a baby, and the baby smiled back? That happens because the baby has started to look for joy in people's eyes.[18]

Scowls, frowns, and unhappy faces deplete that little child's joy center. That's one issue created by the mask mandates during the COVID pandemic. With adults and children wearing masks, babies were prevented from seeing smiling faces, and that depleted their joy centers.

Colbert explains that the limbic system is the emotional center of the brain. At fifteen months of age, a baby's limbic system myelinates, which turns on the power of fear and anger. Children who have not developed their joy center tend to go down the tracks of fear, anger, or both. But Colbert says at eighteen months of age, the baby's joy center attempts to grow a neurological ring around all the other emotional centers and unify control over those emotions, thus giving them a path back to joy and letting joy reign supreme.

I believe it's important to understand what is happening in our brains.

This kind of knowledge helps us realize these biblical principles about joy and happiness are not only spiritually true, but they have a scientific basis.

Colbert is a physician, but he's also a Spirit-led believer who through his books and public appearances helps other believers understand health matters that otherwise might confuse them. It's good to know that in addition to trusting God for good health, there are practical steps we can take to be healthy. For example, if you're sick and believing for a healing miracle, it's helpful to learn that losing weight by following a healthy diet and exercising can not only improve your health but also make you feel better emotionally.

So how can we turn on joy? Colbert says it's easy to see the lifelong emotional challenges created when babies don't have full joy centers. Conversely, having a full joy center as a baby leads to healthy emotions later in life. When a person who has that neurological ring around their emotions gets angry, sad, down, or whatever, they have a ready access right back to joy and don't get trapped in anger, rage, sorrow, depression, or despondency. They have a literal path back to joy.

However, even if your joy center wasn't filled as a baby, you can fill it now. Jesus said in John 16:22 that no one can take your joy. Paul teaches us in 1 Thessalonians 5:18 to give thanks "in everything" because gratitude, or thanksgiving, literally activates our joy. This means no matter how bad things get in our upside-down world, you can give thanks and activate joy.

Filling the joy center is kind of like filling a tank of gas; smiling, laughing, and dancing activate joy and fill up that tank. And there are other things we can do.

One is gathering with other believers to worship and pray together. You won't believe the difference this will make and the refreshing it will bring to your spirit. This is why Hebrews 10:25 says: "Let us not forsake the assembling of ourselves together."

And here's a surprising tip you need to try: belly laughter. Colbert says there are so many health benefits associated with belly laughter that it should be prescribed for every patient.[19] His list of the ten most powerful health benefits of joy and laughter is in the endnotes.[20]

I wanted to share this information about the healing power of laughter and joy because Spirit-led living doesn't only bear spiritual fruit. It will improve every area of your life—your health, your family, and your sense of fulfillment—and deepen your relationship with God in every way. In a sense, I've sought to do this over the years in the more than a thousand issues of *Charisma* and other magazines and the more than two thousand books I've had the privilege to publish. I hope everything Charisma Media does continues to fulfill our corporate vision of helping people experience the power of the Holy Spirit and radically change their world.

LIVING IT OUT

Read Philippians 4:4:

Rejoice in the Lord always. Again, I will say rejoice!

Think about it:

1. Think about the world in which Paul lived when the Spirit of God instructed him to tell the church to rejoice. How does this change your perspective on rejoicing in the circumstances of your life?

2. Fuchsia Pickett reminds us that what we think of as a time of adversity could be God's preparation for a task we are not yet ready to handle. What character traits do you see the Holy Spirit developing in your life as a result of the trials and tests you've endured? What do you think those trials are/were preparing you for?

3. How will the things Dr. Colbert shared about your brain's joy center and the power of a good belly laugh change the way you go about your day?

4. Floyd Brown said: "With each trial, my relationship with God was changing, growing, deepening." What trials have brought you closer to God?

Chapter 12

SURVIVE END-TIME TRIBULATIONS THROUGH THE SPIRIT

HISTORY IS FULL of times that were difficult for believers—indeed many millions of Christians are being persecuted in our generation. But Christians in America have been living in a sort of bubble. Because of our constitutional rights, we have freedoms not enjoyed in other countries.

There have been terrible times before, but it seems God came through in answer to prayer. Fifty years ago in the hippie era, the Jesus movement (which impacted me) brought millions of rebellious young people to faith in Christ. Then, when America seemed at low ebb during the Jimmy Carter administration, something seemed to shift when hundreds of thousands of Christians humbled themselves and prayed and repented of America's sins at the Washington for Jesus rally in 1980. Ronald Reagan was elected president later that year, and things seemed to shift politically and financially. The Berlin Wall even came down. But now, forty years later, I wonder how much really changed.

We now live in a post-Christian culture. Today, evil is called good, and good is called evil. That's the essence of a culture that's upside down. While many of us believe God raised up America, let's face it, the nation is becoming more and more evil and deserves to be judged.

There's a wonderful promise in Revelation 3:10: "Because you have kept My word of patience, I also will keep you from the hour of temptation which shall come upon the entire world, to test those who dwell on the earth." It's not fun to think about, but we may face persecution in this country. Some Christians already have been cancelled on social media for posting Scripture verses. A few have lost their jobs when they refused to comply with woke policies being enforced.

If we believe the Bible, we know persecution will come. The question is whether we will see it in our lifetime. Christians over the millennia have been expecting Christ to return. Now the world is so upside down it appears what Jesus prophesied about the end of time is happening before our eyes. A one-world government, the rise of the man the Bible calls the Antichrist, and even a mark required to buy and sell seem to be the natural result of the "great reset" the World Economic Forum has called for.

We've looked at the Holy Spirit as the Comforter, and He is. But He's more than a friendly Counselor who can help us with our anger issues or deal with disappointment. He can do those things, and most of this book has been focused on His power to help us overcome in life. But the reality is, we're in a spiritual war. And when the tribulation comes, it will be the war of all wars.

So we must prepare for battle if we are to survive, just as Navy Seals must toughen themselves in a way civilians don't. Because of their training, those Navy Seals stand a better chance of surviving in a combat situation than you or I would!

Dr. Stella Immanuel is a general practitioner in Houston, Texas. I've seen that she is a powerful woman of the Spirit who believes in spiritual warfare and leads Fire Power Ministries in addition to managing her medical practice.

She was among the group of America's Frontline Doctors who stood on the steps of the US Supreme Court in 2020 and said the government and Centers for Disease Control were lying about alternative treatments such as hydroxychloroquine being ineffective against COVID-19 and masks being necessary to curb the spread of the virus. She believes the government used the health emergency to introduce nanotechnology as a means of furthering their cause of controlling our lives.

She considers mRNA technology a bioweapon—a messenger that modifies your DNA. She notes that the mRNA "vaccines" have caused blood clots and even death in some people. That's a problem, of course, but the bigger issue is that there are those predicting that as the public accepts this and technology advances, someday we will be required to have chips implanted that enable the government to control every area of our lives.

Dr. Immanuel says it's like the Bible says in Psalm 2:2, "The kings of the earth set themselves, and the rulers take counsel together, against the LORD and against His anointed." Current leaders have "taken counsel against the Lord and against the earth; they've taken counsel against the people of the world," she says.[1] To some this sounds like conspiracy theories. But whenever the world's elite billionaires discuss solving the world's problems, population control always seems to come up.[2] This is scary stuff.

Yet the Bible says when we hear this to rejoice and look up because our redemption is nigh.

A man who has been sounding the alarm is my friend Clay Clark, founder of the ReAwaken America Tour. Clark is exposing schemes that are almost beyond comprehension, things most of us don't encounter when we go to work, attend church, or interact with our families.

I believe Clark is what the Bible calls a watchman on the wall,[3] one who wants to alert the Christian community and others of dangers from those who are anti-God and proposing schemes that are dangerous to mankind, such as government surveillance, especially the idea of implanting surveillance devices known as biosensors under the skin.

One man he exposes is Yuval Noah Harari, an Israeli intellectual who seems to have great influence over the technological and business elites and the World Economic Forum. When Harari talks about the potential of advances in info-technology and biological sciences, it sounds as if he's describing the mark of the beast. For example, in one interview published in the summer of 2020, Harari said:

> We are witnessing the creation of new surveillance systems all over the world, by both governments and corporations. The current crisis might mark an important watershed in the history of surveillance. First, because it might legitimate and normalize the deployment of mass surveillance tools in countries that have so

far rejected them. Secondly, and even more importantly, it signifies a dramatic transition from "over the skin" to "under the skin" surveillance.

Previously, governments and corporations monitored mainly your actions in the world—where you go, who you meet. Now they have become more interested in what is happening inside your body. In your medical condition, body temperature, blood pressure. That kind of biometric information can tell governments and corporations far more about you than ever before.[4]

Other quotes from Harari make it easy to see how the stage is being set for the end-time and the rise of the Antichrist. Sadly, it's likely just a matter of time before these ideas begin to affect each of our lives.

- "Ideally the response to COVID should be the establishment of a global healthcare system, a basic healthcare system for the entire human race."[5]

- "COVID...legitimizes the deployment of mass surveillance even in democratic countries, and it makes surveillance go under your skin."[6]

- "History began when humans invented gods, and will end when humans become gods."[7]

- "The most important thing to know about living in the twenty-first century is that humans are now hackable animals."[8]

- "Humans are developing bigger powers than ever before. We are really acquiring divine powers of creation and destruction. We are really upgrading humans into gods."[9]

When asked about religion's role in society, Harari said, "So far in history, in order to organize humans on a large scale, you always had to have some story, some fiction which humans invented, but which enough humans believed in order to agree on how to behave."[10] In other words, Harari believes the Bible and the resurrection of Jesus are just a shared fiction used to help us behave better.

I've watched some of Harari's videos, and it seems to me that he is deceived about many things. I agree with Clark on the evils of the great reset and the danger of globalism. Whether Clark is right about Harari's dark influence on powerful people remains to be seen. Here's what I do know: As a Christian, I must judge every new quote, every new philosophy, and every new teaching in the light of Scripture as a whole.

With Scripture as my standard, I know humans are not just hackable animals. We're made in the image of God. I know there's only one God, and He's not me. And I know the Bible and the resurrection of Jesus are not just shared fictions to help me behave better. Both are powerful realities in my life every single day.

Notice what the Bible says about the one "who opposes and exalts himself above all that is called God or is worshipped, so that he sits as God in the temple of God, showing himself as God." He is the one "whom the Lord will consume with the breath of His mouth, and destroy with the brightness of His presence."[11]

We also see God's judgment on display in Genesis 6:

> When men began to multiply on the face of the earth and daughters were born to them, the sons of God saw that the daughters of men were fair and took as wives any they chose. The LORD said, "My Spirit will not always strive with man, for he is flesh; yet his days will be a hundred and twenty years."
>
> The Nephilim were on the earth in those days, and also after that, when the sons of God came in to the daughters of men, and they bore children to them. These were the mighty men who were of old, men of renown.
>
> The LORD saw that the wickedness of man was great on the earth, and that every intent of the thoughts of his heart was continually only evil. The LORD was sorry that He had made man on the earth, and it grieved Him in His heart. So the LORD said, "I will destroy man, whom I have created, from the face of the

earth—both man and beast, and the creeping things, and the birds of the sky, for I am sorry that I have made them."[12]

The world seems to be raging out of control, and most of what's happening seems beyond our understanding. We know everything is upside down, but we don't know what to do. Some have compared this to the time in Germany when Jews knew something was seriously wrong, but the Nazi agenda was too horrific for anyone to believe it could actually happen. They hoped the furor would blow over. But it didn't; in fact, it got worse.

According to the US Holocaust Memorial Museum, six million Jewish men, women, and children, along with eleven million members of other groups, were murdered by the Nazi regime.[13] People like Corrie ten Boom lived through that time, and the story of how her Christian family hid Jews to save their lives is told in the book *The Hiding Place*. Some Jews survived, such as Viktor Frankl, who wrote the classic *Man's Search for Meaning*, in which he tells how he sought meaning during that time of utter hopelessness and how finding meaning helped him survive.

Another man who has experienced untold pain and unfair treatment is televangelist Jim Bakker, who was sent to prison on what turned out to be trumped-up charges. Did he do anything wrong? He wrote a book titled *I Was Wrong*, which I've read. But I've known Bakker for years, and in my opinion, the things he was accused of in court were minor, especially when compared to what many get away with. Bakker has been vindicated by the courts, but in the interim, he lost his huge ministry, his reputation, his freedom, and even his wife.

When he was in prison, however, something wonderful happened. He got into the Word of God. He studied the Bible as never before—especially the Book of Matthew, where Jesus predicted what would happen at the end of time.

PREPARING FOR WHAT LIES AHEAD

Bakker received a word from the Lord in 2012 that warned of five stages for the days ahead. After almost a decade, based on events that had transpired, he felt we were about halfway through the stages, and he wrote about it in his book *You Can Make It*, which we published in 2021. Like me, he believes there is a massive cultural shift taking place. "When the church is unable to act as a check and balance to society," Bakker warned, "civilization will act as directed by the evil one."

The first stage was confusion, which he explains is the same as instability or disorder—perfect descriptions of the United States in the last few years. Bakker believes the unrest in our culture is due to the church being lulled to sleep instead of keeping a watchful eye on society. "The church stood on the sidelines when prayer was removed from our schools. We've seen the Ten Commandments removed from courthouses." He believes if Christians continue to do nothing, many will fall away from the faith and it will become increasingly hard to evangelize.

Bakker says the Lord told him that explosions were the second stage. Rather than literal explosions of bombs or other weapons, he believes the term refers to rapid expansions of the confusion of stage one, along with explosions of corruption, perversion, and ultimately persecution.

Stage three is deception, and according to Bakker, we were unmistakably in this stage when he wrote *You Can Make It*. He cited the corruption of modern media such as television, movies, and even social media as just one example. He believes that because of the massive deception going on, some Christians are already signing up for the antichrist system, pointing out that Revelation 19:20 says those who received the mark of the beast were deceived into doing so.

Bakker says the deception of our age will eventually cause depression, which is stage four. Not only will people be in deep personal depression, but "we will also see a tremendous global economic depression." I agree with Bakker that we've been in this stage since the end of 2020. There's no denying the economic downturn since the last presidential election cycle. Stage five will be collapse. Bakker believes a worldwide economic collapse is coming. Indeed, we can look around and see that we are already teetering on the brink and about to fall into this abyss. Bakker believes this ultimate financial collapse is the final prerequisite before the Antichrist can be revealed on the earth.

He says Christians should heed this warning and stand up against the things of the world rather than conforming to them. "The key to our survival is threefold: remain in Christ, keep His commandments, and remain in His body, the church. Escape is not an option. Endurance is our goal."

Bakker follows up these ominous words with chapters that explain a great global shaking, which he believes is coming as a series of events that will be carefully orchestrated to mete out God's judgment on the entire earth. He wrote that earthquakes, fires, floods, and asteroid strikes are coming, and coming soon.

But he strongly believes all these apocalyptic events described in the Book of Revelation are not about despair; they are about hope. "God did not give us the Book of Revelation so that we would fear the end of the world. He gave it to us so we could save those around us from being on the wrong side of judgment. God wants us to be mentally, physically, and spiritually prepared for all that is coming!"

He offers practical advice on food storage and how to care for your family, extended family, neighbors, and community during coming

Facing the Giants

Many people came to know me from a viral video from April 2021 where I kicked out Canadian authorities who came to our church Easter weekend, demanding that we shut down. They claimed we were violating COVID-19 health orders by holding church services and that we disregarded rules on mask-wearing and physical distancing. But they were the ones breaking the law. In Canada, we have a constitution that gives us fundamentally protected rights. But during the pandemic, it seemed we had no rights whatsoever.

As someone who fled communism in Poland in search of freedom in Canada, I was shocked to find myself being arrested in the middle of the highway in May 2021 and charged with inciting people to come to church and participating in an illegal gathering as a pastor. I was told that I had broken two court orders, which brings a potential of four years in prison. Also, in May 2021, my then-twelve-year-old daughter asked me to baptize her for her birthday. So I baptized my daughter, and for that "crime" [of violating COVID restrictions by baptizing her], I faced another two years in prison.

While I was facing those gigantic problems, I decided to go to the United States to tell my story and warn the American people. They came for me, times of famine and food scarcity. He provides checklists of essential emergency items he believes could be the difference between life and death in a disaster.

He also offers advice for how to prepare spiritually, which corresponds with the message of this book. He encourages believers to do the following.

- Draw upon the Holy Spirit, make sure you know His voice, and know what He says is coming.

- Avoid the great falling away from the faith by strengthening yourself in the Lord.

- Pray fervently for revival and reformation based on true repentance and commitment to Jesus Christ.

- Let go of anger, bitterness, and unforgiveness.

- Devour the Word of God and stay strong in your faith.

so be sure of it; they will come for you as well unless you rise up and stand up. You have two choices: You can bow and perish, or you can stand up and fight the tyranny. The founding fathers were willing to die for America to be the land of the free. Now I think it's time for this generation to rise up and fight for freedom as well.

When I visited the United States in 2021, I was invited to stay there and be safe. But I had to go back, no matter what I might face, and I was arrested on the tarmac when my plane landed at Calgary International Airport. That was just one of five arrests I've endured since the start of the COVID pandemic—all for doing my job as a pastor and exercising my God- and state-given rights. In 2022, I was jailed for more than fifty days. Fortunately, I have not been convicted of any criminal charges, but as I write these words, I am still under house arrest and facing more than ten years in prison for participating in a border blockade organized by truckers opposed to vaccine mandates.

As the end-time draws near, the kind of persecution I've faced may increase. The good news is that God is still bigger than the enemy. No matter what happens, if we read the Bible, we know how the story ends. We win because God wins.

—ARTUR PAWLOWSKI, PASTOR, STREET CHURCH, CALGARY, ALBERTA

Bakker says, "Only by knowing the Word, knowing our Father's voice, can you navigate the tumultuous waters we are currently sailing in. Stay in your Bible every day. Devour it as you would a hearty meal or rich dessert. If you can, get a Bible with excellent study notes or even a thick concordance."[14]

In his book, Bakker shares that on July 1, 1994, shortly before his release from prison, he began to write a series of commitments he would make to Jesus daily. "These commitments," he says, "have enabled me to maintain my walk with Him in the last twenty-seven years." Bakker encourages everyone to keep a similar list and follow it each day because we will need to remain deeply committed in the days ahead. His list reminds him to walk in humility before God, meditate on God's Word, to daily crucify his flesh, not judge others and to exhibit the fruit of the Spirit. You may be inspired by his list of fifteen daily commitments so I added them to the endnotes.[15]

Bakker says: "This is the last season to get prepared. The stroke of midnight is near, and the clock can no longer be stopped. We do not act in fear, but we continue to move forward in the authority of our Lord and Savior, Jesus Christ. He will return very soon for those who love Him....God will not forsake you in the days to come. I've been on the highest of mountains and the lowest of valleys, so I can say with confidence that you can make it through the valley of the shadow of death. God will be there right beside us, and we shall emerge victorious."[16]

I agree. We must be prepared. I believe everyone must go through the tribulation, or the period leading up to the reign of the Antichrist. Like Bakker, Dr. Stella Immanuel believes times are going to get hard. She believes we are already in Revelation 6, which describes six seals.

1. The Conqueror

2. Conflict on Earth

3. Scarcity on Earth

4. Widespread Death on Earth

5. The Cry of the Martyrs

6. Cosmic Disturbances

She believes the Conqueror was released in 2020. "It's conquered whole world; the whole world is under this craziness," she told me. "The second thing that was released is the sword; the sword is fighting among each other. The third thing right now is famine, with food shortages the result of war in the Ukraine, the breadbasket of Europe, as well as drought and supply chain disruptions as a result of the COVID pandemic."

Now is the time to prepare physically, financially, and spiritually. Dr. Immanuel says in the same way Joseph in the Book of Genesis stored up food to prepare for lean times, you can set aside long-shelf-life food (as we have done at the Strang household).

Even though she believes things are going to be "really bad," she told me this: "If you're in Christ, you don't have to be afraid. If you look at Revelation, the full course of the apocalypse is death and hell, and people are going to die from famine, pestilence, or war. So you can die, but you don't have to go to hell. You don't have to be in the death-and-hell group; you can be in the death-and-seen-at-the-throne-of-grace group. So there is hope."

Each of us must decide. If half the world is going to die as is prophesied, we don't need to be afraid if we've given our lives to Christ. That's the message we must proclaim: When things get bad, call on the name of Jesus, because the Bible says whoever calls on His name shall be saved.[17]

Though the world seems to be careening toward the last days, this is not the time to become discouraged. We have the Holy Spirit, and He will never leave us nor forsake us.[18] As Moses told Joshua, "The LORD, He goes before you. He will be with you. He will not fail you nor forsake you. Do not fear, nor be dismayed."[19]

God is our only hope. As Michael Youssef, pastor of The Church of The Apostles in Atlanta, says in his book *Is the End Near?*: "Being a Christian in the end-time will be incredibly difficult. It will mean being hated and persecuted for your faith. But I guarantee that even if you are hunted down, abused, and killed for your faith in Jesus, it will have been worth it. You will have eternal life with Jesus in heaven. When He returns, you will be full of joy at His appearing while the unsaved world despairs. Only Jesus offers true security in a collapsing world."[20]

As we've seen throughout this book, the Holy Spirit can empower us to stand up to all the evil in the culture and fill us with joy, contentment, and vision even in the midst of it. I sincerely believe it's possible to experience God's power to not only survive but thrive, even when the world is upside down.

The Holy Spirit can give us discernment about all that is happening leading to the end of time. But sadly, too many Christians are not pressing into God and are missing the real opportunity to lay hold of the victory and fullness of life available to us in Him. But it's not too late to access this power. You can be filled with the Spirit—or filled anew—and experience His power and presence at a greater measure than you ever thought possible.

LIVING IT OUT

Read Revelation 3:10 (NKJV):

> Because you have kept My command to persevere, I also will keep you from the hour of trial which shall come upon the whole world, to test those who dwell on the earth.

Think about it:

1. The Holy Spirit is more than a friendly Counselor who can help us manage anger issues or disappointments. How do you think the Holy Spirit will help you as you face end-time events?

2. Jim Bakker believes the apocalyptic events in the Book of Revelation are not about despair; they are about hope. How does reading about them motivate you to prepare mentally, physically, and spiritually for what lies ahead?

3. Consider the following steps of spiritual preparation and write how each step applies to your life.

   - Draw upon the Holy Spirit, make sure you know His voice, and know what He says is coming.
   - Avoid the great falling away from the faith by strengthening yourself in the Lord.
   - Pray fervently for revival and reformation based on true repentance and commitment to Jesus Christ.
   - Let go of anger, bitterness, and unforgiveness.
   - Devour the Word of God and stay strong in your faith.

Conclusion

FACING THE FUTURE WITHOUT FEAR

T HIS BOOK WAS written to help encourage you to be entirely led by the Spirit in new and fresh ways—to launch out into the deep[1] and experience the power and strength that come only from knowing Christ in a deep way.

Yes, the world is upside down. But it was upside down before we were born, and it will be upside down until Christ comes to set up His kingdom during the millennial reign written of in the Book of Revelation, which I discussed in the last chapter.

In recent years many Christians, including me, thought if we could just vote in leaders who shared our values, the trajectory of the nation would improve. But we've had setback after setback. With rising inflation, crime, transgenderism being taught in schools, and socialistic policies gaining sway, things were so bad on so many levels it seemed change was inevitable. Many of us had high hopes for the midterm elections, as a number of conservative politicians—many of them Christian leaders—seemed poised to win. Some political pundits and even some Christian prophets said there would be a red wave, meaning conservatives would be elected and implement policies more in tune with a biblical worldview.

But the red wave didn't happen, and millions of Christians who believed God would answer their prayers and the tide would turn were suddenly saying, "God, where were You?"—as if He were asleep.

Right after the election, Barry Meguiar, a successful businessman and the author of *Ignite Your Life*, wrote an outstanding editorial on charismanews.com suggesting that our desire for America to become a godly nation is not God's will because it would be out-of-step with His judgment on America and end-time prophecies. Had God-honoring candidates and issues prevailed in the midterms, he says, it would have interfered with God's trajectory for America.

"America has earned God's judgment a thousand times over, and we know America isn't even mentioned in last-days prophecies," Meguiar says. "In two short years, America has lost the world's respect and our nation's confidence. The idea of turning our allegiance to a global leader (the Antichrist) is now a *fait accompli*. It's going to happen, and we deserve it to happen. God is no longer going to allow anything to slow down our race to judgment."

He reminded us God gives us the rulers we deserve, not the ones we want. Sadly, in every obscene category America is, by far, the major purveyor of wickedness worldwide.

"If you love God and still live for this world and the things of this world, these elections are your worst nightmare," Meguiar says. "But if you love God with eyes fixed on the world to come, the darker it gets, the closer you are to the rapture and actually seeing Him face to face."

For those who wonder if we are close to the end of time, there's no question; we're getting really close. But that is no reason to despair. Jesus told us, "When these things begin to happen, look up and lift up your heads, for your redemption is drawing near."[2] And when Paul describes the rapture of the church, he says, "Comfort one another with these words."[3]

So let's be encouraged! As Meguiar wrote, "Rather than allowing the events of these days to drag you down and discourage you, use them as your launching pad to move everyone, every day closer to Jesus—before it's too late and they're left behind."[4]

The spiritual and eternal, not the political or cultural, are most important. We have a mission to spread the gospel, and as Alton Garrison, former assistant general superintendent of the Assemblies of God, points out now is the time to reach the lost and disciple newly converted Christians so they don't become what he calls "casual Christians." Part of our mandate as believers is to help others embrace a Spirit-led life and fulfill the Great Commission of going into all the world to preach the gospel to everyone.

"The ultimate goal of our faith journey is to relate to the person of Jesus—the One who spoke the Great Commission. Our relational connection to Jesus will produce Christlikeness and spiritual growth. His instruction was to 'teach these new disciples to obey all the commands I have given you,'" Garrison writes.[5] "We need to become disciples who make disciples who make disciples."

Sadly, discipleship doesn't happen often, and when it does, it calls on the disciple to learn about the Bible or how to behave. Garrison says: "Concentrating on what we should know, if taken to the extreme, can make us arrogant. Behavioral effort (doing more or behaving better), taken to the extreme, minimizes grace."

We understand that knowledge and behavior are essential to Spirit-led living, but alone, they do not transform! Instead, we must love Jesus deeply.

"The primary purpose of Spirit empowerment is to carry out the transformative mission of God among the lost," Garrison writes. "With the challenges facing us today, it would be senseless to attempt to affect a change in the lives of people by merely utilizing our own ingenuity, intellect, and human effort. God has not abandoned us to that fruitless recourse. When we take hold of the Spirit's power, we are fully equipped and emboldened to confront our lost world with the hope of the gospel.

"Our forefathers got it right. The last sentence in the Assemblies of God Statement of Fundamental Truths reveals the Pentecostal understanding of the importance of Baptism in the Holy Spirit. The language is important. It speaks of something extra, something added on: 'With the baptism in the Holy Ghost come such experiences as...overflowing fullness...deepened reverence...intensified consecration...more active love.' A key word here is *MORE*."[6]

In what areas do you long for more? You can begin that pursuit by seeking more of the Spirit's power in your life.

THE HOPE OF VICTORY

I've mentioned that Romans 8 is one of my favorite chapters in the Bible and if one were to give it a title, "Life in the Spirit" would be fitting. When I consider how far our nation has drifted from biblical truth and how close we must be to the end-time, I find myself gravitating to Paul's words in that chapter. This world may be upside-down, but we don't have to live as victims.

Paul writes that "for as many as are led by the Spirit of God, these are the sons [and, I might add, the daughters] of God. For you have not received the spirit of slavery again to fear. But you have received the Spirit of adoption, by whom we cry, 'Abba, Father.'"[7]

He goes on to say: "The Spirit Himself bears witness with our spirits that we are the children of God, and if children, then heirs."[8] Isn't that fantastic news?

Yet Paul continues, "...if indeed we suffer with Him, that we may also be glorified with Him. For I consider that the sufferings of this present time are not worthy to be compared with the glory which shall be revealed to us."[9] This allows us to step boldly into the future without fear. As the *FireBible* commentary notes, sickness, pain, disappointments, injustice, mistreatment, rejection, sorrow, persecution, and trouble of any kind are considered small when compared with the blessings, privileges, and glory that will be given to every believer as we spend eternity with Him.[10]

Then Paul not only promises the Holy Spirit will help us in our weakness, but he makes one of the most significant biblical promises to the Spirit-led Christian—that "the Spirit Himself intercedes for us with groanings too deep for words."[11] We call this praying in the Spirit, as we discussed in chapter 3, and it's something I've done many times, especially when I have a deep need for the Lord's intervention and don't even know how to articulate my request.

God knows the mind of the Spirit, who intercedes for us according to the will of God.[12] We can know we pray according to the will of God when we pray in the Spirit.

Romans 8 contains another powerful promise that changed my life when I heard the late Doug Wead preach on it when I was in my twenties. Paul says in verses 24–25, "For we are saved through hope, but hope that is seen is not hope, for why does a man still hope for what he sees? But if we hope for what we do not see, we wait for it with patience."

I'd never noticed the insight Wead shared. The passage says we are saved by hope. We know the scripture that we are saved by faith, not by works, lest any man should boast.[13] But these Bible truths tie together. Hebrews 11:1 says faith is the substance of things *hoped* for, the evidence of things unseen. So hope comes *before* faith. I'd never seen that.

Wead had a way of making things so simple. He said some of the leaders who were teaching people to confess the Word in dire circumstances where it was hard to believe were putting burdens on believers they couldn't bear. For example, if someone has cancer and is saying in faith that the cancer is gone, the person might feel she is lying, which is not helpful when you're praying for a miracle.

Wead used to say, "Faith says, 'It is,' but hope says, 'It's possible.'" Anything is possible. Today, somewhere in the world, someone is getting healed of cancer, a divorce is being reversed at the last minute, a wayward child is coming to Christ, and someone is receiving a financial miracle. I've been in some situations where I was only able to say, "It's possible," but that led to faith, which led to a miracle.

I love Romans 8, and I've encouraged many people over the years with this insight. Now I am able to share it here.

Near the end of Romans 8, verse 28 says, "We know that all things work together for good to those who love God." How comforting that verse is, and I confess it often, as recently as this week. Yet there is more to that scripture than we typically include when we quote it. It's a phrase whose importance Meguiar made clear in his new book *Ignite Your Life*.

The promise that all things work together for good is "to those who are called according to His purpose"—and His purpose is for all to come to know God. In other words, God's will is that we bring people to Christ "because He does not want any to perish, but all to come to repentance."[14]

In his amazing book, Meguiar tells of the joy he's found in sharing his faith each day, and his story is inspiring for the rest of us.

Paul's message in Romans 8 is not just that you can be saved from your sins and avoid hell and eternal separation from God but that you can live a life in the Spirit—and that, as verses 37–39 say: "In all these things we are more than conquerors through Him who loved us. For I am persuaded that neither death nor life, neither angels nor principalities nor powers, neither things present nor things to come, neither height nor depth, nor any other created thing, shall be able to separate us from the love of God, which is in Christ Jesus our Lord," even in an upside-down world!

LIVING IT OUT

Read Romans 8:16–17:

> The Spirit Himself bears witness with our spirits that we are
> the children of God, and if children, then heirs.

Think about it:

1. Barry Meguiar wrote: "Rather than allowing the events of
   these days to drag you down and discourage you, use them
   as your launching pad to move everyone, every day closer
   to Jesus." How do you to focus on the spiritual and the
   eternal, not the political or cultural, in this upside-down
   world?

2. The world seems to be careening toward the end of time,
   and if you focus only on that you can become discouraged.
   How does the Holy Spirit help you face this reality?

3. Doug Wead said we are not only saved by faith; we are
   saved by hope. Explain why you do or don't agree with that
   statement in light of Hebrews 11:1, "Now faith is the substance of things hoped for, the evidence of things not seen."

4. Spirit-led living will improve your life and deepen your
   relationship with God in every way. Write what you can do
   to press into God and embrace every opportunity to experience the Holy Spirit's power.

EPILOGUE

BILLY WILSON, CURRENT President of Oral Roberts University, is a man with a big vision. As the global co-chair of a Pentecostal-Charismatic networking group called Empowered21, he's working to realize their bold vision to see every person on earth have an authentic encounter with Jesus Christ through the power and presence of the Holy Spirit by Pentecost Sunday 2033.

That's a big goal, considering the world population just passed eight billion and 2033 is a mere decade away. But just as we celebrated the two thousandth anniversary of the birth of Christ, 2033 marks an even more significant date—the two thousandth anniversary of the birth of the church.

Did you catch that? The year 2033 marks two thousand years since AD 33, when Jesus was crucified, rose from the dead, and ascended to heaven. And one of the largest Charismatic relational networks in the history of Christianity has commenced with a vision of seeing every person on earth have an authentic encounter with Jesus Christ through the power and presence of the Holy Spirit that year.

"We have a philosophy that the prayer of Jesus for unity is not only relational, but it's also missional," Wilson says. Empowered21 is mobilizing movements and churches and encouraging the body of Christ to work toward making the next decade the greatest time of Great Commission effort in the history of the church.

Technological advancements over the years have opened doors to reach people in ways the global church once never thought possible.

"Jesus over and over again would reach out to an individual and by seeing that individual converted would open an entire region like [He did with] the woman of Samaria," Wilson says.

I first met Billy Wilson when he led the great centennial of the Azusa

Street Revival in Los Angeles in 2006. Tens of thousands of Pentecostal Christians came from around the world to celebrate the revival that had swept the world.

Aware that it's easy to be overwhelmed by the masses—eight billion people sounds like a lot of people—Wilson was on a prayer retreat and asked the Holy Spirit, "How are we going to give every person on earth an opportunity to know You over the next decade?"

When I interviewed Wilson about this, he said, "I really felt like the Holy Spirit said to me, 'One person at a time'—that if we'll focus on the one, God will help us ultimately reach everyone.

"Now, Empowered21 is calling everyone in the church to get involved just in sharing their faith and loving people in praying for the lost. There's another initiative going on, where we're seeking to pray for every person on earth by name over the next ten years as well. And we believe as we pray for people, God will give us an opportunity to share the good news with them. And then they'll have an opportunity to either receive or reject Jesus. This is our goal."

Wilson shared three things that need to happen for the church to move into a moment of acceleration.

1. Listen to the voice of God.

2. Be willing to say yes to the difficult task.

3. Be led by the Holy Spirit to be a witness in your community.

We are blessed with the opportunity to know Jesus and learn about Him openly and freely. Many people around the globe have never had that chance. If every single Christian realized the calling and purpose on their life to spread the light of the world living inside of them, the entire world would be changed.

I wrote this book to help you receive and appropriate the Holy Spirit in your own life. But I want to challenge you to join with tens of thousands of others in spreading this message to a lost and dying world that seems to grow more evil and decadent by the day. Yet we know things can turn around. That little Jewish sect that spread out after the Day of Pentecost ultimately exorcised paganism in ancient Rome and established Christianity in place of the Roman Empire itself.

The same God who poured out His Spirit two thousand years ago is with us today. Through the power of the Holy Spirit, the early Christians "turned the world upside down."[1] We can do the same.

HOW TO RECEIVE JESUS AS YOUR SAVIOR

By Lisa Dean

DID YOU KNOW you don't have to live life alone? Did you know you are loved? Did you know you could have a Father who has everything you'll ever need to live a satisfying and fulfilled life, with nothing missing and nothing broken, inside and out?

The only real answer that will ever be found to these life questions is all wrapped up in the person of Jesus Christ. The Bible tells us in Jeremiah 1:5 that before the foundations of the world He knew you and formed you in your mother's womb. Matthew 10:30 says He even knows the number of hairs on your head! It's like He knows you better than you know yourself. In Jeremiah 29:11, God tells us, "For I know the plans I have for you, plans to prosper you, plans for a hope and a future."

If I didn't already know Him and know that these scriptures have rung true in my own life, I would want to know how to meet Him. In fact, I had cancer and lost all my hair. When God healed me and it all came back, I realized that He really did care for me. He really did know the number of hairs on my head. Most importantly, I knew He had a plan for my life, and He has one for you too! I know it sounds too good to be true. The fact that someone could really love you that much is almost unbelievable.

You might think, "Well, maybe that was just for you. Maybe all this God stuff is just for some people." According to Acts 10:34, that's a lie, because "God is no respecter of persons." I know from personal experience that I'm not anyone special, and my God has been faithful to complete the good work He started in me. That work started the day I accepted Him as my personal Lord and Savior, and I want to invite you to do the same. This is the most important decision you will ever make in life.

God promises in Romans 10:9–10: "If you declare with your mouth, 'Jesus is Lord,' and believe in your heart that God raised Jesus from the dead, you will be saved. For it is with your heart that you believe and are justified, and it is with your mouth that you profess your faith and are saved."

PRAY OUT LOUD

Jesus, I confess that You are my Lord and Savior. I believe with all my heart that God raised You from the dead. By faith in Your Word, I receive salvation now. Thank You for saving me![1]

If you have accepted Jesus as your Savior and Lord, Let's Go Deeper: A Practical Guide to Following Jesus *by J. Lee Grady is an excellent resource to help you grow in your walk with God. You can find it at mycharismashop.com.*

Appendix B

HOW TO BE BAPTIZED IN THE HOLY SPIRIT

By J. Lee Grady

WHEN WE MEET Christ and put our trust in Him, we are "born again"[1] and receive the Holy Spirit in our hearts. This is the most important decision we will ever make. This happened to the disciples of Jesus in John 20:22, which says: "[Jesus] breathed on them and said to them, 'Receive the Holy Spirit.'"

But before Jesus ascended to heaven, He told His disciples to wait in Jerusalem until the "promise of [the] Father" had come. He told them that if they would wait there, they would be "clothed with power from on high."[2] In the Book of Acts, Jesus told His followers that they would receive "power" to be His witnesses.[3]

So the disciples waited in Jerusalem for many days, praying near the temple. On the Day of Pentecost, which was fifty days after Jesus had died on the cross, something amazing happened. The Holy Spirit was poured out on the early church.[4] The Bible says that when the Spirit came, the disciples were filled (another word is *baptized*) with the Spirit.

This shows us that there are two separate experiences we can have with God. One is salvation, in which we receive through God's amazing forgiveness a new nature. The Holy Spirit comes to live inside us, and He becomes our Teacher, our Comforter, and our Helper.

The second experience is the Baptism of the Holy Spirit, in which the Holy Spirit who is already in us overflows. *Baptized in the Spirit* means completely immersed in the Spirit. Jesus never wanted us to rely on our

192

own ability to do the work of ministry. He wants to do it through us. So He fills us with the Holy Spirit in order to empower us with His ability.

When we have this experience, the Holy Spirit's power fills us so full that He spills out. Also when we are baptized in the Spirit, unusual gifts of the Holy Spirit[5] begin to be manifested in our lives. We begin to experience His supernatural power. These gifts include prophecy, discernment, miracles, healing, and speaking in tongues.

When people were baptized in the Holy Spirit in the New Testament church, the Bible says they all spoke in tongues.[6] A lot of people get hung up on speaking in tongues because it seems like a weird thing. It's actually not strange at all. It is a very special form of prayer that any Christian can experience.

When we pray in our heavenly prayer language, we are praising God and also strengthening ourselves spiritually. Speaking in tongues helps us become mighty in the Spirit. The apostle Paul, truly a giant in the New Testament church, told the Corinthian believers, "I thank my God that I speak in tongues more than you all."[7]

Being baptized in the Holy Spirit is not something you have to qualify for. Any Christian can ask, and Jesus is ready to do it. You can pray by yourself, or you can ask someone else to pray for you.

Here are the simple steps you can take to be filled with the Holy Spirit:

1. Prepare your heart. The Holy Spirit is holy. He is compared to a fire,[8] which means He purifies sin and burns up that which is not Christlike in our lives. Make sure you have confessed all known sin and made your heart ready for His infilling.

2. Ask Jesus to baptize you in the Spirit. You do not need to jump through hoops to get God's attention. He is eager to answer your request. Jesus is the One who baptizes us in the Spirit, so ask Him—and expect Him to answer.

3. Receive the infilling. Begin to thank Him for this miracle. The Holy Spirit's power is filling your life. If you feel your mind is clouded with doubts, just praise the Lord. Focus your mind on Him and not on yourself.

4. Release your prayer language. The moment you are filled with the

Spirit, you will receive the ability to speak in your heavenly prayer language. You may feel the words bubbling up inside you. You may begin to hear the words in your mind. Open your mouth and begin to speak, trusting the Lord to give you this new, supernatural language.

Some people ask me, "Do I have to speak in tongues?" Certainly God will not force you to do it, and speaking in tongues has nothing to do with salvation. But I believe He offers this gift to anyone who wants it. It could be considered the least of the gifts—but it serves as a doorway to the supernatural realm and helps usher you into the deeper things of God.

5. Step out in boldness. After you have been baptized in the Holy Spirit, one of the first things you will notice is a new boldness. The Holy Spirit does not like to hide. He wants you to speak about Jesus to those around you—and He will give you surprising courage.[9]

If you prayed to receive the Baptism in the Holy Spirit, Rebuilding the Real You: The Definitive Guide to the Holy Spirit's Work in Your Life *by Jack Hayford is a great resource to help you grow in your relationship with the Holy Spirit. You can find it at mycharismashop.com.*

ACKNOWLEDGMENTS

C OMPLETING A BOOK such as this takes a team, and I'm blessed to have a great team at Charisma Media. Together we've published nearly two thousand books with excellence. But it's different for the team when the author is also the boss. Yet we've worked together well and produced a book I pray will bless you.

My appreciation goes especially to Debbie Marrie, our vice president of content development, who was my collaborator, researcher, and sounding board. Adrienne Gaines, who has edited several of my books, did a great job turning what Debbie and I submitted into excellent prose. I also appreciate the hard work of the others on our book editorial team: Melissa Bogdany, Candace Ziegler, Angie Kiesling, and Ann Mulchan.

Justin Evans and his team of artists did a great job with the cover. Chad Dunlap and his sales team placed the book in all the outlets. Lucy Kurz and her marketing team let readers know this is a book they want to read. My administrative assistant, Christina Schimbeno, helped in myriad ways. Ken Peckett, our controller and executive vice president of operations, and Joy Strang, our CFO, kept the company running smoothly so I could take time to write this.

I admit that writing on current events or cultural wars (as I did in my previous books) is much easier than writing about Spirit-led living. That is partly due to the intense spiritual warfare I experienced as I wrote this. (I don't believe the enemy wanted this book written or published.) In addition, as I wrote, I wondered if my stories would inspire or if my insight communicated more than what so many have said in other ways and other books.

Writing this book forced me to go deep and to depend on the Holy Spirit to lead me into what to write, not just so the writing was excellent or the book would sell well. Instead, I had to have faith that this book would change lives. My goal is to help the Spirit-led community stand up to the attacks from the upside-down world and give readers encouragement during critical and difficult times. And I hope to motivate a new generation to press in to the Holy Spirit as generations of Spirit-led Christians before them have done.

Because of the spiritual nature of the book, I have had a cadre of people I respect pray for me, and while I can't thank everyone, I want to let Ben Inman of Nashville, Tennessee, know I appreciate his encouragement early in the process.

Our prayer warriors back home—Rebecca McInnis, Mary Jo Clouse, Myra Goldfarb, and Joy Strang—regularly lifted me in prayer, gave me feedback, and encouraged me to be bold in what I wrote.

Finally, I want to acknowledge my friend the Holy Spirit, who led me years ago to found a media company that has had as its motto "Spirit-led living" and now has led me to write this book. My prayer is that He will use it to impact your life. If it has touched your life, email me at info@ charismamedia.com.

ENDNOTES

A WORD FROM JACK HAYFORD

1. John 14:16.
2. Acts 2:38.
3. Acts 2:39.
4. Galatians 3:3, NLT.
5. See Romans 8:14.
6. Genesis 1.
7. Genesis 32.
8. Exodus 12.
9. Judges 7.
10. Luke 23.
11. 1 Thessalonians 5:2.
12. Isaiah 60:2.
13. See Psalm 138:8.
14. John 5:14, NLT.
15. Luke 11:24–26.
16. John 8:11.
17. Adapted from Jack Hayford, *Rebuilding the Real You* (Lake Mary, FL: Charisma House, 2009), 15–16, 18–19, 21, 114–115, 196, 207–208, 224.

INTRODUCTION

1. Ephesians 3:20.
2. Romans 8:14.
3. Acts 8:26–28.
4. Mario Murillo, *It's Our Turn Now* (Lake Mary, FL: FrontLine, 2023), 24–25.
5. Shaun Sapp, "How the Covid Vaccines Damage the Body," Brightwork Research & Analysis, December 4, 2022, https://www.brightworkresearch.com/how-the-covid-vaccines-damage-the-body/.
6. See my friend Floyd Brown's book *Counterpunch* for more about the dangers of the great reset put forth by the World Economic Forum in 2020 and outlined in the aptly titled book *COVID-19: The Great Reset*

by Klaus Schwab and Thierry Malleret. See also Michael Rectenwald, "What Is the Great Reset," *Imprimis* 5, no. 12 (December 2020), https://www.imprimis.hillsdale.edu/what-is-the-great-reset/.

7. Joshua Nelson, "Sen. Tom Cotton: 'Cannot Have Liquor Stores and Marijuana Shops Open, but Close Houses of Worship,'" Fox News, May 22, 2020, https://www.foxnews.com/media/sen-tom-cotton-cannot-have-liquor-stores-and-marijuana-shops-open-but-close-houses-of-worship.

8. Hebrews 11:33–35.

9. Hebrews 11:35–39.

CHAPTER 1

1. Alton Garrison, "Spirit-Empowered Lifestyle," Assemblies of God, June 9, 2019, https://news.ag.org/Features/Spirit-Empowered-Lifestyle.

2. Donald C. Stamps, gen. ed., *FireBible: Modern English Version*, "The Doctrine of the Holy Spirit" (Springfield, MO: Life Publishers International, 2014), 1543. See 2 Corinthians 3:17–18, Hebrews 9:14, 1 Peter 1:2, Romans 8:27, Romans 15:30, 1 Corinthians 12:11, and John 14:16–18, 26.

3. Stamps, *FireBible*, 1543.

4. John 14:16.

5. John 16:7; Luke 24:49; Mark 1:8.

6. 1 John 4:19.

7. 1 John 4:8.

8. Kenneth Copeland, *The Word of Faith Study Bible* (Lake Mary, FL: Passio, 2017), 1636.

9. Galatians 5:22–23.

10. Fuchsia T. Pickett, *Walking in the Spirit* (Lake Mary, FL: Charisma House, 2015), 123.

11. D. L. Moody, *Notes From My Bible: From Genesis to Revelation* (New York: Fleming H. Revell Co., 1895).

12. Romans 5:5.

13. 1 Corinthians 13:2.

14. Fuchsia Pickett, *Cultivating the Gifts and Fruit of the Holy Spirit* (Lake Mary, FL: Charisma House, 2004), 110–116.

15. Jack W. Hayford, ed., *NKJV Spirit-Filled Life Bible, Revised and Updated Third Edition* (Nashville, TN: 2018), 1703.

16. Hayford, *NKJV Spirit-Filled Life Bible*, 1702.

17. Genesis 1:1–3.
18. Numbers 27:18.
19. Judges 6:34.
20. Judges 13:25; 14:6.
21. 1 Samuel 10:9–10.
22. Acts 1:5.
23. Acts 1:8.
24. Mark 1:7–8.
25. John Sherrill, *They Speak With Other Tongues*, rev. ed. (Grand Rapids, MI: Chosen, 2004), 45.
26. Sherrill, *They Speak With Other Tongues*, 45.
27. Sherrill, *They Speak With Other Tongues*, 46.
28. Genesis 1:2; Job 33:4.
29. 2 Peter 1:21.
30. John 14:26; 15:26–27; 1 Corinthians 2:10–14.
31. Acts 1:8.
32. Stamps, *FireBible*, 1543.

CHAPTER 2

1. Joel 2:28.
2. Matthew 16:15.
3. 2 Timothy 4:6–8.
4. 2 Timothy 4:8.
5. Mark Batterson, *The Circle Maker* (Grand Rapids, MI: Zondervan, 2016), 15.
6. Benny Hinn, *Mysteries of the Anointing* (Lake Mary, FL: Charisma House, 2022), 28, 30.
7. God's Generals, "Learning to Listen to the Inward Witness || Rev Kenneth Hagin," YouTube, October 9, 2020, https://www.youtube.com/watch?v=3x0SVU34464.
8. John 14:16–17.
9. John 16:13.
10. 1 Thessalonians 5:23.
11. Romans 8:14.
12. Romans 8:16.
13. Proverbs 20:27.
14. Proverbs 20:27, NKJV.

15. Kenneth E. Hagin, "Knowing What to Do and Which Way to Go," Kenneth Hagin Ministries, accessed January 11, 2023, https://www.rhema.org/index.php?option=com_content&view=article&id=1568:knowing-what-to-do-and-which-way-to-go&catid=150.

16. 1 Peter 3:3–4.

17. Romans 7:22; Ephesians 3:16.

18. 1 Peter 3:4.

19. Hebrews 4:12.

20. Kenneth E. Hagin, "Man Is a Spirit Being (How You Can Be Led By the Spirit Of God) | Rev. Kenneth E. Hagin *(Copyright)," YouTube, June 23, 2020, https://www.youtube.com/watch?v=cAajF_RllCs.

21. Psalm 91:1–2, NKJV.

22. Jennifer LeClaire, "10 Ways God Speaks to His People," in *Life in the Spirit*, vol. 3, *Holy Spirit Baptism* (Lake Mary, FL: Charisma Media, 2016), 22–25.

23. Ephesians 4:31–32, NIV.

24. R. T. Kendall, *The Sensitivity of the Spirit* (Lake Mary, FL: Charisma House, 2002), 31–49.

25. Acts 2:2.

26. 1 Thessalonians 5:19.

27. Luke 24:49.

28. 1 Corinthians 14:39.

29. 1 Thessalonians 5:20.

30. 1 Corinthians 1:13.

31. Adapted with permission from J. Lee Grady, "Why We Need to Stop Quenching the Spirit's Fire," *Charisma*, May 24, 2002, https://www.charismamag.com/blogs/fire-in-my-bones/why-we-need-to-stop-quenching-the-spirit-s-fire/.

32. Grady, "Why We Need to Stop Quenching the Spirit's Fire."

CHAPTER 3

1. Gina Z. Zurlo, Todd M. Johnson, and Peter F. Crossing, "World Christianity and Mission 2020: Ongoing Shift to the Global South," *Sage Journals* 44, No. 1 (October 16, 2019), https://www.journals.sagepub.com/doi/10.1177/2396939319880074; Rich Tenorio, "Are the End Times Near? How Pentecostal Christianity Is Taking Over the World," *Times of Israel*, October 15, 2022, https://www.timesofisrael.com/

are-the-end-times-near-how-pentecostal-christianity-is-taking-over-the-world/.

2. Kairos, "Spirit-Empowered Christianity One of Fastest-Growing Global Movements, New Study Shows," Charisma News, February 25, 2020, https://www.charismanews.com/us/80076-spirit-empowered-christianity-one-of-fastest-growing-global-movements-new-study-shows.

3. Acts 17:6.

4. Acts 3:4–5.

5. Fuchsia Pickett, *Stones of Remembrance* (Lake Mary, FL: Creation House, 1998), 26–33.

6. Pickett, *Walking in the Spirit*, 45.

7. NKJV.

8. Romans 8:26.

9. Daniel D. Isgrigg, "Oral Roberts: A Man of the Spirit," *Spiritus* 3, no. 2 (2018): 325–350, https://digitalshowcase.oru.edu/cgi/viewcontent.cgi?article=1093&context=spiritus.

10. Adapted from "Pat Boone Recounts Why He Wrote 'If' for the Ones Who Don't Know God," September 28, 2022, in *Strang Report*, https://strangreport.libsyn.com/pat-boone.

11. Mark Rutland, in communication with the author, December 21, 2022. Portions of this testimony were also shared in Jordan Daniel May, "In Our Own Tongues," *Enrichment Journal*, Winter 2015, https://enrichmentjournal.ag.org/Issues/2015/Winter-2015/In-Our-Own-Tongues.

12. Dan Van Veen, "Holy Spirit Confirms God's Love for Teen," Assemblies of God, April 7, 2017, https://news.ag.org/features/holy-spirit-confirms-gods-love-for-teen. Used with permission.

13. 1 Corinthians 14:6.

14. 1 Corinthians 14:22.

15. Jack Hayford, *The Beauty of Spiritual Language* (Dallas, TX: Nelson, 1996).

16. Galatians 3:2, 14.

17. John 7:37.

18. Adapted from John Rea, ThD, *Charisma's Bible Handbook on the Holy Spirit* (Lake Mary, FL: Creation House, 1998), 160–162.

19. 2 Timothy 1:7.

CHAPTER 4

1. Mike Bickle, *Growing in the Prophetic* (Lake Mary, FL: Charisma House, 1996, 2008), 36.
2. Wayne Grudem, *The Gift of Prophecy in the New Testament and Today*, rev. ed. (Wheaton, IL: Crossway Books, 2000), 18.
3. Bickle, *Growing in the Prophetic*, 35–37.
4. Jamie Buckingham, *Where Eagles Soar* (Grand Rapids, MI: Chosen Books, 1980), 60.
5. Proverbs 15:23.
6. 1 Corinthians 14:3.
7. 1 Corinthians 14:5, 31.
8. Bickle, *Growing in the Prophetic*, 169–171, 178.
9. Hubie Synn, *The Tales of a Wandering Prophet* (Lake Mary, FL: Charisma House, 2015), 10–20.
10. Adapted from David Tyree with Kimberly Daniels, *More Than Just a Catch* (Lake Mary, FL: Charisma House, 2008), 115, 120–123.
11. Kim Clement, "April 4th, 2007—Redding, CA—Media, Trump, Gatekeeper, New York, Praying President," YouTube, March 3, 2017, https://www.youtube.com/watch?v=6Aa2vFjuQCo&list=PLvt06LwIld OLwZ_kXHmYCxELC5uBvk_G_&index=107&t=33s.
12. Rob Poindexter, "Kim Clement Prophesying About Donald Trump 2007," YouTube, January 11, 2023, https://www.youtube.com/watch?v=eFfFtqlfljY.
13. Kim Clement, "Prophecy: February 10th, 2007—Scottsdale, AZ—Praying President, Hot Blood," YouTube, February 21, 2017, https://www.youtube.com/watch?v=PU3MKt5h1wo.
14. Donné Clement Petruska, "Kim Clement Prophecy—Supreme Court, Drain the Swamp," YouTube, March 12, 2018, https://www.youtube.com/watch?v=Xqae12Otunk&t=4s.
15. Petruska, "Kim Clement Prophecy—Supreme Court, Drain the Swamp."
16. Revelation 19:10.
17. Revelation 12–13.
18. 1 Timothy 3:15.
19. 1 Chronicles 12:32.
20. 1 Corinthians 12:10-11.
21. Bickle, *Growing in the Prophetic*, 69–74.

CHAPTER 5

1. Isaiah 11:2–3.
2. Romans 12:6.
3. Walter A. Elwell, "Gifts of the Spirit," *Baker's Evangelical Dictionary of Biblical Theology*, accessed December 26, 2022, https://www.studylight.org/dictionaries/eng/bed/h/holy-spirit-gifts-of.html.
4. Derek Prince, *Foundational Truths for Christian Living* (Lake Mary, FL: Charisma House, 2006), 300.
5. Derek Prince, "The Gifts of the Holy Spirit," Derek Prince Ministries, accessed December 26, 2022, https://www.derekprince.com/teaching/99-3.
6. Stamps, *FireBible*, 1662.
7. Steve Strang, "The Incredible Kathryn Kuhlman," *Florida Magazine* (*Sentinel Star*), April 27, 1975, https://www.newspapers.com/newspage/224580822/.
8. Reinhard Bonnke, *Evangelism by Fire* (Lake Mary, FL: Charisma House, 2011), 185–186.
9. Sid Roth, "Over 1,000 Mostly Jewish People Make Professions of Faith During Supernatural Healing Meeting," June 19, 2019, in *Strang Report*, podcast, https://www.charismapodcastnetwork.com/show/strangreport/c58b073a009a4083a01f6af19dc68306/Over-1%2C000-Mostly-Jewish-People-Make-Professions-of-Faith-During-Supernatural-Healing-Meeting.
10. Romans 12:3.
11. Hebrews 11:1.
12. J. Lee Grady, "Embrace the Gifts of the Holy Spirit," *in Life in the Spirit*, vol. 3, *Holy Spirit Baptism*, 18–19.
13. Matthew 17:20; Mark 11:23.
14. KJV.
15. Habakkuk 2:4.
16. Stephen Strang, "Kenneth Copeland," *Charisma*, June 1979, https://charismamag.com/spriritled-living/church-ministry/kenneth-copeland/.
17. Kathryn Kuhlman, *I Believe in Miracles*, rev. ed. (Alachua, FL: Bridge-Logos Publishers, 1992), 201–205.
18. Heidi Baker, *Birthing the Miraculous* (Lake Mary, FL: Charisma House, 2014), 110–112.

19. Larry Keefauver, *Ministering in the Gifts of the Spirit* (Lake Mary, FL: Creation House, 1997), 30–31.
20. 1 Corinthians 14:1, NIV.

CHAPTER 6

1. Galatians 5:19–21.
2. Geffrey B. Kelly and F. Burton Nelson, *The Cost of Moral Leadership: The Spirituality of Dietrich Bonhoeffer* (Grand Rapids, MI: Eerdmans, 2002), 81.
3. I have an interest in this because my ancestors were Huguenots who fled France in 1685 because of intense persecution, some of the worst in European history. My family actually came to America for religious freedom.
4. In Houston, a young Black woman named Lucy Farrow, the niece of the famous abolitionist Frederick Douglass, pastored a Black Holiness church. Farrow was receptive to Parham's message and turned her church's pastorate over to Seymour so she could return to Kansas with the Parhams as their governess. While staying in the Parham home, Farrow experienced the Baptism in the Holy Spirit and spoke in tongues. She returned to Houston with the Parhams in the fall of 1905 and encouraged Seymour to enroll in the college Parham planned to open there on January 1, 1906. Jim Crow laws mandated racial segregation, but Parham arranged for Seymour to sit in an adjoining room and listen to classes through an open door. Despite these circumstances, Seymour absorbed Parham's teaching on the Baptism in the Holy Spirit with the evidence of speaking in tongues and began earnestly seeking this gift. The next month, Seymour accepted an invitation to pastor a storefront Holiness church in Los Angeles. He had not yet received the Baptism in the Holy Spirit, but he was desperately hungry for it and prepared to preach it without compromise.
5. Seymour introduced the Baptism in the Holy Spirit during his first service, but the elders were not receptive and decided he was preaching false doctrine. When Seymour arrived for the evening service, the doors were padlocked. Less than a week after moving to Los Angeles, Seymour found himself without a church. Some of the storefront church members took pity on him, and Seymour was invited to stay first at the home of Edward Lee and then later with Richard Asberry, who lived at 216 Bonnie Brae Street in Los Angeles. Now driven by an

almost overwhelming hunger for the power of the Holy Spirit, Seymour spent nearly all his time in prayer. Because of Seymour's devotion to prayer, the Asberrys opened their home to evening prayer meetings. Seymour told the group about Lucy Farrow, who had introduced him to the idea of the Baptism in the Holy Spirit. They took an offering to pay for her train fare and invited her to come. When she arrived, Edward Lee asked her to pray for him to receive the Baptism of the Holy Spirit. She laid hands on him, and he fell out of his chair and began speaking in tongues. When Lee and Farrow went to the prayer meeting that night, as Lee walked through the door, he raised his hands and broke out in tongues. Immediately, almost everyone present began speaking in tongues. Jennie Moore, who had never had a piano lesson, began to play the piano and sing in tongues. She would later become Seymour's wife. According to an eyewitness, they shouted for three days and nights. People came from everywhere, and as soon as they entered the house, they would fall under the power of the Holy Spirit. Sick people were healed, and sinners were saved. So many people came that the house's foundation collapsed, but no one was hurt. Realizing the Asberry home was too small to contain the crowds, the prayer meeting was moved to 312 Azusa Street.

6. Zurlo, Johnson, and Crossing, "World Christianity and Mission 2020."

7. R. A. Torrey, a respected leader and then-head of the famous Moody Bible Institute in Chicago, once wrote a booklet calling for Baptism in the Holy Spirit. But after the Azusa Street Revival, which was known for exuberant worship and speaking in tongues, he rejected this and called the Pentecostal movement "emphatically not of God." G. Campbell Morgan, pastor of Westminster Chapel in London and one of Torrey's contemporaries, went so far as to call it "the last vomit of Satan." See R. A. Torrey, *The Baptism With the Holy Spirit*, rev. ed. (Overland Park, KS: Digireads.com, 2022), and David Cloud, *The Pentecostal-Charismatic Movement* (Port Huron, MI: Way of Life Literature, 2012).

8. While the Azusa Street Revival was in progress, a new denomination grew out of the Holiness movement called the Pentecostal Church of the Nazarene. Several groups merged in 1907, and one had Pentecostal in its name. Later, when Pentecostalism became associated with speaking in tongues, the denomination seemed to reject tongues-talking Pentecostals so much that they dropped the word Pentecostal and today are known as the Church of the Nazarene.

9. In the early 1950s when a dairy farmer from California named Demos Shakarian (whom I interviewed before he died in 1993) founded a network for businessmen, he called it the Full Gospel Businessmen's Fellowship International. *Full gospel* is a term Charles Parham also used before the Azusa Street Revival.

10. Bill Bright, the founder of Campus Crusade for Christ (now called Cru) and a man I knew personally, objected to Pentecostals using the term *Spirit-filled* because Evangelicals such as him felt excluded. He was among those who made the point that all believers have the Spirit living inside them. Because of my respect for Dr. Bright and because he was right, I've avoided using the term *Spirit-filled*.

11. "The Renewalists: Pentecostal and Charismatic Evangelicals," Infinity Concepts and Grey Matter Research, accessed January 11, 2023, https://www.infinityconcepts.com/wp-content/uploads/2022/08/The-Renewalists-Downloadable.pdf.

12. NKJV.

13. Derek Prince, *Foundational Truths* (Lake Mary, FL: Charisma House, 2006), 269.

14. Ephesians 1:13–14.

15. Prince, *Foundational Truths*, 270.

16. John 4:24.

17. Stephen Strang, "Join Sid Roth in Praying in Tongues on Yom Kippur," September 22, 2020, in Strang Report, podcast, https://www.charismapodcastnetwork.com/show/strangreport/5f994ab4-b574-44f7-a314-d8425dba488f/Join-Sid-Roth-In-Praying-in-Tongues--for-Our-Nation-on-Yom-Kippur.

18. Strang, "Join Sid Roth in Praying in Tongues on Yom Kippur."

19. Ezekiel 47:1–12.

20. Destiny Image, "Jonathan Cahn's Urgent Warning to America: They've Returned!," YouTube, August 19, 2022, https://www.youtube.com/watch?v=C-yKy-65m_c.

21. Destiny Image, "Jonathan Cahn's Urgent Warning to America: They've Returned!"

22. Stephen Strang, "Sid Roth Explains How Jonathan Cahn's 'Return of the Gods' Is a Start of God's Glory Rising," September 6, 2022, in Strang Report, podcast, https://www.charismapodcastnetwork.com/show/strangreport/e14f2b09-a20e-47e8-a681-efc3522cfe0e/Sid-Roth-Explains-How-Jonathan-Cahn's-%22Return-of-the-Gods%22-Is-a-Start-of-God's-Glory-Rising.

23. "Testing Prophecies Together: Smith Wigglesworth's 1947 Prophecy," Prophecy Today UK, May 6, 2016, https://prophecytoday.uk/study/prophetic-insights/item/389-testing-prophecies-together-smith-wigglesworth-s-1947-prophecy.html.

24. Frank Sumrall Global Ministries, Facebook, December 3, 2018, https://www.facebook.com/franksumrallministries/photos/here-is-the-word-given-by-smith-wigglesworth-to-lester-sumrall-in-1939smith-wigg/1985983311481535/.

25. Sid Roth, "Sid Roth Prophesies This End-Times Outpouring Will Be Uncontainable," March 5, 2019, in Strang Report, podcast, https://www.charismapodcastnetwork.com/show/strangreport/699876a8a832 46769a0bb774e0eaf91b.

26. Sid Roth's It's Supernatural!, "Sid Roth in 1972 Interview With Kathryn Kuhlman on 'I Believe in Miracles,'" YouTube, February 15, 2017, https://www.youtube.com/watch?v=28o3xIPCoZE.

27. Destiny Image, "Jonathan Cahn's Urgent Warning to America: They've Returned!"

28. 1 Corinthians 2:9.

29. Roth, "Sid Roth Prophesies This End-Times Outpouring Will Be Uncontainable."

30. Karl Strader, "Don't Criticize Charismatics," *Charisma*, January/February 1976, 14–15.

31. Jeremiah 29:13.

CHAPTER 7

1. Romans 7:24.

2. Romans 8:2.

3. Stamps, *FireBible*, 1613–1614.

4. John Lindell, *Soul Set Free* (Lake Mary, FL: Charisma House, 2019), 155–162.

5. Romans 8:5–8.

6. Stamps, *FireBible*, 1614.

7. Romans 8:13.

8. Michael L. Brown, PhD, *The Grace Controversy* (Lake Mary, FL: Charisma House, 2016), 59.

9. Some people confuse the conviction of the Holy Spirit with condemnation. But there is a vast difference between the two. Conviction is the Holy Spirit's way of letting us know we've done

something bad; condemnation is a lie from the devil telling us we are bad. Dr. Michael Brown writes in *The Grace Controversy*: "Condemnation says, 'You have sinned. Get away from me!' Conviction says, 'You have sinned. Come near me,'" Brown writes. "…The Lord never pushes us away but always calls us near. That's how you can distinguish the convicting voice of the Spirit from the condemning voice of the enemy or even the condemning voice of your own mind (or of religious tradition)….Satan condemns, but the Spirit convicts." (See Brown, *The Grace Controversy*, 68.)

10. Romans 3:23.

11. Psalm 53:3.

12. Harry Emerson Fosdick, *Twelve Tests of Character* (New York and London: Harper & Brothers Publishers, 1923), accessed January 2, 2023, https://www.religion-online.org/book-chapter/chapter-6-minding-ones-own-business.

13. Ephesians 6:12.

14. David Wilkerson, *The Cross and the Switchblade* (Grand Rapids, MI: Chosen Books, 1986), 151–155.

15. Alton Garrison, "Spirit-Empowered Lifestyle," Assemblies of God, June 9, 2019, https://news.ag.org/Features/Spirit-Empowered-Lifestyle. Used with permission.

16. "The Duquesne Weekend," Catholic Charismatic Renewal, accessed January 2, 2023, http://www.ccr.org.uk/about-ccr/about/the-duquesne-weekend/.

17. David Kinnaman, "The Porn Phenomenon," Barna Group, February 5, 2016, https://www.barna.com/the-porn-phenomenon/.

18. "Marriage and Cohabitation in the U.S.," Pew Research Center, November 6, 2019, https://www.pewresearch.org/social-trends/2019/11/06/marriage-and-cohabitation-in-the-u-s/.

19. John 8:36.

CHAPTER 8

1. Mark Fackler, "The World Has Yet to See…," *Christianity Today*, accessed January 2, 2023, https://www.christianitytoday.com/history/issues/issue-25/world-has-yet-to-see.html.

2. 2 Corinthians 3:18.

3. Matt Weinberger, "Microsoft CEO Sataya Nadella Bothered by Bill Gates' Mission," Business Insider, February 21, 2017, https://www.

businessinsider.com/microsoft-ceo-satya-nadella-bothered-by-bill-gates-mission-2017-2.

4. Jason Law, "God Wants You to Have a Vision and a Dream!—Dr Yonggi Cho of Yoido Full Gospel Church, Korea," Christianity Malaysia, April 15, 2015, https://christianitymalaysia.com/wp/god-wants-you-to-have-a-vision-and-a-dream-dr-yonggi-cho-of-yoido-full-gospel-church-korea/.

5. Myles Munroe, *Understanding Your Potential* (Shippensburg, PA: Destiny Image, 1992), 64–65.

6. Bill Winston, *Revelation of Royalty* (Lake Mary, FL: Charisma House, 2021), 172.

7. Patrick Morley, "54—Second Wind for the Second Half," Man in the Mirror, December 10, 2008, https://maninthemirror.org/2008/12/10/54-second-wind-for-the-second-half/.

8. Patrick Morley, *Second Wind for the Second Half* (Grand Rapids, MI: Zondervan, 1999).

9. Morley, *Second Wind for the Second Half*, 174–175.

10. Romans 4:19–22.

11. Romans 4:23–24.

12. Batterson, *The Circle Maker*, 180.

13. 1 Corinthians 9:22.

14. 1 Corinthians 9:25–26.

15. Matthew 9:29.

16. Psalm 119:49.

17. James 2:18.

18. John 6:29.

19. Ephesians 3:20.

20. Luke 11:8.

21. Matthew 19:26.

22. Dan Arnold, "Why It's Important to Set Faith Goals," in Steve Strang, "Take My Challenge: Set Some Huge Faith Goals in 2015," *The Strang Report* (blog), January 16, 2015, https://charismamag.com/blogs/the-strang-report/take-my-challenge-set-some-huge-faith-goals-in-2015/.

23. Mark Batterson, *The Circle Maker*, 197.

24. Matthew 28:20; Hebrews 13:5.

CHAPTER 9

1. Steve Warren, "New Barna Survey: More Americans Believe in Satan Than Believe in God," CBN News, April 24, 2020, https://www1.cbn.com/cbnnews/us/2020/april/new-barna-survey-more-americans-believe-in-satan-than-believe-in-god.
2. Mark 16:15–17.
3. Adapted from Sherry Andrews, "The Deliverance of James Robison," *Charisma*, December 1983, 34–41.
4. 2 Corinthians 10:4–5.
5. Mark 16:17–18.
6. Matthew 10:8.
7. Zechariah 4:6.
8. 2 Corinthians 10:5, NLT.
9. See Philippians 2:12–13.
10. Matthew 12:44–45.
11. 2 Corinthians 10:3–5.
12. Eckhardt writes: "*Power* is the Greek word *dunamis. Authority* is the Greek word *exousia.* Authority is the legal right to use power. We have been given authority to use the power supplied by the Holy Spirit." See John Eckhardt, *The Deliverance and Spiritual Warfare Manual* (Lake Mary, FL: Charisma House, 2014), 88.
13. Eckhardt, *The Deliverance and Spiritual Warfare Manual*, 86–90.
14. Ramirez writes: "Nothing can explain the power of Jesus' name better than this: 'For this reason also [because He obeyed and so completely humbled Himself], God has highly exalted Him and bestowed on Him the name which is above every name, so that at the name of Jesus every knee shall bow [in submission], of those who are in heaven and on earth and under the earth, and that every tongue will confess and openly acknowledge that Jesus Christ is Lord (sovereign God), to the glory of God the Father' (Phil. 2:9–11, [AMP])." See John Ramirez, *Fire Prayers* (Lake Mary, FL: Charisma House, 2023), 26–27.
15. Ramirez, *Fire Prayers*, 26–27.

CHAPTER 10

1. 1 Peter 1:6–7.
2. Bethel Church—Inspire, "Bill Johnson's Message 3 Days After Beni's Passing Away/How to Process Loss and Disappointment," accessed January 3, 2022, https://www.youtube.com/watch?v=bBPolLt3TJg.

3. Bill Johnson, "The Healing Power of Grief," *Charisma* (January–February 2023).

4. Bethel Church—Inspire, "Bill Johnson's Message 3 Days After Beni's Passing Away."

5. 1 Thessalonians 4:13, emphasis added.

6. Johnson, "The Healing Power of Grief."

7. Ephesians 4:14.

8. Habakkuk 3:2.

9. Psalm 31:24.

10. Psalm 33:22.

11. Psalm 62:5–6.

12. James 1:2, NKJV.

13. Blue Letter Bible, s.v. *"chara,"* accessed January 8, 2023, https://www.blueletterbible.org/lexicon/g5479/kjv/tr/0-1/.

14. James 1:3.

15. 1 Corinthians 10:13.

16. James 1:12.

17. See Isaiah 9:6.

18. Joe Suro, "He Shall Be Called: Wonderful Counselor," sermon, City Church FL, accessed January 3, 2023, https://www.youtube.com/watch?v=Q0zn0nOWZjg. See Proverbs 3:6, Philippians 4:6, James 1:5, and Romans 5:8.

19. Psalm 23:4; Suro, "He Shall Be Called: Wonderful Counselor."

CHAPTER 11

1. James 5:10–11.

2. Philippians 4:11.

3. Fuchsia Pickett, *Walking in the Spirit* (Lake Mary, FL: Charisma House, 2015), 122–123, 139–141.

4. 1 Peter 5:10.

5. Hebrews 10:36; James 1:3; Psalm 30:5.

6. Job 1:9–12; 2:3–7.

7. John 9:1–3; 11:1–4.

8. Philippians 3:10.

9. 2 Corinthians 1:3–7.

10. 1 Peter 2:20; Hebrews 12:5–9.

11. As in Genesis 22; Nancy Missler, "Why Trials and Suffering? Never Give Up! The Fruit of Longsuffering," Koinonia House, January 1, 2006, https://www.khouse.org/articles/2006/626/.

12. Bill Johnson, *Born for Significance* (Lake Mary, FL: Charisma House, 2020), 15.

13. Stephen E. Strang, *God and Cancel Culture* (Lake Mary, FL: FrontLine, 2021), 39–41.

14. 2 Corinthians 11:24–29.

15. See Isaiah 54:5–6.

16. Floyd Brown, "A Purpose for Restoration," *Charisma*, March–April 2023, https://charismamag.com/mar-apr-2023/a-purpose-for-restoration-taking-hold-of-new-rules-for-spirit-filled-believers-to-land-a-peaceful-counterpunch/.

17. James 1:2.

18. Tamas Ungar, MD, "Neuroscience, Joy, and the Well-Infant Visit That Got Me Thinking," *Annals of Family Medicine* 15, no. 1 (January 2017): 80–83, https://www.ncbi.nlm.nih.gov/pmc/articles/PMC5217849/; Silvan S. Tomkins, *Affect Imagery Consciousness*, vol. 1, *The Positive Affects* (New York: Springer Publishing,1962), 369–395.

19. Don Colbert, "A Talk on Joy Unlike You Ever Heard," February 16, 2022, in *Divine Health With Dr. Don Colbert*, podcast, https://divinehealth.libsyn.com/website/a-talk-on-joy-unlike-you-ever-heard.

20. Dr. Colbert's top ten health benefits of laughter: 1. Laughter relieves stress and tension and helps one to relax. It also helps people sleep if they have insomnia. 2. Laughter relieves pain. Norman Cousins, editor of the *Saturday Review* magazine, had a very painful, incurable condition called ankylosing spondylitis. He started watching funny films and TV shows and found that ten minutes of belly laughter would give him at least two hours of pain-free sleep. So he started practicing regular belly laughter, and he believes he was able to reverse his incurable disease. 3. Laughter is great for your marriage. Couples who laugh together, stay together. If you can, start watching comedians or funny movies or television shows with your spouse. 4. Laughter is good for your brain. Those concerned about Alzheimer's, dementia, Parkinson's, age-associated memory impairment, and cognitive memory impairment should take note. 5. Laughter can improve problem solving and creativity. So if you're having difficulty solving a problem or experiencing a creative block, take a thirty- to sixty-minute "belly laughter break" and watch some funny videos. 6. Laughter improves anxiety and depression

by helping raise neurotransmitter levels, especially the feel-good
chemicals serotonin and dopamine. 7. Laughter improves the
immune system and increases the natural killer cells that protects us
against cancer, bacteria, and viruses, including COVID. 8. Laughter
decreases adrenaline, a stress response that causes our arteries to
constrict, raises our blood pressure, and makes our hearts pound
faster. 9. Laughter helps us lose weight. Belly fat usually starts to be
burned when laughter is combined with exercise. One belly laugh
for about twenty seconds is equivalent to about three minutes of
rowing, according to one study. 10. Laughter increases longevity.
One of the common traits of people who live into their eighties and
nineties, and even a hundred is that they practice joy and laughter
frequently and don't take life too seriously. See Lawrence Robinson;
Melinda Smith, MA; and Jeanne Segal, PhD, "Laughter Is the Best
Medicine," HelpGuide, December 5, 2022, https://www.helpguide.org/
articles/mental-health/laughter-is-the-best-medicine.htm; Norman
Cousins, *Anatomy of an Illness as Perceived by the Patient* (Boston: G.
K. Hall, 1980), 43; Matt Kaplan, "How to Laugh Away Stress," *Nature*,
April 7, 2008, https://www.nature.com/articles/news.2008.741; Arwa
Mahdawi, "Laughter Therapy," *The Guardian*, July 5, 2008, https://
www.theguardian.com/lifeandstyle/2008/jul/06/healthandwellbeing4.

CHAPTER 12

1. Stephen Strang, "Frontline Doctor Stella Immanuel Shares How to
   Prepare for the Challenges to Come," December 14, 2022, in *Strang
   Report*, podcast, https://directory.libsyn.com/episode/index/show/
   strangreport/id/25326996.
2. Bill Gates, "A Conversation With Bill Gates: Population Growth,"
   GatesNotes, February 18, 2012, https://www.gatesnotes.com/about-bill-
   gates/a-conversation-with-bill-gates-population-growth; Paul Harris,
   "They're Called the Good Club—and They Want to Save the World,"
   The Guardian, May 30, 2009, https://www.theguardian.com/world/2009/
   may/31/new-york-billionaire-philanthropists; Matthew Herper, "With
   Vaccines, Bill Gates Changes The World Again," *Forbes*, November
   2, 2011, https://www.forbes.com/sites/matthewherper/2011/11/02/the-
   second-coming-of-bill-gates/?sh=4d28c69b13fd.
3. Isaiah 62:6.

4. "Yuval Noah Harari: 'Every Crisis Is Also an Opportunity,'" The UNESCO Courier, July–September 2020, https://en.unesco.org/courier/2020-3/yuval-noah-harari-every-crisis-also-opportunity.

5. Thrivetime Show, "CBDCs | 'Is This What the Future Looks Like?,'" Brighteon, accessed January 9, 2023, https://www.brighteon.com/0946f6d1-2884-4d7e-b829-dfffed766150.

6. Thrivetime Show, "CBDCs | 'Is This What the Future Looks Like?'"

7. Home Page, Yuval Noah Harari, accessed January 6, 2023, https://www.ynharari.com.

8. "Yuval Noah Harari: Humans Are Now Hackable Animals," CNN, accessed January 6, 2023, https://www.cnn.com/videos/world/2019/11/26/yuval-noah-harari-interview-anderson-vpx.cnn.

9. Thrivetime Show: The ReAwakening versus The Great Reset, "Yuval Noah Harari | 'We Are Upgrading Humans Into Gods,'" Rumble, accessed January 6, 2023, https://rumble.com/vy126n-yuval-noah-harari-we-are-upgrading-humans-into-gods.html.

10. "Yuval Noah Harari: '21 Lessons for the 21st Century' | Talks at Google [Full Transcript]," Scraps From the Loft, July 7, 2019, https://scrapsfromtheloft.com/culture/yuval-noah-harari-talks-at-google-transcript/.

11. 2 Thessalonians 2:4, 8.

12. Genesis 6:1–7.

13. "Documenting Numbers of Victims of the Holocaust and Nazi Persecution," United States Holocaust Memorial Museum, accessed January 4, 2023, https://www.encyclopedia.ushmm.org/content/en/article/documenting-numbers-of-victims-of-the-holocaust-and-nazi-persecution.

14. Jim Bakker, *You Can Make It* (Lake Mary, FL: FrontLine, 2021), 130, 134, 143, 150, 166, 187.

15. Fifteen of Jim Bakker's daily commitments: (1) I will humble myself and walk daily in humility before God; (2) I will seek my God daily and do nothing without consulting Him; (3) I will read, study, and meditate on God's Word daily and implement it; (4) I will have no other gods or idols or place anything before my God; (5) I will love, trust, praise, and worship my God with all my heart daily; (6) I will show mercy, forgive all, and love my neighbor as myself; (7) I will abide in Christ and allow His Word to abide in me and keep His commandments; (8) I will crucify my flesh and die to it daily, fleeing temptation and sin; (9) I will accept the trial of my faith as more

precious than gold, knowing whom God loves He chastises; (10) I will always confess that Jesus Christ is Lord, my Master, Owner, and Possessor; (11) I will keep my heart right toward God, confessing my sins and never lying to the Holy Spirit; (12) I will live by the total counsel of God's Word; (13) I will not judge others, lean on my own understanding, or trust the arm of the flesh; (14) I will demonstrate love, joy, peace, long-suffering, gentleness, goodness, faith, meekness, and temperance; (15) I will keep my eyes on heaven, the mark of the prize of the high calling in Christ Jesus. See Bakker, *You Can Make It*, 203–214.

16. Bakker, *You Can Make It*, 202; see Psalm 23:4.
17. Romans 10:13.
18. Deuteronomy 31:6; Hebrews 13:5–6.
19. Deuteronomy 31:8.
20. Michael Youssef, *Is the End Near?* (Lake Mary, FL: FrontLine, 2022), 179–180.

CONCLUSION

1. See Luke 5:1–11.
2. Luke 21:28.
3. 1 Thessalonians 4:18.
4. Barry Meguiar, "Were the Midterm Results an Indication of God's Judgment on America?," Charisma News, November 14, 2022, https://www.charismanews.com/us/90676-were-the-mid-term-results-an-indication-of-god-s-judgment-on-america.
5. Matthew 28:20, NLT.
6. Garrison, "Spirit-Empowered Lifestyle."
7. Romans 8:14–15.
8. Romans 8:16–17.
9. Romans 8:18.
10. Stamps, *FireBible*, 1613–17.
11. Romans 8:26.
12. Romans 8:27.
13. Ephesians 2:8–9.
14. 2 Peter 3:9.

EPILOGUE

1. Acts 17:6.

APPENDIX A

1. Lisa Dean, "Receive Jesus as Your Savior," in *Life in the Spirit*, vol. 2, *In His Presence* (Lake Mary, FL: Charisma Media, 2016), 79.

APPENDIX B

1. John 3:3.
2. Luke 24:49.
3. Acts 1:8.
4. Acts 2:1–4.
5. 1 Corinthians 12:8–10.
6. Acts 2:1–4; 4:31; 10:44–48; 19:1–7.
7. 1 Corinthians 14:18.
8. Matthew 3:11.
9. J. Lee Grady, "How to Be Baptized in the Holy Spirit," in *Life in the Spirit*, vol. 3, *Holy Spirit Baptism*, 38–39.

ABOUT THE AUTHOR

STEPHEN E. STRANG, the founder of Charisma Media, is a fourth-generation Pentecostal. He has had an interest in writing and journalism since high school and graduated from the College of Journalism and Communications at the University of Florida, where he won the prestigious national William Randolph Hearst Journalism Award. He began his career in 1973 as a government and general-assignment reporter for the *Sentinel Star* (now the *Orlando Sentinel*).

Being excited about and wanting to report on the fast-growing Charismatic movement, at age twenty-four he founded *Charisma* in 1975 at a large Orlando, Florida-area church. From those humble beginnings he believes the Holy Spirit empowered him and his wife, Joy, to create a platform that has influenced millions and given him influence he never would have dreamed possible.

He was cited by *Time* magazine in 2005 as one of the twenty-five most influential Evangelicals in America, and he has had the privilege of interviewing four US presidents and speaking at the United Nations. In recent years he has appeared on major media such as Fox News, MSNBC, and CNN, and been written about in *Politico* and the *New York Times*.

He has been married to the love of his life, Joy, for fifty years, and they have worked together at Charisma Media for the past forty-two years. Their oldest son, Cameron, is the founder of *Relevant* magazine. Their youngest son, Chandler, is a musician and entrepreneur. At the time of this writing, their grandson, Cohen, is in seventh grade.

Besides writing hundreds of articles in print and online, Stephen Strang hosts the *Strang Report* podcast, available on all the major podcast platforms and YouTube. This is his ninth book.

To keep up to date with the latest content related to
Spirit-Led Living in an Upside-Down World, scan the QR
code or visit SteveStrangBooks.com/spirit-led-resources.